*cha
Clans.*

The Short C

Italy in the Early Middle Ages

The Short Oxford History of Italy

General Editor: John A. Davis

Italy in the Nineteenth Century
edited by John A. Davis

Liberal and Fascist Italy
edited by Adrian Lyttelton

Italy since 1945
edited by Patrick McCarthy

Early Modern Italy
edited by John Marino

IN PREPARATION, VOLUMES COVERING

Italy in the Later Middle Ages 1000–1300
Italy in the Age of the Renaissance 1300–1550

The Short Oxford History of Italy

General Editor: John A. Davis

Italy in the Early Middle Ages

476–1000

Edited by Cristina La Rocca

OXFORD

UNIVERSITY PRESS

OXFORD
UNIVERSITY PRESS

Great Clarendon Street, Oxford OX2 6DP

Oxford University Press is a department of the University of Oxford.
It furthers the University's objective of excellence in research, scholarship,
and education by publishing worldwide in

Oxford New York

Auckland Bangkok Buenos Aires Cape Town Chennai
Dar es Salaam Delhi Hong Kong Istanbul Karachi Kolkata
Kuala Lumpur Madrid Melbourne Mexico City Mumbai Nairobi
São Paulo Shanghai Singapore Taipei Tokyo Toronto
with an associated company in Berlin

Oxford is a registered trade mark of Oxford University Press
in the UK and in certain other countries

Published in the United States
by Oxford University Press Inc., New York

British Library Cataloguing in Publication Data
Data available

Library of Congress Cataloging in Publication Data
Data available

ISBN 0–19–870047–4 (hbk)
ISBN 0–19–870048–2 (pbk)

10 9 8 7 6 5 4 3 2 1

Typeset in Adobe Minion
by RefineCatch Limited, Bungay, Suffolk
Printed in Great Britain by
T. J. International, Padstow, Cornwall

General Editor's Preface

Over the last three decades historians have begun to interpret Europe's past in new ways. In part this reflects changes within Europe itself, the declining importance of the individual European states in an increasingly global world, the moves towards closer political and economic integration amongst the European states, and Europe's rapidly changing relations with the non-European world. It also reflects broader intellectual changes rooted in the experience of the twentieth century that have brought new fields of historical inquiry into prominence and have radically changed the ways in which historians approach the past.

The new *Oxford Short History of Europe* series, of which this *Short History of Italy* is part, offers an important and timely opportunity to explore how the histories of the contemporary European national communities are being rewritten. Covering a chronological span from late antiquity to the present, the *Oxford Short History of Italy* is organized in seven volumes, to which over seventy specialists in different fields and periods of Italian history will contribute. Each volume will provide clear and concise accounts of how each period of Italy's history is currently being redefined, and their collective purpose is to show how an older perspective that reduced Italy's past to the quest of a nation for statehood and independence has now been displaced by different and new perspectives.

The fact that Italy's history has long been dominated by the modern nation-state and its origins simply reflects one particular variant on a pattern evident throughout Europe. When from the eighteenth century onwards Italian writers turned to the past to retrace the origins of their nation and its quest for independent nationhood, they were doing the same as their counterparts elsewhere in Europe. But their search for the nation imposed a periodization on Italy's past that has survived to the present, even if the original intent has been lost or redefined. Focusing their attention on those periods— the Middle Ages, the *Renaissance*, the *Risorgimento*—that seemed to anticipate the modern, they carefully averted their gaze from those that did not, the Dark Ages, and the centuries of foreign occupation and conquest after the sack of Rome in 1527.

Paradoxically, this search for unity segmented Italy's past both chronologically and geographically, since those regions (notably the South) deemed to have contributed less to the quest for nationhood were also ignored. It also accentuated the discontinuities of Italian history caused by foreign conquest and invasion, so that Italy's successive rebirths—the *Renaissance* and the *Risorgimento*—came to symbolize all that was distinctive and exceptional in Italian history. Fascism then carried the cycle of triumph and disaster forward into the twentieth century, thereby adding to the conviction that Italy's history was exceptional, the belief that it was in some essential sense also deeply flawed. Post-war historians redrew Italy's past in bleaker terms, but used the same retrospective logic as before to link fascism to failings deeply rooted in Italy's recent and more distant past.

Seen from the end of the twentieth century this heavily retrospective reasoning appears anachronistic and inadequate. But although these older perspectives continue to find an afterlife in countless textbooks, they have been displaced by a more contemporary awareness that in both the present and the past the different European national communities have no single history, but instead many different histories.

The volumes in the *Short History of Italy* will show how Italy's history too is being rethought in these terms. Its new histories are being constructed around the political, cultural, religious and economic institutions from which Italy's history has drawn continuities that have outlasted changing fortunes of foreign conquest and invasion. In each period their focus is the peoples and societies that have inhabited the Italian peninsula, on the ways in which political organization, economic activity, social identities, and organization were shaped in the contexts and meanings of their own age.

These perspectives make possible a more comparative history, one that shows more clearly how Italy's history has been distinctive without being exceptional. They also enable us to write a history of Italians that is fuller and more continuous, recovering the previously 'forgotten' centuries and geographical regions while revising our understanding of those that are more familiar. In each period Italy's many different histories can also be positioned more closely in the constantly changing European and Mediterranean worlds of which Italians have always been part.

John A. Davis

Contents

List of contributors

CLAUDIO AZZARA is professor of medieval history at the University of Salerno. Publications: *Venetiae. Determinazione di un'area regionale fra antichità e altomedioevo* (Treviso, 1994); *L'ideologia del potere regio nel papato altomedievale (sec. VI–VIII)* (Spoleto, 1997); 'Pater vester clementissimus imperator. Le relazioni tra i franchi e Bisanzio nella prospettiva del papato del VI secolo', *Studi medievali*, 3rd ser., 36 (1995), pp. 303–20.

ATTILIO BARTOLI LANGELI is professor of Latin paleography at the University of Padua. Publications: 'Scritture e libri. Da Alcuino a Gutemberg', in G. Ortalli (ed.), *Storia d'Europa*, iii: *Il medioevo (secoli V–XV)* (Turin, 1994), pp. 935–83; 'Gli scritti di Francesco. L'autografia di un illitteratus', in *Frate Francesco d'Assisi. Atti del XXI convegno internazionale di studi francescani* (Spoleto, 1994), pp. 101–59; *La scrittura dell'italiano* (Bologna, 2000); *Gli autografi di frate Francesco e di frate Leone* (Turnhout, 2000); 'Le forme dei documenti italiani tra alto e basso medioevo (secoli VI–XI)', in G. G. Fissore (ed.), *Storia del medioevo italiano*, vii: *Scritture e memoria del potere* (Rome, in press); editor of *Nolens intestatus decedere. Il testamento come fonte per la storia religiosa e sociale* (Perugia, 1985).

FRANÇOIS BOUGARD is maître de conférence at the University of Paris X–Nanterre. Since 1996 he has been director of medieval studies of the École Française de Rome. Publications: *La Justice dans le royaume d'Italie de la fin du VIIIe siècle au début du XIe siècle* (Rome, 1995); *Paul Diacre, 'Histoire des Lombards'. Traduction, présentation et notes* (Turnhout, 1994); 'Palais royaux et impériaux de l'Italie carolingienne et ottonienne', in *Palais royaux et princiers au moyen âge. Actes du colloque international tenu au Mans les 6, 7 et 8 octobre 1994* (Le Mans, 1996), pp. 181–96.

FLAVIA DE RUBEIS teaches medieval epigraphy at the University 'Ca' Foscari' of Venice. Publications: 'La scrittura epigrafica in età longobarda', in C. Bertelli and G. P. Brogiolo (eds.), *Il futuro dei longobardi. L'Italia e la costruzione dell'Europa di Carlo Magno. Saggi* (Milan, 2000), pp. 71–83; 'La tradizione epigrafica in Paolo Diacono', in

P. Chiesa (ed.), *Paolo Diacono. Uno scrittore fra tradizione longobarda e rinnovamento carolingio* (Udine, 2000), pp. 139–62; 'Le epigrafi dei re longobardi', in F. Stella (ed.), *Poesia dell'alto medioevo europeo: manoscritti, lingua e musica dei ritmi latini. Atti delle Euroconferenze per il Corpus dei ritmi latini (IV–IX sec.)* (Florence, 2000), pp. 223–40.

RICCARDO FRANCOVICH is professor of medieval archaeology at the University of Siena and director of *Archeologia medievale*. Publications: *Rocca San Silvestro* (Rome, 1991); *La ceramica medievale a Siena e nella Toscana meridionale* (Florence, 1982); *Le ragioni di un parco alle radici dell'archeologia mineraria*, (Venice, 1994); editor of *Archeologia e storia del medioevo italiano* (Rome, 1987); editor (with D. Manacorda) of *Dizionario di archeologia* (Rome, 2000).

STEFANO GASPARRI is professor of medieval history at the University 'Ca' Foscari' of Venice. Publications: *La cultura tradizionale dei longobardi* (Spoleto, 1986); *I milites cittadini. Studi sulla cavalleria in Italia* (Rome, 1994); *Prima delle nazioni* (Rome, 1996).

SAURO GELICHI is professor of medieval archaeology at the University 'Ca' Foscari' of Venice, and president of the Society of Italian Medieval Archaeologists. Publications: *Introduzione all'archeologia medievale. Storia e ricerca in Italia* (Rome, 1997); (with G. P. Brogiolo) *La città nell'alto medioevo italiano. Archeologia e storia* (Rome, 1998).

CRISTINA LA ROCCA is professor of medieval history at the University of Padua and joint editor of *Archeologia Medievale*. Publications: *Pacifico di Verona. Il passato carolingio nella costruzione della memoria urbana* (Rome, 1995); *Da Testona a Moncalieri. La dinamica del popolamento nella collina torinese* (Turin, 1986); with D. Modonesi she is the editor of *Materiali di età longobarda nel veronese* (Verona, 1989).

WALTER POHL is director of medieval studies of the Austrian Academy of Sciences in Vienna, and teaches medieval history at the University of Vienna. Publications: *Die Awaren* (Vienna, 1988); *Die Germanen* (Vienna, 2000); *Le origini etniche dell'Europa* (Rome, 2000); *Werkstätte der Erinnerung. Montecassino und die Gestaltung der langobardischen Vergangenheit* (Vienna, 2001).

CLAUDIA VILLA is professor of medieval philology at the University of Bergamo. Publications: *La 'Lectura Terentii' da Ildemaro a Francesco Petrarca* (Padua, 1984); 'Trittico per Federico II *Immutator mundi*',

Aevum, 71 (1997), pp. 331–58; 'Die Horazüberlieferung und die "Bibliothek Karls des Großen". Zum Werkverzeichnis des Handschrift Berlin, Diez B.66', *Deutsches Archiv für Erforschung des Mittelalters*, 51 (1995), pp. 29–52.

CHRIS WICKHAM is professor of early medieval history at the University of Birmingham. Publications: *Early Medieval Italy* (London, 1981); *Land and Power* (London, 1995); *Community and Clientele* (Oxford, 1998); *Legge, pratiche e conflitti* (Rome, 2000).

Abbreviations

Introduction

Cristina La Rocca

The identity of a distant past

An introduction to this volume on Italy in the early medieval period has to start by explaining how historical approaches to this period have changed in recent years. This is not a question of discussing more general shifts in historical interpretation or the influence of different historiographical schools, but rather of positioning the essays that make up the volume in their specific historiographical context, since each of the topics addressed in this book has been deeply influenced by new research, by the new methods that have been adopted, and by the conclusions that have been drawn from them.

In fact, the early medieval period is now one of the most interesting and innovative fields in European historical writing in Italy in general, and perhaps the one that has been most open to new interpretations. The scale and quality of recent research has been impressive; the new interpretations that are beginning to emerge are only partly the result of the use of new and much wider types of source, and have more to do with the new perspectives that historians have brought to the study of the early Middle Ages. The very varied backgrounds of the scholars currently studying the early medieval period in different European countries has been an excellent antidote to the exclusively national perspectives in which each European society had previously studied its own early medieval past. In those perspectives, the early Middle Ages were invariably treated as the moment when the national history of each society began, and in which the distinctive features of the modern national society were already formed and visible. Put another way, the early Middle Ages often simply served as a mirror to the cultural and political aspirations of nineteenth-century elites.[1] But although the period between the fifth and the tenth centuries has been studied as fully in Italy as elsewhere in Europe, and despite the importance and quality of recent research and the new archaeological excavations on urban and rural sites that have been started since the 1980s, this period continues to be considered as one of only minor interest in Italy.

The fact is that ever since national unification in the mid-nineteenth century the Italians have looked on the early medieval period with diffidence. For writers of the *Risorgimento*, the period from the fifth and the tenth centuries was associated primarily with the dispersion and fragmentation of the territorial unity that had been achieved in earlier Roman times as a result of the invasions by 'barbarian' and 'foreign' peoples who destroyed the political freedom of the local inhabitants and took the place of the Romans as rulers of Italy. In this way the rhetoric of *Risorgimento* associated Italy's lost territorial unity with the suffocating presence of the foreign invaders and oppressors. The 'Germans' were held to have been responsible for the decline in every aspect of Italian society and for the political subjection of the 'Italians'. In fact, the early medieval period came to represent the condition of Italy before Unification and independence, so that while other European nations looked to the early Middle Ages as the period from which they had originated, in Italy, by contrast, the period was seen simply as one of abject subordination and decline.[2]

Despite new research and changing attitudes this ideological matrix has gone unchallenged for a very long time, and has continued to condition the ways in which Italian medieval historians viewed the early medieval past. Had they been asked to define the distinctive features of Italian history in this long period of time, they would have replied unequivocally in one of two ways. Either they would have stressed the continuity with earlier Roman traditions that was evident in the survival of lively urban centres as well as in many other aspects of institutional and material life, or they would have regretfully

[1] A. Banti, *La nazione del Risorgimento. Parentea, santità e onore alle origini dell' Italia unita* (Turin, 2000); E. Artifoni, 'Il medioevo nel Romanticismo. Forme della storiografia tra Sette e Ottocento', in G. Cavallo, C. Leonardi, and E. Menestò (eds.), *Lo spazio letterario del Medioevo, i: Il Medioevo latino*, iv (Rome, 1997), pp. 175–221.

[2] C. Wickham, 'Problems of comparing Rural Societies in Early Medieval Western Europe', in *Land and Power: Studies in Italian and European Social History, 400–1200* (London, 1994), pp. 201–26.

insisted on the total nature of the break with the past that followed
the Lombard invasions of 568 or 569 which marked the true beginning of the 'Dark Ages'. This clash of opposites was epitomized in the
image of the encounters between the civilized locals (the Romans)
and uncouth and ignorant barbarians (the Lombards) that would
over time result in what was termed a process of 'acculturation' (a
term first used by anthropologists and then adopted by archaeologists
to describe the fusion of formerly separated and distinct traditions).
The argument was that the Lombards learned from the Romans to
appreciate and exploit the external forms and apparatus of power
(first of all the use of Latin in its written form) while Italian society
would become structured hierarchically along 'typically Germanic'
models that derived from a military lifestyle. The fusion between
Romans and Lombards was complicated by the successive Carolingian domination in northern Italy, and by the Byzantine and Muslim
presences in central and southern Italy. This would finally be the
cause of the crisis of the tenth century (the 'iron century', as it was
significantly termed) when these internal contradictions would
finally explode in ways that enabled Roman legal traditions to
resurface, paving the way for the recovery of the original and 'civilized' features of Italian society. In this perspective, however, the early
Middle Ages in Italy were simply a long and painful period of labour
during which the new elements of civic consciousness and institutional maturity that would characterize the Italian *comuni* from the
late eleventh century onwards were emerging.

Even though the terms have obviously changed since the nineteenth century, the period continued to be portrayed in ways that
underlined the distinctions between the traditions and cultures of the
'invaders' and of the 'invaded' and relied on adversarial dichotomies:
Romans and Germans; Arians or pagan Lombards and Catholic
Romans; 'rural' Lombards and 'urban' Romans; and so forth. Driven
by the desire to separate the two distinctive souls of early medieval
'Italian' society, historians were more interested in juridical institutions than in society itself, in norms rather than practice, in terminology rather than substance, and finally in the period that followed
the Lombard migration rather than that which preceded it.[3] As a

[3] G. Tabacco, 'Problemi di popolamento e di insediamento nell'alto medioevo',
Rivista storica italiana 79 (1967), pp. 67–110; G. Tabacco, 'Latinità e germanesimo nella
tradizione medievistica italiana', *Rivista storica italiana* 102 (1990), pp. 691–716.

result they turned the early Middle Ages into a remote and incomprehensible past, a time when foreign, 'typically Germanic', and deeply alien mentalities and institutions were forced on the native populations, in the process sacrificing the distinctive 'indigenous' features of local cultures. This also meant that the period from the fifth to the tenth centuries was studied and evaluated primarily in moral terms.

Although the period attracted a considerable amount of research, especially in the years immediately after national unification and again after the Second World War, this was largely concerned with constructing a 'reality' that no longer bore any relation to fact. Yet these studies became a sort of academic testing ground, and no one could progress in the academy without being able to show that they understood the intricacy of the mysterious 'Germanic' universe, even though the belief that this period was of any significance for understanding the origins of contemporary society was rapidly waning. This was evident, too, in the terrible monotony of the subjects studied and the very limited variety of the sources used. While it is true that there was a radical decline in the number of written sources that began in the sixth century and got worse in the seventh century, for a long time historians continued to rely almost exclusively on just two passages from Paul the Deacon (who was writing at the end of the eighth century) and a few paragraphs from Tacitus' *Germania* (written in the first century AD) to describe the status of the subjugated Romans and the destruction of their elite during the Lombard invasion. From these narrow and anachronistic sources historians drew images that emphasized on the one hand the survival of 'ancestral' and immutable customs and habits and on the other the prevailing conditions of violence and destruction to portray the melancholic landscape of a decaying society.

The repetitive nature of this research went hand in hand with a total lack of interest in uncovering, never mind editing or analysing, new written or material sources for the early medieval period. Although from the beginning of the eighth century onwards the repertory of documentary sources became wider and more varied for Italy than for anywhere else in Europe, publication of editions of royal charters and private documents did not start until the 1920s, and even then was done without any real system and not always to the highest scholarly standards, while the editions of private documents still remained far from complete. But that was not all: even during the heyday of nineteenth-century positivism, interest in the materials found in 'barbarian' tombs with grave-goods—which in other European countries provided the evidence around which the material culture of these societies was reconstructed—also declined before completely disappearing in the Fascist era. The problem was that the archaeological sources did not seem to answer the key questions posed by historians: How many types of 'invader' had there been? How could they be distinguished from 'Italians'? What were their 'strategies' in occupying the territory? Since archaeologists seemed unable to give any clear and satisfactory answers, these sources were deemed to be of no public interest and of relevance only for purely local history or for historians of the minor arts.[4] These distinctions between national and 'official' and 'local' and amateur studies gave rise to a dual, albeit hardly compatible, set of classifications. For academic historians the early Middle Ages were considered a part of the past to be dispensed with as quickly as possible, whereas at a local level the sites and documents from the period were a source of civic pride, making some king or queen, lord or bishop, or benefactor or founder of a monastery an illustrious fellow citizen and hence a 'local hero' who by association boosted the community's status.[5]

Gian Piero Bognetti's reworking of the early Middle Ages

The idea that the Lombard era marked a break between what preceded and what followed it (since Theoderic's Goths had been forgiven and accepted within the 'civilized' world, because of their generally respectful behaviour and the homage they paid to the Roman world) was given a new lease of life during the 1950s by the work of Gian Piero Bognetti. As historian of the legal institutions in

[4] C. La Rocca, 'Uno specialismo mancato. Esordi e fallimento dell'archeologia medievale italiana alla fine dell'Ottocento', *Archeologia medievale* 20 (1993), pp. 13–43.

[5] E. Artifoni, 'Ideologia e memoria locale nella storiografia italiana sui Longobardi', in G. P. Brogiolo and C. Bertelli (eds.), *Il futuro dei longobardi. Saggi* (Brescia 2000), pp. 219–27.

the early medieval period, Bognetti became known as the 'inventor of the Lombards' because in a number of influential studies he argued that the Lombards had created a completely new society that was quite different from the past. According to Bognetti, the great innovation of the Lombards was to get rid of the corrupt, bureaucratic, and decrepit society based on Roman and Byzantine models, and replace it with one that was youthful and vigorous, primitive and naive but therefore also strong and lively. The traditional contrast between the two rival souls of early medieval 'Italian' society as a result not only became sharper but was now also the basis for measuring the long-term political and social consequences of the invasion.

Bognetti's concern was not to measure what had been lost from the past, but to gauge what had been gained from the infusion of the new 'Germanic' elements that now became a part of Italian history and survived down to the late Middle Ages and beyond. The historian's task was to identify what was 'new' and what was 'old' in every aspect of society, and what had survived in the long term. This meant addressing new questions and using new types of evidence to reconstruct the primitive and original world from which the new had originated. This had often to be invented. The strong Catholic convictions of Bognetti and his followers, for example, led them to argue that the conversion of the Lombards to Catholicism was the principal source of stability in their 'new' society, and to attribute a fundamental and active role to the papacy in shaping the organization of Lombard society. Insisting on the stubborn and primitive features of Lombard paganism, and especially Arianism, Bognetti described the difficult and praiseworthy intervention of the Roman church and its unrelenting efforts at evangelizing to the point of proposing genuine 'missions' of conversion, similar to those of Boniface in Germany, whose success would lead to the founding of new churches built on former Arian or heathen shrines and dedicated to saints that 'specialized' in this symbolic function. Through the fundamental teachings of the papacy and the bishops, the primitive strength of the Lombard thus became an 'educated' and enduring strength.

From a methodological point of view, Bognetti's work focused attention on the search for the roots of Lombard society and culture through the study of the linguistic, terminological, and institutional traces that had survived in documents of later times, so that both 'local' and national historians now redrew the 'Dark Ages' from late medieval sources. Despite the great variety of local contexts and of written documents, these reconstructions followed the lines already set out by Bognetti himself.[6] In every location it was claimed that the Lombards had settled 'strategically' next to a road, a river, or a border, taking as proof of this terms like *fara* and *sala* which were typically Lombard and therefore certainly originated from the period of their rule (while, in fact, these were two quite common terms that quickly became part of everyday language), or the churches dedicated to St George, St Martin, or, better still, St Michael, the foundation of which could be safely dated beyond doubt.

Emphasis on the uniform character of the Lombard settlements in every region of Italy gave rise to an unspoken assumption that everything had now been said on the subject of Lombard culture and society. Research on early medieval Italy based on written sources therefore shifted to later periods, taking the innovatory character of the Lombard era for granted and of relevance only for tracing the prehistory of later phenomena. The strong local perspective of the surviving Italian documents also encouraged the study of the institutional organization of the local societies that had originated after the Carolingian conquest of the Lombard kingdom, and these studies focused primarily on the development and transformation of territorial organization and on the shift from public to private power with the rise of new dynastic properties among the seigneurial elite which was completed during and after the eleventh century.[7]

Back to the sources

The turning point in academic research on early medieval Italy took place in the 1970s, and was driven by a much more thorough and direct use of the sources. In the case of written sources, this took the form of much closer analysis of familiar materials. In palaeography, for example, it meant returning to the originals of preserved documents

---

[6] G. P. Bognetti, 'I loca sanctorum e la storia della Chiesa nel regno dei Longobardi', in *L'età longobarda*, iii (Milan, 1967), pp. 305–45; on Bognetti's historiography, see G. Tabacco, 'Espedienti politici e persuasioni religiose nel medioevo di Gian Piero Bognetti', *Rivista di storia della Chiesa in Italia* 24 (1970), pp. 504–23.

[7] e.g. G. Sergi, *I confini del potere* (Turin, 1995).

and the careful study of their external as well as their intrinsic features (that is to say their form, the graphic materials, and the language used) in addition to their contents and the formulas they used. The study of codices as material objects also led researchers to consider them not as separate single texts but rather as groups of texts connected to each other, and as objects designed to be ordered, read, and preserved. A catalogue of the rich epigraphic materials that had previously been completely ignored is currently being compiled, and will enable these materials to be analysed in ways that are both formalistic (with reference, for example, to the writing techniques used) and also oriented towards the purchasers and the uses to which epigraphy could be put. Inscriptions are now studied as products whose purpose was to express—through their graphic form and their texts—the social status of the purchasers.

As well as new ways of studying the wealth of written sources, the new ways of writing the history of the early Middle Ages have been made possible by the veritable explosion of new data derived from archaeological sources. It has been the birth of medieval archaeology as an academic discipline distinct from Christian archaeology, which traditionally has been concerned primarily with studying the monumental traces of early Christianity, that has given the strongest impulse, in Italy as elsewhere in Europe, to the study of early medieval history. The new archaeological research has followed two main paths. It has enabled historians to reconsider subjects that had previously been studied only on the basis of written sources. But it has also brought to light new questions and offered new ways of understanding the history of early medieval Italy. The study of towns, for example, has now been completely freed from the old question of continuity and discontinuity with earlier Roman structures, and is set instead in the perspective of different patterns of regional transformation and above all in the shifting relations between political and economic organization, The fundamental importance of archaeological evidence can also be seen in the new questions being asked about the differing organizational patterns of the rural landscape, which can be reconstructed through the study of the changing functions of buildings and settlements, changing economic resources, types of land use and farming. It has also made possible study of the role played by the aristocracy in founding residential buildings and monasteries, while information on the circulation of certain types of ceramics has made possible the study of commercial and economic activities.

All these examples illustrate the fundamental importance of archaeology in stimulating new historical debates, which increasingly engage archaeologists as well as historians. This does not mean, however, that the conclusions and interpretations reached by archaeologists and historians on the basis of their own particular sources are always compatible. More often than not, as can clearly be seen in the essays in this volume, they are not compatible at all. But these disagreements and the alternative explanations to which they give rise are in themselves a measure of the vitality of current research and debate on this period. The great expansion of the source materials thanks to new archaeological data has made a major contribution to every field of research, and archaeological data have made a fundamental contribution to the ways in which all the topics and themes addressed in this volume are now studied. Even when it comes to questions like the changing nature of public power, or that of ecclesiastical institutions and the papacy, the sources used in the past can now be augmented by information derived from the material manifestations of power (such as the symbols of power, the material wealth, the siting and organization of solemn public meetings, and the types of building associated with power). Taken together with the data on the institutional and juridical dimensions of power, these sources enable us to study not only institutional changes but also of the reasons that lay behind them and the context in which they took place.

Two more aspects deserve to be mentioned in terms of new perspectives and the demise of established traditions. The first is the question of 'ethnicity', which has now been replaced by the study of the cultural and social identities of the elites. Secondly, contemporary research has by and large abandoned the idea that the lay and ecclesiastical spheres were rigidly separated, and has shown instead the considerable degree of interlinkage between the two, especially in terms of family strategies. On the other hand, recent studies have also challenged the widely accepted view that a written culture that emanated exclusively from the ecclesiastical world was the single vehicle of cultural transmission, taking evidence from the study of epigraphs, codices, and private charters to demonstrate the existence of alternatives.

There is a great deal still to be done, however. To justify at least in part the thematic and regional gaps that will be evident in this volume, it has to be said that the new research has been more vigorous in central and northern Italy, while in southern Italy and the islands institutional themes like the structure of monarchy and of vassalage continue to dominate. These essays will also show how the period with which this volume ends—the one around the turn of the millennium—is studied in ways that look forward towards the development of the more complex ecclesiastical institutions that accompanied the later Reformation of the eleventh- and twelfth-centuries. In the case of the reconstruction of settlement patterns and rural landscapes, however, the cut-off point is, by contrast, the tenth century. These different chronologies relate in part to the timing of changes in particular areas. But it is not a matter of chance that the tenth century emerges in a somewhat fragmented and irregular form. It has an ambiguous status, being both the last century of the early Middle Ages and the beginning of the central part of the Middle Ages. Depending on each scholar's field of specialization, it is as a result either a period of final breakdown or the point of departure. Almost certainly it will be on this century that future research in all the fields discussed in this volume will come to be focused.

As this volume goes to print, I would like to take the opportunity to thank John Davis for his unfailing assistance with every aspect of the book's preparation, as well as Andrew MacLennan, Fiona Kinnear, Jo Stanbridge, and Matthew Cotton for their technical support and their great professional skills, the translators: Andrea Pennacchi (Introduction), Antonio Sennis and Nichola Anderson (chapter 2), Geraldine Ludbrook (chapters 3, 4, 5, 7), Jeremy Scott (chapter 8), Richard Davis (chapter 9), Eric Ingaldson (chapter 10), John Davis (chapter 11), and finally, all the authors for their punctuality and willingness. I hope that this volume will play a part in bringing to an end both the ethnic prejudice against the 'German invaders' and the more contemporary ethnic *topos* reflected in the words of an anonymous reviewer of this project: 'Italian scholars are not usually renowned for their brevity and even the most laconic of scholars would find it difficult to do justice to some of these complex topics in 5,000, 7,500 or even 9,000 words.'

Padova, October 2001

Invasions and ethnic identity

Walter Pohl

Romans and barbarians in late Roman Italy

To modern eyes Roman Italy had a very distinct identity, and its Romanness was expressed in numerous cultural features: architecture and crafts, mosaics and inscriptions, institutions and law, literature and education. Indeed, few pre-modern societies have left such lasting marks on the landscape, and in the memories of many generations to come. Still, as Andrea Giardina has argued, Roman Italy had not quite achieved an identity of its own; his book is appropriately titled *Roman Italy: Histories of an Incomplete Identity*. Early Rome had conquered an ethnically heterogeneous country, with *Veneti* and Celts in the North, Etruscans in the Centre, several regional peoples in the South, and Greeks along some of the coastlines. The Romans, in turn, cherished their mythical Trojan origins. Paradoxically, it was the very success of Roman expansion that left little room for the development of an ethnic Roman-Italian identity. In 48 AD, when the emperor Claudius opened the senate to non-Italians a ferocious debate ensued about the value of Italian *consanguinitas*, blood relationship, which proved to be too artificial to be convincing for many contemporaries.[1] As a result, Romanness remained what it had always been: a political identity that easily accommodated those who had the means, and the conviction, to live by its rules. It was precisely this

---

[1] A. Giardina, *L'Italia romana. Storie di una identità incompiuta* (Rome, Bari, 1997), pp. 3–10.

tension between a strict definition of what it meant to be Roman, and a considerable flexibility as to who could become Roman, that made the Roman model so successful, even in times of crisis (for instance, in the third century). It also coexisted perfectly with civic, regional, or even 'ethnic' identities, many of which survived, however transformed, the centuries of Roman rule in Italy. Thus, for instance, Greek identities in the South going back to the pre-Roman *Magna Grecia* could provide a basis for Byzantine rule up to the eleventh century.

The barbarian invaders of Italy constitute another clear-cut image in the modern mind: fair-haired and blue-eyed heavy-drinking and riotous Germanic warriors, clad in filthy furs, whose plain but violent ways replaced the decadent sophistication of late Rome. The modern image of the barbarian goes back to the long tradition of ethnocentric stereotypes and perceptions in antiquity. The word 'barbarian' itself is of Greek origin, and meant those who could only mutter indistinct gibberish instead of speaking proper Greek. It was then used simply to describe non-Romans, so that barbarians came to be seen as uncivilized, violent, and treacherous, although critics of Roman decadence such as Tacitus and later critics of Christian sinfulness sometimes depicted them as uncorrupted and noble savages.

Like Gibbon watching the sun set over the Roman forum, generations of Europeans have wondered why Rome fell to those barbarians. Down to the present, historians remain divided, with Italian, French, and Spanish historians speaking of 'invasions', while German and English scholars call the same process 'migrations'. Did Rome 'decline and fall', or was it destroyed by invading barbarians? A less controversial and more inclusive concept is the 'transformation of the Roman world'. In this perspective the antagonism between Romans and barbarians was not the key issue as it had been in ancient, medieval and modern thought, and newer approaches have placed greater emphasis on the more complex processes through which the barbarians were integrated into changing late Roman societies. These processes were full of contradictions, conflict, and bloodshed; but more often than not the conflict was not between invaders and others, but developed along different lines.

Italy, as the heart of the empire, had always been a focus of migrations and communications in the Mediterranean and beyond. Italy needed its barbarians: it imported and attracted them. The number of foreign slaves who came to Italy in the centuries of Roman rule can only be guessed at, but there is no doubt that their manpower was essential to the ancient economy. Prisoners of war were regularly sold as slaves; entire groups of defeated barbarians were settled as *laeti* or *dediticii* in late antique Italy and in other provinces. At the imperial court in Rome (and later, Milan and Ravenna), noble barbarians lived as hostages or refugees, and barbarian soldiers played an important role in the emperor's bodyguard. In fact, it was in the army that barbarians were increasingly welcome. Here, in late antiquity, soldiers of barbarian origin could also rise to the highest ranks. By the time of Theodosius I (d. 395), a majority of 'Roman' officers were in fact barbarians. The most successful among them, the Vandal Stilicho, became consul and patrician and dominated politics in the west after the death of Theodosius. From the third century onwards, internal conflicts and the needs of defence against barbarian incursions had increased Rome's need for soldiers, and many barbarians were prepared to face any risk in return for a share in Rome's goods and prestige. In times of relative peace, Italy saw little of its barbarian defenders. But slowly, they moved closer to the inner circles of power.

The gradual militarization of the Roman world meant that civil society increasingly lost its control over the armed forces. But much of the inner unrest of the fifth century was also due to the attempts by senatorial aristocrats to expand their power. The leading senators still enjoyed a unique position, with huge estates scattered across the empire, traditional careers in the civil service that gave access to the inner circles of power, and political networks that could be the basis for far-reaching alliances. But parallel to the conservative outlook of this ruling elite, a different Roman-barbarian culture of power also came into being. For a long time the army had been an agent of Romanization, but now it also encouraged the rise of sub-imperial identities. The *esprit de corps* cultivated in Roman army units paradoxically encouraged the growth of new ethnic identities within the late Roman system. As political control over the army declined, these more particular loyalties gradually became more important than obedience to the empire. The power of many commanders, for example the fifth-century Roman general and warlord Aetius, was now based on the personal devotion of their soldiers in ways that had some precedent in earlier Roman history. But when they died or were removed from their commands, the armies they had built around their personal leadership were disbanded. Their position in court politics was also precarious and when Stilicho was overthrown in 407 a massacre of barbarians followed and the core of his troops joined Alaric's armies. Because Alaric, a Roman general of Gothic origin, succeeded in attracting different ethnic loyalties to his army, it proved less vulnerable to defeat or to a change of leaders.

The Goths were the most successful of these groups. Even though the two strongest Gothic powers north of the lower Danube and the Black Sea had succumbed to the Huns around 375, the Goths enjoyed an unrivalled prestige as barbarian soldiers because they were both ferocious fighters and willing to adapt to Roman ways. Whether derived from genealogy, tradition, or imitation, Gothic identity opened the door to military careers in the empire. After the emperor Valens had lost the battle of Adrianople (378) against a Gothic-led alliance of recent immigrants, Rome had been forced to accommodate groups of Goths as quasi-autonomous federates in Roman provinces. Technically, these were components of the Roman army, but at the same time they were able to improve their position through negotiation and blackmail. Alaric, king of the Goths, who moved to Italy around 400 and sacked Rome in 410, was the first barbarian leader who successfully built up an autonomous, albeit precarious non-Roman power base in Italy which enabled him to negotiate a key role in western Roman politics for his Goths. But even his dazzling victories were not sufficient to guarantee a secure hold in the shifting sands of the Italian balance of power; his heirs would prove more successful elsewhere, establishing the Visigothic kingdom in Aquitaine and Spain. In Italy the political elite carefully avoided allowing the Goths to become too strong as a single group, although this required occasional purges in the army.

Other barbarian leaders chose a different strategy. They raised large and heterogeneous armies, and marched into Italy. This was the case of the Goth Radagaisus, whose forces were crushed by Stilicho at Fiesole in 406. Better known is Attila's invasion in 452, after his attack on Gaul had been halted at the Catalaunian Fields in the previous year. Attila assembled a huge army of several tens of thousands of Huns, Goths, Gepids, Heruls, and others, besieged and took Aquileia, and marched as far as Milan, which offered no resistance. Nobody in Italy could have stopped him at this point. But disease and lack of supplies became a problem, while his warriors were already laden with booty. The example of Alaric, to whom the sack of Rome had brought little lasting success, may have served as a warning, but in any case Attila decided to return to Pannonia, where he died soon after. Papal propaganda soon attributed this to Pope Leo's intervention—a legend that has stuck (the scene can be admired on Raphael's fresco in the Vatican). The Huns had long been pictured by Christian preachers as the apocalyptic people of Magog who were sent as a scourge by God to punish the sinful—more a moral drama than a political event in fact. The incursion of Attila's Huns thus became one of the best-known events of the period, although it was in reality little more than an episode whose outcome showed that even an extraordinary concentration of military force was not sufficient to take control over late Roman Italy (which was almost certainly not Attila's aim anyway). Cities abounding in riches could still easily be plundered, as the Vandal king Geiseric proved when he mounted a sudden raid on Rome from the sea a few years later, in 455. But to gain mastery of the old heartland of the empire, it was necessary to employ the machinery that had been set up by the Romans to govern it.

Odoacer and the kingdom of Italy

From 395 until 476, the western emperors were at the mercy of mainly barbarian commanders (the Vandal Stilicho, the Suevian Ricimer, the Burgundian Gundobad), and often the only option the emperors had was to play their generals off against each other. These barbarian generals held the title of *magister militum* as commanders of the field army as well as that of *patricius*. They received yearly subsidies that allowed them to entertain a large retinue of personal followers, called *buccellarii* after the superior type of bread they received compared to ordinary soldiers. In the highest ranks of this military aristocracy the difference between Romans and barbarians was slight; their families intermarried, and they used similar strategies to compete for the same positions. The 'barbarian' Stilicho celebrated his consulate in the traditional Roman way on an elaborate ivory consular diptych, whereas Aetius, the 'last Roman', as Procopius called him, owed much of his success to a devoted retinue of Huns. The only difference was that according to a tacit assumption, barbarians could not become emperors themselves. This was hardly a serious disadvantage, given that most emperors quickly met violent deaths, and the barbarian *patricii* often had the opportunity to 'make' new ones.

Before 476, the neighbouring powers tried in turn to draw this unstable political system into their orbit of power: the Burgundians and the Visigoths in Gaul, and of course the eastern Romans. But it was significant that Odoacer, the first barbarian to consolidate his rule over Italy, had no distinctive political allegiance or ethnic identity. Historians have debated whether he was a German or a Hun, a Herul or a Thuringian. But that is to miss the main point, which is that the ambiguity of the contemporary sources in this respect demonstrates that Odoacer's ethnic identity reflected the heterogeneous character of the Italian field army that he commanded. Odoacer came from Attila's court in Pannonia, a bustling power centre where aristocrats of very different origin, Huns, Goths, Gepids, and many other barbarian peoples as well as Romans, came together and established a network of power that would outlast Attila's death in 453 and the collapse of the empire of the Huns. Odoacer's father, Edica, was one of the notables at the Hunnic court, as were the fathers of Odoacer's predecessor (Romulus Augustulus, the last western emperor) and his successor (Theoderic the Ostrogoth). After 453, Edica established a small kingdom of the Sciri along the middle Danube; when the Ostrogoths shattered it in 469, Odoacer went to Italy, his brother Hunulf to Constantinople. After serving as an imperial bodyguard, Odoacer became commander of the federate troops in Italy, to a considerable extent composed of barbarians who had been conscripted from Pannonia.

In the summer of 476 the federate troops overthrew emperor Romulus Augustulus and his father, Orestes, and made Odoacer their king. The rebellion was not intended to overthrow the empire as such; Odoacer was simply another barbarian king striving for power within the Roman system. But there was a difference: the king sent the imperial insignia to Constantinople, stating that an emperor was no longer needed in the west since his authority no longer extended beyond Italy. Although still nominally subject to the eastern (or Byzantine) empire, Odoacer as a result became the supreme authority in Italy. But his kingdom, which had been set up by a federate army, had no specific ethnic identity. *Odoacer rex* as a result acted as king of Italy, and took up residence in the imperial palace of Ravenna.

Until very recently, modern historians have seen 476 as a critical moment in the fall of the Roman empire in the west, and hence as the point where antiquity came to an end and the Middle Ages began in Italy. But contemporaries showed no awareness of any fundamental change. Odoacer maintained the form and content of the Roman administration of Italy; there was little that was 'Germanic' about his kingdom except for the remote origins of many of his troops (which contemporaries simply called 'barbarian'). It was not until the sixth century, in the reign of Theoderic, that the Romans who for one reason or another opposed him turned to the emperor in Constantinople for support, and began to refer to the barbarian kings in Italy as an anomaly and as a threat to the identity of the Romans. It was at that time that the origins of the problem were dated to Odoacer. Jordanes, who wrote in Constantinople in the 550s, even described the coup of 476 as if it had been a fully-fledged barbarian invasion.[2] The truth was that Odoacer had brought a period of relative peace to Italy; and by contrast it was the emperor who in the end plunged Italy into another bloody war. Theoderic, king of the Goths, was one of his generals who had built up a powerful position in the Balkans at the head of his federate army; in order to remove this threat the Emperor Zeno ordered him to depose Odoacer and rule Italy in his name. Theoderic raised a huge multi-ethnic army and invaded Italy in August 489. After a siege lasting three years Theoderic entered Ravenna, where he treacherously murdered his predecessor and became king in Italy.

Theoderic and the Goths

Who were the Goths? Traditional scholarship assumed that the Goths probably were of Scandinavian origin, lived in modern Poland in the first two centuries AD, then moved to the steppes north of the Black Sea, where they split into Visigoths and Ostrogoths. At the end of their long migrations, the former established kingdoms in southern

[2] Jordanes, *Getica* c. 46, ed. Th. Mommsen (Berlin, 1882), p. 120.

France and Spain, the latter in Italy. But thanks to the ground-breaking work of Herwig Wolfram, we now know better. Numerous different groups of barbarians were referred to as Goths between the third and the sixth centuries: they included raiders and pirates in the Aegean, traders in the Crimea, peasants in the Balkans, enemies and allies of the Huns, units of the Roman army, and, last but not least, the followers of the dynasties that established the two Gothic kingdoms on Roman territory. These groups fluctuated, drew in people of very diverse origin, grew with success and waned with failure, and were in turn supported, kept at bay, or wiped out by the Romans. The term 'Goth' was frequently used by Roman writers, and in late antiquity it was often used for any non-Hunnic peoples who came from the eastern steppes. They were not regarded as Germans but were classed as Scythians, like the Huns. Then nineteenth-century philologists claimed that Gothic was a Germanic language, and consequently a new concept of Germanness was created that determined the ways in which the historical role of the Goths was interpreted.

Recently, it has been suggested that the term 'Goth' may have been just a convenient label for a privileged military elite enjoying the benefits of the Roman system rather than the inherited and carefully preserved identity of thousands of Ostrogothic soldiers. It is hard to imagine that the Goths were simply an invention, and if individual Goths were not explicitly called Goths in our sources this was probably because that would have been unnecessary. On the other hand, it is unclear how many of the Italian Goths of the sixth century were descended from Attila's Goths in the fifth, or even from Black Sea Goths in the fourth century. Their history was deeply fragmented, and Goths had fought (and died) in the front line on both sides in almost all of the major battles of the age (for instance, on the Catalaunian Plains). The prestige and privilege of the Goths drew new bands of barbarians to join them at different times. But knowing exactly where the parents and the grandparents of the Goths who followed Theoderic to Italy came from would tell us less about them than traditional scholarship assumed, because in Italy, to be a Goth was associated primarily with specific social roles that conferred privileges and gave rise to certain expectations.

The army with which Theoderic had conquered Italy probably consisted of some 30,000 soldiers, and when the women, children and slaves are included may have risen to some 100,000 people. In Italy it was joined by some of Odoacer's troops. The Goths and their barbarian allies were, therefore, a small minority in a country whose inhabitants amounted to several millions. Why the huge Roman population accepted being governed by barbarians is beside the point, however. For a long time Roman armies had been largely composed of barbarians, while Roman tax collectors were widely seen as oppressors, so we can assume that the majority of the people had stopped worrying about who exactly governed them. Although the Roman aristocrats despised the barbarians, many also believed that they could use them to their own purposes. Indeed, Theoderic sought the support of the senators and employed Roman specialists in civil administration (like Cassiodorus and Liberius) to help the Goths to settle and guarantee their supplies.[3] Historians have recently debated whether the Gothic soldiers, who were mainly garrisoned in the cities, received allocations from tax revenues or land. It seems likely that initially the Goths were supported from tax revenues, but in the long run many of them also acquired landed property.[4]

Theoderic and his Roman advisers looked to create a lasting cultural mix in which the Goths would preserve their special status and prestige while adapting to the customs and culture of Roman society. A great deal of effort went into curbing any outrages that Gothic warriors might commit and to reassuring the Roman population that life would continue as before. There were only certain areas where the Goths refused to adapt. They continued to adhere to the Arian creed, referred to as the *lex Gothica* or Gothic law in our sources. It is no coincidence that the only extensive text in Gothic that has survived is the so-called Codex Argenteus, a sumptuous Gothic bible, which is the earliest known long text in any Germanic language. Goths had their own Arian churches (as can still be seen in Ravenna), and surviving documents written by clerics show that Gothic was spoken there.

Theoderic's reign (493–526) gave Italy a period of peace and relative prosperity. But consensus among the senators slowly eroded and as Justinian (527–65) consolidated his authority over the Byzantine

[3] Cf. Cassiodorus, *Variae*, trans. S. J. B. Barnish (Liverpool, 1992).
[4] See W. Goffart, *Barbarians and Romans, A.D. 418–584: The Techniques of Accommodation* (Princeton, NJ, 1980) and W. Pohl, 'The empire and the Lombards: treaties and negotiations in the sixth century', in W. Pohl (ed.), *Kingdoms of the Empire: The Intergration of Barbarians in Late Antiquity* (Leiden, 1997), pp. 75–134.

empire the opposition in Italy began to look to him for support. When in 535 King Theodahad deposed his co-ruler, Theoderic's daughter Amalasuntha, Justinian took this as a pretext to attack. The Gothic war lasted for almost twenty years, and ruined a considerable part of the Roman infrastructure in the peninsula. The historian Procopius was an eyewitness to many of these events, and his detailed history of the war is one of the liveliest accounts of the situation in Italy in the period.[5] Procopius showed that as the war raged on the Byzantines came to be regarded as foreigners: not Romans any more, but Greeks. In their own propaganda the Ostrogoths depicted the Byzantines as invaders, and stressed that their army was an amalgam of barbarians: Heruls and Huns, Goths and Slavs, Armenians and Persians, Gepids and Lombards from Pannonia and Isaurians from Asia Minor.[6] Franks, Burgundians, and Alamans began to raid Italy on their own account. By 540 it seemed that the Byzantines had won the war; but the administrators and tax collectors from the east soon provoked such discontent that the defeated Goths were able to launch another successful offensive. The war dragged on in a seesaw of sieges; when a city was taken, the soldiers were usually granted safe conduct or even changed sides, but (as happened in Milan) there were many massacres of the civilian population.

By the time that the Gothic kingdom finally collapsed in 552/53, Italy was impoverished, and waves of plague continued to depopulate the country. Regional resistance continued, usually led by local barbarian commanders and often supported by the Franks, who had extended their control over almost the whole range of the Alps. It would soon become evident that this reflected a fundamental change in the political culture of Italy. The unity established by Rome that had firmly drawn together the different regions of Italy was fading away, and the Byzantine state, with its tax collectors and its barbarian soldiers, was incapable of maintaining it. Before the Roman legions changed things, Italy had been a conglomerate of cities and rural areas with widely differing climates, economies and deep-rooted regional and local identities. Now the senatorial elite with its wide-ranging interests had lost power. During the Gothic war townspeople

[5] Procopius, *History of the Wars*, vols. iii–v, ed. and trans. H. B. Dewing (London, 1953–4).
[6] Ibid. 8, 30, vol. v, p. 367.

all over Italy had learnt that what little peace and security they could enjoy was sheltered behind their city walls. It may seem paradoxical that in a period in which most of the old cities were in decline, with ruins and empty spaces expanding inside the walls, their political weight should have grown. But their impoverishment necessarily diminished the resources that could be transferred to any central government, be it Byzantine or barbarian. The formidable military machinery that the late Roman empire had set up, and that had finally won back the old heartland of the empire after the Gothic war, could no longer be maintained without excessive taxation. As in all other provinces of the western empire, the simple fact that barbarian government was less expensive made Roman (by now, Byzantine) rule untenable.

The Lombards

The failure of Byzantine rule to establish solid roots in Italy soon provoked another barbarian invasion. In 568, the Lombards under their king, Alboin, raised an army in Pannonia that also included Gepids, Suebians, Sarmatians, Bulgars, Saxons, Roman provincials, and others. With its multi-ethnic composition, its size, and the route it took to Italy it resembled Theoderic's army of some eighty years before. But unlike the Ostrogoths, the Lombards hardly encountered any serious resistance; although paradoxically Alboin's rule, and that of his successors, would be limited to a part of northern Italy only. The reason was that, without resistance, there was no need for the army to stay united and it dissolved: the Saxons went home, others began to raid Frankish Gaul, while two other groups marched off to the South and eventually founded the independent Lombard duchies of Spoleto and Benevento in the mountainous inland areas of the peninsula. The rest settled in the cities of the North, such as Cividale, Trento, Brescia, or Turin, where powerful dukes established strongholds with armed followers that represented a force any monarch would have to reckon with. The ethnic ties between the Lombards certainly did not result in unity: and for decades after 568 the Lombard dukes joined the Byzantines or the Franks as they pleased for short-term political benefits. For ten years there was no king, until a concerted Byzantine-Frankish offensive prompted the restoration of the kingdom.

In contrast to earlier Roman or Gothic rule, the new structure of power limited the power of the king (and thus has often been interpreted as a structural weakness of the kingdom) while at the same time strengthening local ties and civic identities. This was reflected in the growing importance of the role of the bishops as civic leaders. In 594, for instance, 'the bishop and the citizens of Brescia', in a dogmatic controversy, directly challenged Pope Gregory the Great by requiring an oath that he would not condemn the so-called Three Chapters.[7] At about the same time, although independently, the dukes and cities of Bergamo, Verona, and Padua rebelled against King Agilulf (590–616). Elsewhere, both the 'Lombard' duke and the 'Roman' bishop supported the king, for instance in Trento, which was always threatened by Frankish attacks. Whereas Theoderic had relied on the Roman central administration to govern the country, the Lombards could only cooperate with those structures of civic administration that were still in place.

What happened to the Romans under Lombard rule? Many historians believe that Roman landowners were killed or driven into exile, and that the Roman population was enslaved by the new lords. There is little evidence to support that interpretation. In the cities of the kingdom, church organization continued to function as before, and funerary inscriptions provide evidence of the survival of many well-to-do citizens and artisans. In the years after 568 the level of violence and raiding was high, but the Lombards had come to stay, and to do so they employed the existing infrastructures. Instead of a few tens of thousands of Lombards commanding millions of Roman slaves, we should think in terms of local societies that became ethnically mixed. The principal change was that the civil lay aristocracy disappeared, a change that was taking place in all western European countries. In the long run, only two models for the elite remained: that of the warrior-landowner claiming some prestigious barbarian identity, and that of the 'Roman' cleric. Roman landowners may also have decided to rise into the ranks of the Lombard aristocracy, although that is a process that is better documented for Frankish Gaul and Visigothic Spain. Others could seek protection by the bishop, donating their estates

---

[7] Gregorius Magnus, *Registrum epistolarum* 4, 37, ed. D. Norberg (Turnhout, 1982).

to the Church and receiving them back as a permanent loan. Roman traders and artisans continued in business and came to be protected by royal legislation (for instance the *magistri commacini*, the builders). The court also needed Roman specialists in administration (like Secundus of Trento, the faithful adviser and historian of Queen Theodelinda); Latin continued to be the language of state. At the lower end of the social scale, there were both Roman and Lombard slaves between whom the Edict of King Rothari (643) decreed only minor differences in status.[8]

On the whole, most of the population, and especially the peasants, may have been better off under Lombard rule than before. Systematic taxation ceased, and the relative shortage of manpower eased the pressure on rural labour. The army was no longer financed through taxes, but was now supported directly from landed property. This meant that, for better or worse, the warriors were much harder to control, but it also meant that their interests as landowners eventually got the upper hand over their needs as warriors. The mobile mercenaries of the fifth century had been veritable soldiers of fortune, for whom armed conflict was the only source of income. That was why the Gothic armies repeatedly forced their reluctant leaders to start yet another war. In the eighth century, on the other hand, the Lombard kings had to introduce severe penalties for Lombard *milites* who did not follow the call to arms. An eighth-century Lombard nobleman in Tuscany even converted his house into a monastery and took his vows, apparently to avoid having to fight the Franks.[9] Lombard aristocrats now had a lot to lose. They still went about armed even in peacetime, unlike Roman aristocrats in times of empire, and drunken brawls or even complicated feuds might break out at any time. Lombard kings legislated against all sorts of probable and improbable infringements of public order (including throwing somebody from his horse, stealing a woman's clothes while she was bathing, or street-fighting in which women took an active part). But after the consolidation of the kingdom in c.600 times were relatively peaceful, and wars for the most part remained short and regional.

But the kingdom was now inseparable from the identity of the Lombard people. Whereas Theoderic's title had simply been *rex*, the

[8] *Rothari* 144 (builders); 194 (Roman slaves), pp. 75, 89.
[9] *Vita Walfredi*, ed. K. Schmid (Tübingen, 1991).

full title of the Lombard king was *rex gentis Langobardorum*. Written
histories and wall-paintings celebrated the deeds of the *gens* (the
people), including the pagan myth of their origins that explained
how the god Wodan had given them the name of 'longbeards' (for the
seemingly paradoxical reason that their women had lined up on the
battlefield wearing their long hair like a beard).[10] But apart from these
abstract notions, what actually defined the Lombards is hard to say.
Some Lombards wore beards and others did not; Paul the Deacon, the late eighth-century Lombard historian, noted that they had
completely changed their dress since 600. By 650, burials with grave-
goods had also been abandoned. Christianity had grown in influence
even before the Lombards came to Italy, and by the end of the seventh
century most Lombards were Catholics (perhaps with a tinge of
syncretism in many cases). Churches and monasteries, most of them
quite small, were now founded by the dozen. Although Lombards
notionally lived according to Lombard law, eighth-century legislation
allowed a choice of Roman and Lombard law in certain cases, so that
legal distinctions began to be blurred. This is also attested in charters:
in 758, a *Romana mulier* with the Lombard name Gunderada sold
property with the consent of her husband (who had a Roman name)
as Lombard law required.[11] Gradually Lombard language began to
fade away; it is remarkable that no contemporary observer took any
notice of this process, which must mean that it had no bearing on
Lombard identity. For a long time, Lombard names remained an
obvious sign of identity. But they were not used to perpetuate ethnic
divisions but simply to delineate social status. Paul the Deacon, who
was born into a noble Lombard family in Friuli in the 720s, was given
the Latin name Paulus because he was destined for an ecclesiastical
career, whereas his brother, the heir to the family estate, was given a
Lombard name. While Lombards became Romanized, Lombard identity became more broad and spread to include inhabitants of many
different origins. The result was that by about 1000, 'Lombardia' and
'Romania' had become regional identities within the otherwise relatively homogeneous Italian-speaking populations in different parts of
the Po basin.

[10] Pauli, *Historia Langobardorum*, 1, 7–8.
[11] B. Pohl-Resl, 'Legal practice and ethnic identity in Lombard Italy', in W. Pohl and
H. Reimitz (eds.), *Strategies of Distinction: The Construction of Ethnic Communities,
300–800* (Leiden, 1998), p. 210.

Byzantine Italy

The region around Ravenna, still called Romagna today, remained the centre of Byzantine rule in Italy for almost 200 years after Alboin's invasion; it fell to the Lombard king Aistulf only in 751. In the late sixth century Byzantine possessions were still extensive, and included almost the entire coastline from Istria and the Venetian lagoon on the northern Adriatic to Apulia and Calabria in the South, the islands, and the west coast up to Liguria. Rome, and its hinterland, was the second Byzantine centre. Only gradually were some of these regions lost to the Lombards. But it was typical of the delicate balance of power in the peninsula that throughout the period the Byzantines should have maintained control of the overland communications between Rome and Ravenna through a chain of fortresses along the road that ran through Narni and Perugia and which also marked the border between the Lombard duchies of Tuscia (which owed allegiance to the king) and Spoleto (which followed a more independent course). Exact territorial demarcations of the different powers were more often the result of negotiated settlements than of sieges and wars.

In the North, only a few Byzantine border towns, such as Oderzo or Brescello, suffered lasting damage in war. In the Centre and the South, where there were numerous smaller cities, the first decades after the Lombard invasion caused many of them to decline, and several bishoprics had to be abandoned. Here anti-Lombard rhetoric tended to assume sharper tones, as for example in papal letters: 'the enemies of God, the most sacrilegous Lombards' was the standard formula. Pelagius II (579–90) still hoped they would soon 'disappear like smoke'. But Gregory the Great (590–604) took a more realistic stance, and pressed the lay authorities to negotiate peace. He repeatedly had to ransom prisoners taken in the course of Lombard raids, who would otherwise have been sold off as slaves.[12] Still, in many regions under Byzantine control the disruption was minimal.

Until the beginning of the eighth century, the emperor maintained strict control over his remaining Italian possessions through the

---

[12] Gregorius Magnus, *Registrum*. Cf. Pohl, 'The empire and the Lombards'.

exarch (or governor, usually a Greek) and an elaborate hierarchy of officials. Unlike Lombard Italy, the tax system was retained, primarily to finance the army. Numerous Greek inscriptions show that there was an important Greek minority. Nonetheless, in many respects social changes in the exarchate were similar to those in the territories under Lombard rule. The senatorial aristocracy with its widely dispersed estates had virtually disappeared, and the ownership of landed property tended to become more regional. A new leading group composed of military officials with considerable (but still comparatively modest) landed property began to emerge. The civil lay aristocracy was in decline, while the Church, above all the bishop of Rome, took responsibility for an increasingly wide variety of administrative duties. This suggests that the impact of the Lombards on social change in Italy may have been more limited than has often been thought, but also that we should not exaggerate the long-term effect of Byzantine rule either.

In fact, no 'Byzantine' identity emerged. The Byzantines continued to call themselves Romans, *Rhomaioi*, with the result that the term *Romani* came to mean many different things: the Byzantine state and its agents; its Italian subjects; the citizens of the city of Rome; and the Romance-speaking population of Italy. No contemporary felt a need for more precise definition. When the Lombard king Aistulf, before he attacked Ravenna in 751, introduced penalties for any commerce with 'Romans', the intention was clear, but he did not specify which Romans he meant.[13] To the Italians, the Greek-speaking Byzantines were Greeks, like the Greek inhabitants of southern Italy. But otherwise ethnic designations were of little use in describing the complicated political geography of Italy. When King Ratchis warned his subjects in the 740s not to send unauthorized missions to foreign powers, he specified the foreign *gentes* as the Franks, the Bavarians, or the Avars, whereas in Italy he listed cities instead: Rome, Ravenna, Spoleto, and Benevento.[14]

As the Byzantines gradually lost control of Italy in the eighth century, a number of cities began to emerge as more or less independent powers. The largest and at the same time the most complicated case was the city of Rome, which had been defended by the popes against Lombard attacks using a mix of spiritual rhetoric and Frankish

[13] *Aistulf* 4, p. 228.
[14] *Ratchis* 7, p. 220.

support. The *res publica*, as the popes called it, was intended to represent a restored Roman state with authority in much of Italy under secular papal rule. Other cities were more modest. Long-distance trade gave the city-states of Naples, Amalfi, and to some extent also Gaeta the means to resist their neighbours throughout the ninth and tenth centuries. In the North, Comacchio and Venice controlled the regional salt trade, and towards the end of the ninth century Venice overcame her rival and, under the protection of the relics of St Mark, which had been stolen from Egypt in the 820s, established herself as the principal meeting point between central Europe and the Levant.

Frankish rule and its impact

Soon after Clovis had created a powerful Frankish kingdom around 500, the Franks began to take an interest in Italian affairs. During the sixth century, in the period between the Gothic war and the consolidation of the Lombard kingdom under king Agilulf, there were repeated Frankish interventions in Italy. But with the decline of Merovingian rule, Frankish influence also faded, and it was only in the mid-eighth-century that the popes brought the Franks back into Italian power politics in their search for allies to block Lombard expansion. In the 750s Pippin III repeatedly intervened in Lombard northern Italy. In their annual campaigns against neighbouring peoples, the Carolingians had built up a military potential and dynamic that none of the neighbours could equal. Some, like the Saxons, resisted the Frankish attacks for a long time, but others, including the Lombards, quickly capitulated. Because of the pressure he tried to apply against papal Rome, the last Lombard king, Desiderius, provoked a Frankish invasion that early in 774 led to the capitulation of Pavia and the fall of the Lombard kingdom. Now Charlemagne (768–814) was crowned king of the Lombards. Carolingian rule was diligently established, and irresistibly gained ground in most of Italy. The pope regained some degree of autonomy for his 'Republic of St Peter' while the southern Italian duchy of Benevento accepted Frankish overlordship but remained virtually independent except for the rare occasions when Frankish armies were near.

Carolingian rule in Italy did not constitute a very coherent whole. For most of the ninth century, since Charlemagne had installed his son Pippin as king of the Lombards, the kingdom of Italy was ruled as before from Pavia. At first Lombard nobles continued to have some say in public affairs, but increasingly aristocrats, warriors, adminis-trators, and intellectuals from north of the Alps occupied the key positions. These were Franks, but there were also many Alamans, Bavarians, and others. Many of them continued to own estates and had relatives in other parts of the Carolingian empire, such as Eberhard, who governed Friuli for some decades in the mid-ninth century. He commissioned a Frankish intellectual, Lupus of Ferrières, to compile a comprehensive law-book for administrative use. Like several other collections, this one contained the different Lombard, Frankish, Ala-mannic, and Bavarian law codes, reflecting the heterogeneity of the new ruling elite in northern Italy. The Carolingian empire had intro-duced the principle that wherever they went its subjects could be judged according to their native law. Italians often did not distinguish between the different ethnic backgrounds of the agents of Caroling-ian rule. They simply called them *theotisci*, those who speak the ver-nacular, the language of the people (*theod*). This was the origin of what became the German self-designation, *deutsch*, but also the mod-ern Italian term for the Germans, *tedeschi*. It excluded the Lombards (most of whom no longer spoke a Germanic language); only if one referred to the language they once had spoken was it called *lingua todesca*, as it was in the tenth-century *Chronicon Salernitanum*.[15]

Modern historians depict the period of Charlemagne and his suc-cessor to the empire, Louis the Pious (814–40), as an age of reform and of systematic attempts to make Carolingian government effective throughout the empire. That interpretation is based on the evidence of numerous capitularies, royal edicts, many of which were specific-ally issued for Italy; on the church councils and reform synods; on the *placita*, court proceedings for the settlement of disputes; and on the letters in which intellectuals and politicians discussed the needs and consequences of reform. Not only ideologically, but also in pragmatic ways, the Church became an integral part of the state. But how was Carolingian rule perceived in Italy? Italy played an ambiguous part in the political culture of the time. On the one hand, it was on the

---

[15] *Chronicon Salernitanum*, c. 38, ed. U. Westbergh (Stockholm, 1956), p. 39.

periphery of the empire, and in some ways came to be treated like colonial territory. On the other hand, it was a source of prestigious traditions and skills that were central to Carolingian self-representation: the imperial tradition with its symbols and its representative architecture; the papacy as a source for Christian legitimacy; Montecassino as the cradle of Benedictine monasticism; manuscript collections that opened up unique ways of access to ancient culture and erudition; and relics of martyrs and saints that conferred unparalleled spiritual treasures on the Frankish churches that acquired (and often stole) them. Thus, Frankish reformers often came to Italy to tell Italians to do what in fact the Franks had learnt only in Italy. And Frankish judges sent by the Frankish *rex Langobardorum* sat in judgement over Lombards using the Lombard law code. Carolingian rule and culture were familiar in many ways; it was its flavour of high-handedness and moral urgency that might give offence to the inhabitants of Italy.

The image of the Franks in contemporary Italian sources is therefore ambiguous. Some, such as Paul the Deacon in his history of the Lombards, subtly argued that the Lombard kingdom had already worked very well along the lines of Carolingian reform before the Franks came. Others, such as Andreas of Bergamo in the 870s, glorified insignificant Lombard rebellions that had happened about a century before.[16] Southern histories, such as the *Chronicon Salernitanum*, picture Charlemagne as a great and noble ruler, but place the resistance of Benevento on a higher moral ground. One case when tensions became apparent occurred in the late eighth century when there was a conflict between Lombard and Frankish monks in the monastery of S. Vincenzo al Volturno that at one stage even involved Charlemagne and the pope.[17] Many Franks may have despised the Lombards, but it is no coincidence perhaps that no source is so explicit in voicing prejudice as a letter by Pope Stephen III, written in 770/71, in which he protested against young Charlemagne's planned marriage with a Lombard princess, calling the Lombards 'perfidious and fetid', a people that did not merit to be counted among the peoples of the world and whose only kin were the lepers.[18] Such invectives may or

[16] Andreas of Bergamo, *Historia*, ed. G. Waitz (Hanover, 1878), pp. 222–30.
[17] *Codex Carolinus*, ep. 66 and 67, ed. W. Gundlach (pp. 583–7).
[18] Ibid., ep. 45, p. 561.

may not have been uttered occasionally by drunk warriors; but only papal rhetoric incorporated it in political discourse.

Towards ethnic diversity: regional powers and invaders in the ninth and tenth centuries

In the course of the ninth century, aristocratic families that had come from north of the Alps rooted themselves firmly in their Italian environment. As Carolingian rule faded away some of them were prepared for a bid to take over the kingdom of Italy, and even the empire, among them the Unruochings, descended from Eberhard of Friuli, who came to power with Berengar I, and the Widonians, the family of the dukes of Spoleto. From the end of the ninth century, these and other families (partly from southern France) got involved in a series of regional conflicts and rebellions. The political instability of the *regnum Italiae* around 900 led to another invasion by the Hungarians (also called Magyars). They had occupied the Pannonian plain, modern Hungary, in the last years of the ninth century, and soon started raiding in Italy. Later writers, among them Liutprand of Cremona (d. 972), accused the last Carolingian emperor, Arnulf, of having incited them against his enemies.[19] They also depicted the Hungarians in terms of the apocalyptic images once used for the Huns: the biblical peoples of Gog and Magog let loose on the world in divine punishment. For some decades, Hungarian war bands regularly marched along the old Roman road through Venetia, soon called *strata Hungarorum*. But they were often also used as allies in one of the frequent episodes of internal strife. In 922 they marched as far as Apulia. But they were not invaders who came to stay or to conquer, they were raiders in search of booty and ransom. Yet unlike the many bands of steppe warriors before them, their power did not disappear when their raids stopped. Soon after Otto I had inflicted a decisive defeat on them in Bavaria in 955, their Christianization began. Theirs had been the last 'barbarian invasion' in the north of Italy.

In southern Italy, the powerful principate (as it was now called) of Benevento gradually gave way in the course of the ninth century to a

---

[19] Liutprand of Cremona, *Antapodosis* 1, 13, ed. J. Becker (Hanover, 1915).

number of conflicting regional and local powers. The Lombard aristocracy, proud as it still was of its old ancestry, exhausted itself in endless petty wars. Naples and Amalfi took advantage of the situation; the Byzantines re-established themselves as a major power in the region. But yet another force was now preparing to exploit the chaotic situation: the Saracens. This, like 'Agarenes', was a biblical name given by Christians; in reality, they were Arab-led Muslim warriors of mixed origin based in North Africa. During the 840s they completed their gradual conquest of Byzantine Sicily and in 846 a major force sacked Rome, an event which had repercussions similar to those of the Gothic conquest of 410. For several decades a Muslim emirate controlled Bari and its hinterland. At the same time Saracen mercenaries were being employed in most of the regional conflicts among the Lombards. Their war bands did the most damage, and from a stronghold near Gaeta they sacked the wealthy monasteries of S. Vincenzo al Volturno and Montecassino. It was not until the tenth century that the raids subsided. The amount of disruption caused by Magyars and Saracens which also affected north-western Italy varied, however. Their raids were part of a general power struggle that was in many respects more ruthless than in the preceding period, but the damage done by the pagans was highlighted for several reasons; for instance, monasteries and churches regularly referred to it when they solicited confirmation of property or new donations from their lords.

It is no surprise that contemporary authors usually depict the Saracens as ruthless pagans, although sometimes a more differentiated image may emerge. When the emperor Louis II had reconquered Bari in 871, the emir was kept prisoner at Benevento, and soon seems to have been respected as adviser and friend by the Lombard *princeps*, who eventually even imprisoned the emperor.[20] In fact, chroniclers of the time do not present overbearing Franks, treacherous Byzantines, and greedy Lombards (with rare exceptions) in a much more favourable light than the Muslims. Erchempert (*c*.890), a Lombard monk from Montecassino, paints a bleak picture of a world full of enemies always capable of the most villainous deeds.[21] To him, all powers, including the pope and the emperor, had lost their authority.

[20] *Chronicon Salernitanum*, c. 121, ed. Westerbergh, p. 122.
[21] Erchempert, *Historia Langobardorum Beneventanorum*, ed. G. Waitz (Hanover, 1878), pp. 234–64.

The tenth-century Italian historians like Liutprand of Cremona and
the author of the Salerno Chronicle sounded almost as pessimistic,
and a far cry from the high-sounding rhetoric of reform voiced
around 800.

Italian identities in the period were often attached to cities, and
frequently implied a strong sense of rivalry against other cities in the
neighbourhood—Capua and Naples, Salerno and Amalfi, Siena and
Arezzo are all cases in point. Broader ethnic identities remained
rather uncertain, as a famous text by Liutprand of Cremona shows.[22]
Rejecting the western claim for empire, the Byzantine emperor Nice-
phoros challenged Otto I's ambassador, Liutprand: 'You are not
Romans, but Lombards!' Liutprand replied: 'We, that is, Lombards,
Saxons, Franks, Lotharingians, Bavarians, Suavians and Burgundians,
regard "Roman!" as one of the worst insults.' This is, however, an
expression of 'imperial' rather than Italian identity. In a similar catalogue (c. 54), Liutprand lists *Itali* instead of Lombards—'Lombards'
had become another name for the inhabitants of Italy as a whole.
Whereas the Franks, and the population of the empire, consisted of
Latini, Latin speakers, and *Teutoni*, speakers of the German vernacular (cc. 33, 37, 40), no such language divisions were important among
the inhabitants of Italy. Soon (and for the first time, in John the
Deacon's *Historia Veneticorum*, written soon after 1000), *Teutonici*
would become a collective name for all the people from north of the
Alps. Liutprand's praise of them in deference to Otto I was only one
side of the coin. Paradoxically, both the Saxon and the Byzantine
emperors claimed dominance in Italy on the grounds that they represented Romanness. Both were met with a mix of flattery, prejudice,
acquiescence, and enmity. They were not simply invaders, for they
relied on a long-standing network of rights and claims, of alliances
and strongholds in Italy. But likewise, they continued to be regarded
as outsiders whose involvement in Italian politics was due to
weakness and discord among the Italians.

Italy was in reality a complicated mosaic of competing powers.
That did not necessarily impinge too heavily on the lives of its
inhabitants (though with some it did). But it influenced perceptions.

[22] Liutprand of Cremona, *Relatio de legatione Constantinopolitana* 12, ed. J. Becker
(Hanover, 1915); for an excellent analysis, see G. Gandino, *Il vocabolario politico e sociale
di Liutprando da Cremona* (Rome, 1995), pp. 257–70.

Neither natives nor invaders nor foreign powers managed to create stable political configurations or corresponding identities. This is paradoxical since the legal and administrative foundations for statehood were well developed.[23] Still, the *regnum Italiae* (and more so, the Christian empire) had ceased to inspire much hope or respect, and regional powers had hardly been able to fill the gap. This instability would continue to attract foreign intervention. In the South, Norman mercenaries gradually established their power in the course of the eleventh century. From the second half of the tenth century onwards, a series of interventions from north of the Alps brought the Italian kingdom, and the holy Roman empire, under foreign control: Otto I, the eastern Frankish king, was the first of a series of 'Teutonic' rulers who descended on Italy to lay hold of its crowns, but who otherwise made their rule felt only indirectly for most of the time. In the precarious balance of power between invaders and local lords, the cities gradually expanded their political influence: the 'communal age' was dawning. In an Italian perspective, difference made itself felt much more than identity.

[23] C. Wickham, 'Lawyer's time: history and memory in tenth and eleventh century', in C. Wickham, *Land and Power: Studies in Italian and European Social History, 400–1200* (London, 1994), pp. 275–94.

Public power and authority

François Bougard

Royalty and its transmission

Historians have generally argued that whereas various forms of 'private' power dominated most of the rest of early medieval Europe, in Italy the presence of the state remained by contrast relatively strong. But even if we had a clear understanding of what is meant by terms such the 'state' or distinctions between public and private power when applied to the early Middle Ages, this generalization would probably be too sweeping. Italy's political fortunes, like those of Europe as a whole, changed constantly during the period, but even so the idea of the sovereign nature of public authority was stronger than in other parts of Europe. With the exception of the periods of invasion and moments of weak authority, kings and emperors rarely found it difficult to make their authority recognized, while they and their representatives continued to be treated as the natural and undisputed fount of authority. The prestige of the kings derived in part from their association with the empire, and the increasing importance of the role of the queen was also modelled on Byzantium. The well-established symbolic role of the royal palace gave royal authority an institutional base that exercised a greater force of attraction than anywhere else in Europe, even after the palace was destroyed by the inhabitants of Pavia in 1024. Royal justice issued directly from the royal palace and was widely sought after. Even though this authority waned over time, especially in the rural areas, every effort was made to bring disputes for judgement before the tribunal of the royal palace. At the same time royal charters from the seventh century onwards also show how gifts of land or rights formed part of a conscious policy of royal munificence that contributed in important ways to enhance the authority of the kings.

In this chapter, therefore, we show how Italy differed in this period from the rest of Europe in the practices of kingship, without attempting to explore regional variations within the peninsula (most often intended as the *regnum Italiae*) that would naturally require a more detailed discussion. But while the Ostrogoths, the Lombards, and the Franks who ruled Italy in succession were all of Germanic origin, their practices of kingship did not form a uniform tradition that was handed down from the earlier Roman precedents described by Tacitus. Some customs and symbols of power did continue to be used over time, but the ways in which these were 'managed' changed. New features acquired prominence, most obviously those associated with Christian forms of consecration, while roles also changed over time, and especially that of the queen.

A king's legitimacy was derived first of all from the army. To be acclaimed by soldiers on the battlefield was the most important way of recognizing an individual's capacity to lead an armed people to victory. This was how Roman emperors had been made or broken, and had nothing to do the growing numbers of officers of non-Roman origins in the army. Those who acquired power in this way in the fifth and sixth centuries were assured of unchallenged recognition, and this was symbolically represented in the act of raising the acclaimed king bodily aloft on a shield, as happened to Witiges, one of the last Ostrogoth kings of Italy, in 536.[1] But acclamation did not rule out the possibility of hereditary or even dynastic successions.

Lombard kingship was also rooted in the tradition of acclamation by the people-army (*populus-exercitus*), but its distinctive mark came from the symbolic role of the spear. For the Lombards, the spear symbolized the act of handing down power, something they shared with other cavalry-based peoples like the Avars. Agelmund was the first king of the Lombards during their migration, and had been chosen because he was a descendant of the *Guingini*, meaning 'from the family of Odin's spear'.[2] He passed his kingship on to Lamissio. According to myth, when Lamissio had been abandoned at birth

[1] Cassiodorus, *Variae*, trans. S. J. B. Barnish (Liverpool, 1992), x. 31.
[2] Prologue of Edict of Rothari; Pauli, *Historia Langobardorum*, i. 14.

in a pond together with his six brothers and sisters by his mother, Agelmund happened by chance to be passing. Seeing the newly born infants he pushed the tip of his spear into the water to investigate further, whereupon it was seized by Lamissio.[3]

Throughout Lombard history the spear retained its central symbolic importance. The assembly that ratified the laws issued by Rothari in 643 was known as *gairethinx*, meaning 'the assembly of the spears', and those present demonstrated their approval by banging their spears against their shields. When in 753 it was feared that the ailing Liutprand would soon die, his nephew was given a spear 'as dictated by custom' to identify him as successor to the kingship.[4] But the legitimation of kingship was made more complex by the use of other symbols. This can be seen in the regal symbols that accompany Agilulf in the decorative plaque of a reliquary found in the Valle di Nievole, and now preserved in Florence. At the centre of a gilded bronze plaque (measuring 6.7 cm × 18.8 cm) the king is seated on a throne and identified by an inscription: he holds a sword in his left hand and is flanked by two spear-bearers, who are in turn flanked by two winged victories, while at each end is a crown surmounted by an orb with a cross on it. The king's hair (pointed beard, drooping moustache, long hair) and the spear are signs of his 'barbaric' and warrior characteristics. But the style of depiction also drew on models found only in late Roman and Byzantine representations.

The significance of the crowns has been interpreted in many different ways. Did they depict a coronation that actually took place in 590? Did they represent the reunification of the crowns of two Italies, one that was by now Lombard and another that had remained Roman, on the same head, constituting some sort of territorial claim that was echoed in the inscription *rex totius Italie* on the crown (now lost) that Agilulf himself donated to the treasury of the basilica of Monza? Were they an allusion to the earlier Gothic and Roman political systems? Or were they simply a result of the artist's desire for symmetry? And what should be made of the cross surmounting the orb?

There are no clear answers to these questions despite the information provided by the images described above and others in the Monza collection, but from this time onwards the crown remained an integral feature of Lombard *regalia*. There was still no clear distinction

---

[3] Pauli, *Historia Langobardorum*, i. 15.
[4] Ibid. vi. 55.

between the votive crown and the royal insignia, however, while the iron crown of the Lombard kings was a much later invention. The crown then acquired new importance in the eighth century, when Liutprand placed one in St Peter's in Rome as an act of homage. But this was a statement of political obedience to the pope and the Catholic Church that did not confer any special symbolic importance on the crown. Nor is there any evidence, despite the image on the plaque of Agilulf, that coronation ceremonies were ever held. The only Lombard 'sovereign' to have worn a crown was Arichis II, and he did so as a sign of the independence of his principality of Benevento from the Franks, who were known to have attached far more importance to such insignia.

With the transition to Frankish rule the symbolism of the spear was abandoned, and the ceremonies of coronation and anointing now followed a model that had been in use on the other side of the Alps since 751. Italy as a result adopted the regime of sacred kingship, and when this was extended to the empire the rulers of the *regnum* often underwent two coronations. In theory, this should have established clearer distinctions between the political roles of Pavia and Rome (the former representing the king, the latter the empire), but in practice things were less clear-cut, as the coronation of the Carolingian and post-Carolingian rulers demonstrated. We do not know that Charlemagne's entry into Pavia was followed by any specific ceremonies to mark the transfer of power, but this seems unlikely in view of his deliberate neglect of the city. Of his successors to the throne of Pavia, only Pippin (together with his brother, the future Louis the Pious) and Louis II were crowned in St Peter's in Rome, respectively in 781 and 844, and it was only during the conflict between Berengar I and Wido of Spoleto in 888–9 that Pavia was again recognized as the site that gave legitimacy to the coronation of a ruler. But coronations were still not standard practice. When Charles the Bald returned from Rome where he had just been crowned emperor, his power was acclaimed in Pavia in 876, but since he had not been declared king there was obviously no reason for him to be crowned. In 900 Louis III was elected in the palace but without being crowned. In the cases of Arnulf of Carinthia, Lambert, and Raoul of Provence, the first was imposed by force, the second was acclaimed apparently without election, and the third was acclaimed by a faction without any other proceedings. Coronations only became a regular practice following the reign of Hugh of Provence in 926 and his son Lothar in 931, while Berengar II and Adalbert (950) were also given the crown. But Otto I took the title of *rex Francorum* and *Langobardorum* without asking the consent of the aristocracy, and when he conferred the empire on Otto II in 967 he did not consider it worthwhile making him partner in his Italian kingship. Otto III was crowned king in Aachen when he was barely three years old, a few days after the premature death of his father (983). Arduin (1002) and Henry II (1004) were the last kings to be crowned in Pavia, and after the destruction of the palace in 1024 Conrad II was instead crowned in Milan.

Running through this list of kings, it is clear that the practice of assuming the title before the ruler actually exercised power in Italy and the tendency to use the imperial title as an alternative prevented the establishment of a tradition of kingship comparable to those associated with Rheims or St Denis. There were some attempts to imitate these Frankish models, however, and when coronations took place in Pavia the officiating prelate was the archbishop of Milan because, as a direct dependant of the pope, the bishop of Pavia was not an ideal candidate for the job. But the kings also increasingly invoked the authority of the papacy as a source of legitimacy rather then popular acclamation. Writing to Constantinople in 871 to assert his authority over the *basileus*, Louis II stated that the pope had put the imperial crown on his head in 850. But except for the case of Arduin of Ivrea, coronations in Pavia were only important in the period between 924 to 962, when there was no claimant to the empire, which offered the opportunity to establish an alternative tradition. This may also explain why the spear briefly reappeared as a symbol of royal legitimacy in this period. But by then the spear was no longer a symbol of power over the Lombards, but merely a symbol of investiture. This was the case of the spear offered by a delegation of noblemen from Italy to Raoul of Provence around 921–2, as a pledge of their submission and as an invitation to become the ruler of the kingdom in opposition to Berengar I. If this gesture made specific reference to the symbolic meaning of the spear under the Lombards this was lost on Raoul, for the spear was now associated with the one that had pierced Christ's side and its religious symbolism completely overshadowed any other association. In any case, Raoul quickly gave the spear to Henry, king of Germany, in exchange for expanding his

PUBLIC POWER AND AUTHORITY | 39

lands north of the Alps, and for the latter's descendants it became part of the imperial regalia. After the Carolingian conquest the Lombard kingdom became peripheral and hence only a secondary seat of royalty. But this is not to diminish the importance of Pavia, which was universally recognized as the capital, or the originality of the Lombard form of kingship which, especially in legislative terms, was carefully preserved in ways that created strong underlying elements of continuity. In fact the new rulers, whose legitimacy and identity derived from elsewhere, skilfully drew on Lombard traditions and had themselves recorded without any sense of discontinuity in the lists of the *reges Langobardorum*.

The role and power of the queen

In the definition of royalty as well as in its function and transmission, the queen played an important role. Although there is a great deal of information about the role of the queen for Italy, this has generally been ignored by historians. The queen's principal role was as bearer and transmitter of royalty, of which she took possession on the death of her husband. This gave rise to an authentic Bavarian 'dynasty' in the late the sixth and early seventh centuries when Theodelinda, the widow of Authari (584–90), handed her power on to her second husband, Agilulf (590–616). This was repeated by her daughter Gundeperga, who after the reign of her brother Adaloald (616–26) transferred power first to Arioald (626–36) and then to Rothari (636–52).

Three centuries later the history of Queen Adelaide again illustrated the importance of the role of the royal consort. Adelaide was the daughter of Raoul of Provence, the king of Burgundy and Italy (922–6). She married Lothar II, son of King Hugh, in 947. When Lothar died in 950 and Berengar II came to the throne, he decided that rather than marry him she should marry his son Adalbert, to whom he had delegated royal powers. Adelaide refused, and as a result was imprisoned first in the palace in Pavia and then on Lake Garda. But she managed to escape and made her way to the fortress of Canossa, where Otto I first set her free and then a few months later married her himself in Pavia. This meant that from Raoul II to Otto

III the kingdom of Italy was almost constantly ruled by the same family, while the marriage of Otto I and Adelaide also marked the beginning of an alliance between the *regnum Teutonicum* and the *regnum Italiae* that would last for centuries. The fact that Adelaide was imprisoned is in itself evidence of the political importance of the king's widow, but in this case there were other factors at stake. As well as her title to power in Italy by marriage, Adelaide also had hereditary rights in the kingdom of Burgundy. She also had Carolingian blood: on her father's side she was descended from King Pepin of Italy, which made her sixth in the line of descent from Charlemagne, and on her mother's side from Judith, the second wife of Louis the Pious.

In the seventh and in the tenth centuries women acted as legitimizers of royalty on criteria every bit as valid as the demonstration of personal military skill on the part of the male heir to the throne. But the role of the queen also changed during these centuries and the significance of Otto's marriage was quite different from that of the earlier 'Bavarian' marriages. When Otto I married Adelaide he was already *totius Italiae possessor*, and no longer needed to prove the strength of an army that, although still perceived to be foreign, had already conquered a *regnum* that he had claimed before his marriage (*rex Francorum et Langobardorum* or *Italicorum*). The story of how he freed a beautiful widow won him romantic popularity, but was also a political master stroke. While posing as a saviour (*captatio benevolentiae*) he neutralized a potentially dangerous adversary and at the same time acquired the considerable dowry left by Lothar.

In the period between the Lombard and Ottonian rulers, therefore, the queen's role in the transmission of titles of royalty gradually became more passive and by the end of the tenth century she was no longer consulted when it came to choosing a new sovereign. By contrast, female participation in royal functions increased and had two distinct but not always separate dimensions: one public, the other private.

In the Lombard period the queen sometimes played a major role in 'international' relations, and might even become solely responsible for them, as was the case of Queen Theodelinda, whose correspondence with Gregory the Great has been preserved. The queen was also frequently associated with the issuing of charters, mostly to monasteries that either had close ties with the rulers or that she herself had founded. Initially these activities were focused on Pavia, as when Rodelinda, the wife of Perctarit, had the monastery of S. Maria *ad Perticas* built in 670 to honour the Lombards who had died far from their families. In doing so she was extending to the whole population the duty of keeper of a family's funerary memories traditionally entrusted to women. Monasteries were founded in other areas where the queen already owned land, such as Brescia, where Ansa and Desiderius founded the monastery dedicated to SS. Salvatore, Michel, and Peter in 759. As well as from Ansa and her family, the monastery was also endowed with properties from the royal fisc, so that it was both the product of a local initiative and a base for royal power outside the capital. The success of this foundation and the closeness of its ties to the institution of kingship suggest that the project had been carefully conceived. As long as the abbesses of S. Salvatore were selected from among the daughters of the royal couple or from among their closest relatives, the division of patrimonies imposed on all the royal monasteries during the Carolingian period reserved a part of the monastery and its properties for the personal use of the queen herself as *rectrix*. Judith, wife of Louis the Pious, Ermengarda, wife of Lothar I, and Angilberga, wife of Louis II, all benefited from this arrangement. When in the tenth century the duties of *abbatissa* and *rectrix* were joined, the position became even stronger and gave the Lombard queens access to the services of the numerous public functionaries whose titles appear in the documents between the years 760–70 (*gasindius, scafardus, antepor, gastaldus*). Although the queen did have some responsibility for the 'domestic' management of the palace, despite what is often claimed she did not have a personal court. Her position was therefore mid way between that of the Franks, where the wife of the king barely played any part in public life, and that of Lombard southern Italy, where as a result of the influence of Byzantium the power of the female sovereign seemed to be almost unlimited, especially once she became a widow. At Benevento, for example, Scaniperga shared the title of *summus dux Langobardorum* with her son, her image appeared with his on coins, and she presided over judicial courts.

After the Carolingian conquest the queens lost their influence and thenceforth were strictly confined to domestic roles. This was partly because of the influence of the Frankish tradition and partly because of the subordinate position in which Italy now found itself. Compared to Charlemagne or Louis the Pious, the Frankish king enjoyed very limited powers and those of their consorts were inevitably weakened as well. The first evidence of this subordination comes from the charters of the eighth century in which the public and masculine epithets that had put the queen on a par with the king (*domna, excellentissima, gloriosa*) disappeared, to be replaced by others that refer simply to the private qualities of the royal consort (*amantissima, dilectissima, dulcissima*). After losing their political role the queens became more deeply involved in private pious activities, like Cunegonda, the wife of King Bernard (d. 816), who founded the monastery of SS. Maria and Alessandro in Parma.

Yet the growing autonomy of the kingdom of Italy and the fact that from the time of Lothar I (817) onwards the duties of king and the emperor were carried out by the same person, once again created new opportunities for strengthening the public role of the queen. In the ninth century the first queen to reap the benefits was Angilberga, the wife of Louis II. By the time of Angilberga the expression *consors regni*, which had originally been used for co-emperors, was commonly attributed to the queen. This had no specific constitutional connotations, and described the day-to-day exercise of power that ultimately resulted from the strength or weakness of individual consorts. But this enabled Angilberga to take advantage of the 'southern years' of Louis II's reign when he was resident in Benevento, engaged in military operations and far from Pavia. The court as a result closed ranks around the emperor and gave her the chance to increase her influence. The *consortium regni* included wide powers. The queen engaged in diplomatic activity at the highest level, including organizing the reconciliation between the pope and the emperor in 864 and the meeting between Louis the German and the pope's representatives in Trento in 872 to negotiate the imperial succession. She took charge of petitions for the issue of charters by Louis II, and hence became a critical intermediary between the emperor and his followers. She presided over a general assembly of the kingdom in the north of Italy while her husband was a prisoner in the south (871), and represented the emperor in Capua during the absence of Louis II (873–4). She presided over court cases and, as in the eighth century, the range of the officials that served her reveal the scale of her personal and patrimonial activities. Although Angilberga was particularly closely involved in the affairs of the monastery of S. Salvatore of Brescia, of which she was patron by virtue of her royal title, she also took the greatest interest in the affairs of the monastery of SS. Sisto and Bartolomeo in Piacenza that she had founded. She acquired the wider symbols of royal power and, for example, was portrayed with her husband on the coins minted in Benevento during their stay in the south of Italy. Via Benevento she drew on Byzantine tradition that was still strong in the South, and was able to develop the powers of the *consortium* to their fullest potential.

Each of the female sovereigns who succeeded Angilberga developed one or other of these attributes. Ageltrud, *imperatrix Augusta*, the wife of Wido of Spoleto, presided at a *placitum* (896), while Bertilla, the wife of Berengar I, presented petitions for charters; Alda, the wife of Hugh of Provence, pleaded the case of the monks of Bobbio before the king and some aristocrats. None of these was able to regain the power held by Angilberga, but the fact that women could exercise power was now firmly established. At a local level there was further evidence of this through tenth-century references to individuals like the *senatrices* Theodora and Marozia in Rome, or the Duchess Berta in Tuscany who is famous for the letter she sent to the caliph of Baghdad in which she referred to herself as 'queen of the Franks' and appeared to ask for his hand in marriage.

When Princess Theophanu, who married Otto II in 972, arrived in Italy a further important development took place. Theophanu brought with her a Byzantine political culture that gave the *basilissa* an eminent position within the state, including the power of dealing with legislative matters. Just as Otto II had become *coimperator* following his association to the empire (967), Theophanu became *coimperatrix*, meaning not only that she was a full member of the *consortium imperii*, but also that she was equal in rank to her husband. Like Adelaide before her, she was even granted an imperial coronation, and because of this she was bestowed with the same sacred quality. The sudden death of Otto II enabled her to establish a regency on behalf of the young Otto III, once she had convinced the aristocracy to abandon their opposition. In this way Theophanu and the others set the scene for equally important female rulers in the eleventh century, such as Beatrice of Canossa, *ductrix et marchionissa* of Tuscany, and her daughter Mathilde.

Yet even though the position of the female sovereign in Italy was stronger than elsewhere (with the exception of Byzantium) in the eighth as in the eleventh century, it was also ambiguous, because it lacked clear institutional definition and ultimately depended on the support of the aristocracy of the kingdom. This probably explains why in the decades that followed the queens would return to the private spheres to which they had first been confined by the Carolingians.

Sites of power

The prologue of the Edict of Rothari of 643, the first written Lombard laws, was dated in the palace of Pavia (*Dato Ticino in Palatio*), as were the laws of Aistulf issued in 750. According to the *Chronicon* of Salerno, an embassy led by the bishop and count of Capua, Landulf, went to Pavia in 872 to seek help against the Arabs. The bishop entered a large reception room at the end of which Louis II was seated on a gold throne with his wife Angilberga, both surrounded by optimates. Landulf wept and lay face down on the ground until the emperor sent his *proceres* over to raise him up and bring him. Still weeping Landulf made his request. Louis called together his *proceres* to organize an expedition, then he had some wine served for the bishop by his cupbearer, and as a gift gave him the gold cup from which he had drunk.

During the summer of 929 the palace of Pavia was the theatre for an even more dramatic episode which was recounted in the miracles of St Columba. Because of the usurpations he had been subjected to by more powerful members of the court, the abbot of Bobbio had turned for help on several occasions to the king, Hugh of Provence. But this had been to no avail, because the king would not risk upsetting the people who had put him on the throne. Nonetheless, the king suggested that St Columba, whose body was in Bobbio's possession, be called upon to help. He suggested to the abbot that he should have the saint's remains brought to Pavia for an assembly to impress the aristocracy. This was done, and the body was placed outside the palace in the church of S. Michele Maggiore, which was dedicated to the Archangel adopted as the patron saint of the Lombard kingdom in the late seventh century, and which was where Hugh had been crowned king.

For a dozen days the saint's body drew great attention from the crowds and performed a series of miracles, while the monks renewed their last attempts to gain satisfaction, but in vain. When the planned assembly opened, the matter was raised in the solemn setting of the reception hall (*aula regia*) of the palace. The king called for Columba's chalice to be brought in and everyone was asked to drink from it after him. Those who opposed the rights claimed by the monks of Bobbio declared themselves by refusing to drink from the cup and leaving the room, while those who accepted defeat did so by placing the stick which symbolized the investiture of the disputed properties on the bag in which the saint had carried his gospels. After a public reading of the pontifical privileges and royal and imperial charters in favour of Bobbio, Hugh finally issued a charter of confirmation of the abbey's patrimony. This had been extremely well prepared: the abbot of Bobbio, Gerlanus, was also the chancellor, and so had been able to consult the archives in Pavia as well as those in his own monastery.

These dates and these two related narratives provide clear evidence that the palace of Pavia was a recognized 'site of power'. Pavia was the natural place of recourse in case of disputes, a function that was embodied by the central feature of the palace, the great reception hall. This housed the royal couple and offices such as the chancellery. It was here that the aristocracy met and where embassies were received, where assemblies were held, cases heard, laws made, and where war and peace were decided on. It was also the setting for many other rituals: petitioning, the intercession of the queen, the formalization of alliances or reconciliations through communal drinking. It was here too that gifts were made, investitures of disputed properties were granted, and public readings of charters and displays of reverence or irreverence towards the relics of saints took place.

Ninth and tenth century sources provide a more complete picture of the palace of Pavia prior to its destruction in 1024. The palace was considered to be sufficiently important to be used to represent the city on the *denarii* minted in Pavia during the reign of Louis the Pious (which showed a building accessed by two steps and flanked by two towers with pointed roofs). Since there is no archaeological evidence it is impossible to describe the precise layout of the palace, but what we do know about its central sections indicate its scale and complexity, which increased following the enlargements and repairs to the damage caused in the city by an the earthquake in 836, a fire started by the Hungarians in 924, and the political disturbances and uprisings of 961 and 1024. The reception hall (*aula regia*) was sited on the first floor and contained an apse decorated with mosaics that depicted Theoderic on horseback. There were possibly anterooms like those in the palace of Salerno, through which the envoys that Charlemagne sent to Arechis II had to pass, and where the prince's followers were ranked in order of age.[5] There were also heated rooms (*caminatae*, some of which were used as bedrooms), porticoed galleries (*laubiae*), an animal and vegetable garden, an enclosed courtyard (*curtis*), and a chapel dedicated to St Mauritius, as well as a prison, the mint, a school and the chancery. The archives were probably kept in the treasury, which held not only precious objects like the silver and gold coins with which the king could make gifts but also objects that were associated with collective memory. One example of this was the skull of the king of the Gepids that had been mounted on a precious cup from which Alboin, the first sovereign of Lombard Italy, had made his wife Rosamund drink, and which remained in Pavia until the beginning of the ninth century.

As well as a variety of service activities, Pavia also included dwellings to accommodate the representatives of the various bishoprics and monasteries during convocations of the kingdom's assemblies and synods. The palace and the king also attracted many holy relics whose number and quality bestowed prestige and authority on their owner. The remains of St Sebastian had been transferred to Pavia from Rome in 680, those of St Augustine were transferred to the church of S. Pietro in Ciel d'Oro during the reign of Liutprand, those of St Appian were brought from Comacchio in the ninth century, and, of even greater value, those of S. George and a piece of the Holy Cross from Byzantium and Jerusalem during the reign of Otto II. The presence of all these items distinguished Pavia as a true capital (which was rare in the Latin west) even at those times, for example during the reign of Charlemagne, when politically it was eclipsed.

By comparison, the royal presence in Rome was much more modest, mainly because it was overshadowed by the *patriarchium* of the Lateran. A palace had been built, possibly at Charlemagne's initiative, and was located right next to St Peter's. It therefore had the advantage of being in immediate proximity to the site where imperial coronations took place, while still remaining outside the walls in

---

[5] *Chronicon Salernitanum* c. 12, ed. U. Westerbergh (Stockholm, 1956), p. 15.

accordance with the donation of Constantine. This building was replaced at the end of the tenth century during the revival of the Palatine, which had been abandoned as an imperial residence after the seventh century until Otto III made it central to his attempts to regenerate the empire (*renovatio Imperii*); but information about these palaces is extremely scarce.

Pavia and Rome were not the only two towns in Italy to have a palace, however. In the early Middle Ages Italy preserved most of its ancient palatial buildings as well as the *praetoria* of the governors. These were easily adapted to new uses because they had the basic structural requirements of any palace: an apse-shaped building whose façade had two towers and was flanked by porticoes and a reception room on the first floor that was sometimes also preceded by an anteroom. Such structures also existed in the rural *praetoria* of the late empire, which were all adaptations based on earlier residential buildings.

Ancient structures survived through a process of incessant trans-formation, restoration, and extension. This was the principal form of building activity during the reign of Theoderic, and although he gained a reputation for being the initiator of many new buildings in Pavia, Milan, and Verona, he was in fact mainly responsible for the painstaking preservation of existing structures. Even the palace of Ravenna, which has often been attributed to Theoderic, was really a case of the grandiose remodelling of a pre-existing *domus*. But Ravenna was visited only rarely by the rulers who succeeded Theo-deric, and the palace fell gradually into disuse after it was pillaged by Charlemagne until a new one was built outside the city walls during the Ottonian period.

The Lombards followed a similar pattern: palaces are known to have been built in Verona (in the 580s), in Milan (in the reign of Agilulf and Theodolinda), and in Pavia and Ravenna (after the reign of Aistulf). Although from the end of the fifth century Pavia was the *sedes regia*, it did not really become a capital until the second quarter of the seventh century under Rothari, while Milan remained the main political and religious focus. Under the Carolingians, Mantua joined this list of important cities, while in the southern duchies Spoleto, Benevento, Salerno and, at the time of Duke Godescalc (*c*.740), Siponto acquired importance.

In a country as heavily urbanized as Italy, the towns were a natural anchoring point for power, and any independent ruler was likely to establish his own capital. The southern principalities (Capua-Benevento and Salerno) and the duchies along the Tyrrhenian coast (Naples, Amalfi, and Gaeta) followed this pattern. Under the reign of Arechis II, palace complexes were built in Benevento and Salerno that showed a strong Byzantine influence and sought to rival the palace in Pavia.

Secondary royal residences were established in other towns too. Monza was famous for its basilica dedicated to St John the Baptist, which soon became the permanent depository for a part of the royal treasure and whose fate was reputedly connected to that of the Lombards themselves (a prophecy recorded by Paul the Deacon linked the condition of the sanctuary to the political survival of the Lombards; the frescoes that decorated the walls of the palace depicted the deeds of the Lombards and were used by Paul the Deacon as a figurative source to describe the customs of his people in the seventh century).[6] Monza also had a palace attributed to Theoderic and was linked to Milan at the beginning of the seventh century through the building work that Queen Theodelinda had done there, while King Liutprand built a rural *domicilium* at Corteolona near Pavia around 730. At Corteolona, Liutprand constructed baths and a monastery dedicated to St Anastasius, whose cult he promoted for political reasons. A second monastery, S. Cristina, was also built, and adorned with columns, mosaics, and marble imported from Rome. When Liutprand died in 744 he had barely had any opportunity to enjoy his creation, but its success as a royal residence during the Carolingian period indicates its importance, and Corteolona was probably among the examples that inspired the construction of the royal palace in Aachen.

In northern Italy the Carolingian and Ottonian kings were often itinerant. spending much of their time outside the peninsula and returning only for short visits at more or less regular intervals. They travelled to attend coronations or for a military campaign, or simply because this was the style of government in use north of the Alps. But these were not disorganized attempts to win control over extended territories, and since the king was always accompanied by his entire court these journeys could not be improvised. Since power emanated

[6] Pauli, *Historia Langobardorum*, v. 6; iv. 22.

from the physical presence of the sovereign, wherever the king was became a 'site of power'.

In Italy, as elsewhere, the term *Palatium* could refer to a building or a group of buildings, or to the area in which those buildings were situated, or to the people who were residing there, or indeed to any place that was sufficiently associated with the king's presence to acquire this label even when there were no prestigious building, reception hall, or service buildings. When a site was described as a 'palace' this was an indication of its political and administrative importance, so it is not surprising that some rural areas were also described as 'palaces'. Eight *curtes* acquired this title in the ninth century in the reigns of Lothar I and Louis II, and it was there that the sovereign would spend most of his time whilst in Italy. The first was Corteolona, where there was a palace in the true sense of the word. But of the seven remaining *curtes*, only Marengo seems to have had any particular structure, which made it possible, as in Corteolona, to host the royal assembly that issued the capitulary in 825.

The title 'palace' could also be a temporary one that was used only during the occasional presence of a king. But when we look more closely we find that the siting of these palaces was far from random. All were situated on the largest estates in the kingdom, hence enabling them to host the king and the court, all were in the Po valley, and particularly in Piedmont and Lombardy, all were close to the main urban centres and routes, and all possessed vast forest areas ideal for hunting, which was closely linked to the exercise of kingship.

There was, in other words, a complementary network of palaces of varying size and importance, and the movements of Louis II (844–75) illustrated how these were integrated into the system of government. Pavia was centrally located, and Louis stayed there at least once a year during his long trips to Italy which he regularly combined with the convocation of a general assembly. Rural palaces were situated around the capital at no more than two or three days' march, and these palaces received petitions for charters that were sent from all around the kingdom. Mantua, to the east, was regularly used as a winter palace from January to April, and it was here that local matters were dealt with. Journeys made by the king and the court were usually limited to the Po valley, whereas trips to Tuscany or to the duchy of Spoleto were more rare and were always combined with a visit to Rome. But these journeys did not reduce the geographical extent of

the king's power in any way, and when Louis II remained south of
Rome between 866 and 872 his authority in the north was never
challenged.

Justice: principles, personnel, and places

The description of the assembly held in the *aula regia* in Pavia in 929
during which the conflict between the monks of Bobbio and their
invasores was resolved brings us to one of the primary functions of
the palace and of royalty: the administration of justice. In the concept
of Christian sovereignty formulated by St Augustine, Isidore of
Seville, and the Carolingian *specula*, justice derived from the king or
was administered on his behalf. *Iustitia* was the first of the cardinal
virtues and was far more important than any of the military virtues.
Indeed, it would have been political suicide not to practise justice,
because the strength of the contract drawn up between the king and
his subjects—a contract expressed by the election with the spear or,
later, by an individual oath—depended on the king's capacity to
judge well according to the law and to give to each what he deserved
on the principle of the biblical partnership of *iudicium et iustitia*.

Most Lombard laws were simply the result of decisions made by
the king that were set out thematically or chronologically as the cases
came before him. That was also true of many Carolingian capitularies. Law and justice was also designed to make life better for the
pauperes, a constant source of concern in the ninth century that was
also mentioned in the Edict of Rothari. Paul the Deacon's description
of how King Aripert II (703–12) went out at night to find out from his
subjects how justice was administered was in keeping with these
ideas in the early eighth century, even if they had not as yet been
specifically formulated.

The administration of justice was, therefore, an aspect of government to which kings paid great attention, in ways that contributed to
the centralization of administration and its identification with the
person of the king. This was especially evident in the Lombard
period, from which some twenty judgements have survived that
throw light on the judicial activity of royal or ducal officers who came
directly from the palace. It was the Carolingians, however, who really

gave structure to royal justice. The forms of judicial meetings varied (although we have information only on those concerned with civil affairs), and included rural assemblies presided over by one of the count's delegates, solemn sessions held before the king and the *comes palatii*, and the *placita* held by the *missi* during their journey through the various regions or during one of the king's journeys.

It is often claimed that justice was administered uniformly throughout the kingdom, which gives the impression that tribunals were ubiquitous and extremely effective. In reality, each area had its own traditions of government. The Po valley probably came closest to the images derived from reading the dispositions in the capitularies; judgements were given as close as possible to the place of a dispute, and the court might even have to travel more than once during a single case. In Tuscany instead, where the Lombard tradition remained strong and the government was more town-centred, the courts did not travel, even if this meant they had to delegate some functions. In the duchy of Spoleto, however, where there were few urban centres, justice was pronounced either in the *placita* held in the palace and or in those held in the open countryside, often near a church.

Court hearings had to be public, for their decisions to be both known and respected. Around 1030 the marquis Boniface of Canossa passed judgements while seated on a boat that transported him from country to country where crowds of people gathered along the banks of the Po River. In civil matters at least, the courts in Italy, as elsewhere in the early Middle Ages, seldom gave clear-cut verdicts, since a judgement could be given only after the defeated party had recognized the rights of the winner with a statement that was ritually repeated and then simply confirmed by the judges. Therefore, the more members of the community that attended the hearing the more difficult it was for the loser later to deny a judgement that had been handed down in front of everybody. This meant that the choice of the site of justice was also of great importance; but there were no strict rules for this, except for churches, so that anywhere might be a suitable place to hear the sentence of the judges. But except for the hearings held at the scene of a dispute, the choice of site followed a clear typology. Starting from that of Pavia, palaces were used routinely for the administration of justice, but the apsed reception hall was reserved for the most solemn occasions only, and justice was commonly administered in one of the heated rooms (*caminatae*) in wintertime or in the gardens during the summer. Like all buildings of the aristocracy the palaces had one or two *laubiae*, that is to say porticoes running around the outside of the building, where people could stand outside the colonnades to attend any hearing taking place inside.

From Charlemagne to the Ottonian emperors, the hearings held in the countryside attracted large crowds. These hearings were presided over either by the king's *missi* or by the *comes palacii* or by the emperor himself, whose regular journeys through the peninsula gave him the opportunity to demonstrate his *virtus*. The cases dealt with on these occasions were carefully selected to 'show off justice'. Political propaganda was generally focused in two directions: to demonstrate control over the aristocracy and to reiterate reminders of the immutability of social conditions. In 804, following protests by 172 representatives of the local population, the duke of Istria had to agree to be judged by three *missi* of Charlemagne and Pepin who were sent there 'for the disputes concerning the properties of God's holy churches, the justice of our lords (i.e. what they could expect to have the right to receive from their subjects), the violence made to the people, the orphans, the widows'. Such a cleverly orchestrated staging was meant to defend a fundamental principle: that the king's justice was accessible for the weak, while the powerful could be punished for evil-doing. There were many cases that showed the opposite, and it was not unusual for large numbers of serfs to be summoned to a judicial assembly to be reminded that they were dependent on some great ecclesiastical landowner and should therefore give up all thoughts of freedom: *liber in libertate, servus in servitute* was a common slogan in ninth-century society.

The different parts of the kingdom were unified by the regular presence of the king's direct delegates, whose role grew stronger between the eighth and the eleventh centuries. The royal *missi* did not travel alone but were accompanied by specialists who contributed to the development of a standardized juridical culture that originated from the palace of Pavia. These specialists began to overshadow the local judges or *scabini* who had been introduced by Charlemagne soon after the conquest. Down to the 840s there was only a handful of judges and notaries, sometimes assisted by vassals, all of whom came from Pavia and continued the Lombard tradition of the *notarii regis*. In the years that followed the title of *iudex domini imperatoris* also began to be used. We know of some twelve to fifteen individuals, some of whom were also described as *iudices sacri palacii* (to state clearly the double bond with the king and Pavia), who held this title during the reign of Louis II. Then at the beginning of the tenth century, Berengar I and Hugh of Provence initiated a reform that caused the *scabini* to disappear, after which all the judges adopted the title that associated them with royal (or imperial) authority. This was not an attempt by the rulers to assert their authority, but was rather a statement of the corporate ties that linked both local and itinerant legal experts with the palace of Pavia and the legal training they had received there. The development of this elite was unique in Europe in this period and has been rightly seen as a key moment in the process that later in the eleventh century would lead to the development of new centres of juridical learning in Tuscany and the Romagna. Under the Ottonian emperors the title of *iudex sacri palatii* again came back into fashion, but was now interchangeable with the title associated with imperial authority. With only a few regional exceptions every judge in the *regnum Italiae* was now referred to by one of these two titles.

But at the end of the tenth century, just as the judges were becoming more closely associated with the palace, physically they were also becoming more distant from it. They travelled around the kingdom less often and, despite their title, fewer of them were trained in Pavia. They were now more closely tied to localities, but this was not a return to the model of the former *scabini*. They had been in the service of local counts, whereas the judges now emphasized their privileged dependence on the king. The Ottonians in fact removed all intermediaries to ensure that justice was administered throughout the kingdom in the name of the king. The number of *missi* with local duties also multiplied, and they were now recruited from the judges rather than from the small group of counts and bishops. As a result, the most mundane matters were now tried by highly ranked judges who used very sophisticated procedures. But the nature of the audience had changed as well, and these more refined juridical procedures no longer involved the *pauperes*. The emergence of new forms of rural lordships therefore began to separate the world of peasants from that of public justice, and while the legal records of the eleventh century tell us a great deal about disputes involving the elites, they say very little about the rest of the rural world.

Royal gifts

One of the qualities of kingship was munificence, and generosity was always an important attribute of power. In political terms this means giving presents in order to create and maintain networks of followers and friends. This extended only to the aristocracy and certain representative individuals, however, because the kings—unlike the popes and bishops, who followed a different tradition of the gift-making inherited from the empire of late antiquity—did not feel vested with a mission of charity towards the people, the concerns they expressed for the condition of the *pauperes* had no material implications.

The gift might be material (an object or a piece of land) or it might take the form of some share in power that might or might not bring material reward. Gifts might be given by the king either on his own initiative or as a response to a request; they might be one-off concessions or part of a more continuous policy of 'government by favours'.

We know little about the practice of giving objects as presents, except that these were an essential element of sociability among the powerful and a necessary feature of all power relations. This was true for individuals and states alike, and conformed to the subtle patterns of exchange that have long been studied by anthropologists. In this Italy was simply one example amongst many, and the establishment of a political alliance with the papacy, or the simple preservation of such an alliance, required some form of gift which when delivered by the king himself became the symbol of kingship. After agreeing on peace with Pope Gregory II in 728, for example, Liutprand placed a belt and sword, a gold crown, and a silver cross in St Peter's in Rome.[7] Two centuries later, on the occasion of his crowning as emperor in 915, Berengar I offered a crown and belt belonging to 'the dukes' (of Friuli), and ceremonial clothing that he had received from his parents, in particular from his father, Eberhard, duke of Friuli.[8] Gifts

---

[7] *Le Liber Pontificalis*, ed. L. Duchesne (Rome, 1955), *Vita Gregorii II*, 22.
[8] *Gesta Berengarii imperatoris*, ed. E. Dümmler (Halle, 1871) IV. v. 192–6.

were also used as tokens of obligations of *amicitia* or of reconciliation during peace rituals. In 860, for example, during a judicial assembly, Ildebertus, the count of Camerino, received a *fastilem optimum aureum* from Louis II 'because of the gifts he had previously given' to his sovereign. This brought the count's rebellion to an end before the assembled aristocracy and re-established the hierarchy of obligation, since the emperor had the last word when it came to the exchange of gifts. In a more peaceful way, Elbuncus, the bishop of Parma and arch-chancellor under Lambert of Spoleto, received from the latter a pair of gold spurs decorated with precious stones which he bequeathed to his cathedral (914). Ten years later Berengar I came to hear of a conspiracy organized by an officer of his entourage called Flambertus who was also his kinsman (he was the godfather of Flambertus' son). Flambertus was summoned by Berengar, who reminded him of his previous good deeds and tried (but in vain, since he was murdered shortly after) to renew his loyalty by offering him a gold cup.[9]

The politics of gift-making depended on the royal treasure, which was essential for the exercise of kingship and whose loss endangered its legitimacy. But kingship became less dependent on the royal treasure after the period of migrations. During the struggles between the Franks and the Lombards in the eighth century, for example, the treasure was used on many occasions until Charlemagne succeeded in entering Pavia in 774 and captured 'King Desiderius, his wife, his daughter and all his palace's treasure', which led to the immediate surrender of the entire Lombard people.[10] The treasure consisted not only of precious objects ranging from royal insignia to tableware, jewellery, clothes, and books, but also gold and silver (either in the form of circulating coins or of those that had been 'hoarded' from collections minted long before) as well as in threads and ingots.

With time, royal gifts more frequently took the form of land and the rights and revenues appertaining to it, which meant a share in the ruler's authority. The land 'treasure' at the king's disposal was the fisc, which could always be replenished through the confiscation of property after legal judgements, especially on those guilty of treason against the royal majesty.

---

[9] Liutprand of Cremona, *Antapodosis* ii. 69–70, ed. J. Becker (Hanover, 1915).
[10] Fredegar, *Chronicarum libri IV*, 37-8, ed. B. Krusch (Hanover, 1888); *Annales regni Francorum*, ad a. 774, ed. F. Kurze (Hanover, 1895).

The charters provide us with information about this. Those issued by the Lombard kings varied in type according to their addresses and their content. This was determined by whether the recipient was a religious foundation or body, such as monasteries or bishopric, or a lay person like Alahis, a Tuscan *gasindius* with close connections with the court who obtained at least seven charters from Liutprand. They varied again depending on whether they were deeds of foundations (as in the case of S. Salvatore in Brescia, founded by Desiderius and Ansa) or for the promotion of monasteries already in existence (Bobbio, Farfa). Others were issued in response to specific petitions or for grants of property that might vary in quantity and type, from a share in a well or a mill to whole domains or large forests. Many charters served simply to confirm previous charters, judgements or private transactions.

In all these, material issues prevailed and charters granting rights or exemption from duties or taxes were rare, even though there were a few examples of what would later become the standard features of royal patronage. This was the case of the right of free election granted to the abbot of Bobbio, together with exemption from the bishop's authority, and to those of Farfa and S. Salvatore in Brescia. Other charters bestowed exemption from taxation or from public services for the serfs belonging to a particular church or monastery (Bergamo, Brescia), or granted revenues that had previously belonged to the palace (like the thirty *librae* of soap granted by Liutprand to the bishop of Piacenza, *ad pauperes lavandum*), or the allocation of free women and their children to the *domini* of the serfs who had married them.

In the Carolingian period Italy became part of a much larger political entity, and its political subordination was evident from the fact that the issuing of charters remained the prerogative of the *rex Francorum* or of the emperor. Neither Pepin nor his son Bernard nor Louis II (before becoming emperor in 850) issued any charter, and they did not even have the authority to issue a capitulary. But since the Lombards formed a particular group within the empire it was also necessary to take account of their interests, and although peripheral, Italy was of great importance when it came to the issuing of charters. More than one quarter of Charlemagne's charters (one in every two after he became emperor) concerned Italy, although as emperor he spent only one tenth of his time there. As a result, the absence of the emperors was counterbalanced by the activities of the chancery, and the issuing of charters established strong links between the heart of the empire and its most far-flung regions.

The content of the charters also change a great deal between the late eighth and the beginning of the ninth century. This did not constitute a fundamental break with the past, since texts of the Lombard period were systematically reconfirmed. But it was by means of new charters that the legal practices of the Frankish territories were introduced in Italy in this period. This was especially true of the charters by which Charlemagne granted immunities and exemptions to monasteries and bishoprics, thereby setting all the churches on the same footing in relation to imperial authority and creating a common identity that in some cases survived long after. When in 998 the abbey of Farfa was involved in a dispute in Rome before the pope and the emperor, for example, it claimed that while it was governed by Lombard law it also enjoyed 'privilege equal to that of the other monasteries of the kingdom of the Franks, that is Luxeuil, Lérins and Agaune'.

The privilege to which Farfa referred to was still 'only' that of exemption. But immunities were also becoming more common, meaning that public officials were prohibited from administering justice or collecting taxes within certain territories. This suspension of ordinary jurisdiction in certain places already carried the seeds of later private systems of territorial justice, but this took a long time to develop and there was no simple mechanism of cause and effect. Nor was the purpose of the original grants of immunity to delegate power, but rather to transfer certain responsibilities to an intermediary. Whoever was granted judicial immunity became responsible for accompanying every free man residing on his properties to the judicial assembly, and for ensuring that all goods and services they owed continued to be paid to the authorities. The granting of immunities was part of a process, therefore, that led to the creation of well-defined administrative territories within which the lower levels of society were screened from direct contact with royal authority.

The charters issued by Charlemagne's successors followed in the same direction. These changes can best be observed in what is known as the period of the 'national kings' (888–962). In this period the number of intercessors (starting from the queen) increased, and their role in the presentation of a petition became more and more important. From this, historians have been able to reconstruct networks of the ruler's friends and followers, as Barbara Rosenwein has done for the reign of Berengar I. Individual recipients now increased in comparison to institutions, and more than a quarter of the charters issued by Berengar I and Hugh of Provence were in favour of individuals. This reflected the increasing power of the intercessors, who made gifts to their own entourage on the pretext of rewarding them for being faithful followers of the king. Grants of land, dwellings, and public rights involving sovereign concessions such as the right to fortify a settlement also increased in number. But this should not be taken as a sign that the rulers were abandoning fiscal rights wholesale, since despite their frequency these exemptions were always on a very limited scale.

From the 960s onwards the delegation of judicial rights began to be institutionalized, so that a territory protected by some fiscal or juridical immunity came to constitute a *districtus* in the true sense of the term. Those who benefited most were the bishops, many of whom now definitely replaced the counts in the administration of justice both in the towns and the immediately surrounding areas. At the same time, the ties with kingship were strengthened because the bishops administered justice as the king's nominated *missi*, in other words not on their own authority but as representatives of the kings. As we have seen, the judges who assisted them were also identified with the emperor through their titles. Therefore, although delegation of royal power was in most cases probably an acknowledgement of fact, there were counterbalancing tendencies as well.

The sharp decrease in the amount of land that was granted and in the number of individuals who received charters was a further indication of the new strength of Ottonian kingship. The central power no longer needed a huge retinue of *fideles*, and was now more capable of selecting its true allies. There is no better proof of this than the fact that the charter had become an authentic instrument of government. It was because of the critical role they played in integrating Italy into the empire, in organizing the kings' followers, and in reinforcing their recently established authority that charters were carefully sought after and preserved, their confirmation being regularly requested at every change of ruler. Their importance for both governors and the governed was the truest gauge of their effectiveness.

3

The aristocracy

Stefano Gasparri

The decline of the senatorial order

The Roman senatorial order was the principal model to which the medieval aristocracies of western Europe looked, because it had been founded on the ownership of land, embodied the concept of nobility, and linked prestige to the exercise of political power and ancient lineage without excluding the promotion of *homines novi*. But it was especially in Italy (and this was only an apparent paradox) that the early medieval aristocracy rose from the end of the old senatorial order.

By 500 AD the Italian aristocracy had a much more conservative profile than its western European counterparts, where senatorial families had by that time cohabited for generations with the military elites of the barbaric tribes that had settled in the former Roman provinces. In Italy, by contrast, this had occurred only more recently, and only after the Goths consolidated power after the accession of Theoderic (493), so that on the Italian peninsula the two groups remained separate. The senators continued in their office without interruption, managed public functions, and continued traditional ways of life in a social, political, and institutional environment which both in theory and also in reality largely preserved the ancient *res publica* unchanged. The official ideology of the reign of Theoderic extolled the civil features of the senatorial aristocracy, who continued to hold the highest bureaucratic offices, the most powerful being that of prefect of the *praetorium* (civil administration) of Italy, in clear contrast to the military task of defending *Romanitas* that was reserved for the Goths. In practice the differences between the two groups was much smaller. On one hand, there were senators who adopted a different way of life and even held military offices, from *comes* Colosseus and Servatus *dux Retiarum*, to the better-known cases of Ciprian and Liberius. On the other, as had occurred in the past, members of the Gothic elite also entered the senate, one example being the *patricius* Tuluin, or Triwila, who was *praepositus sacri cubiculi* (a Palatine, not a military office) and obtained the rank of *vir illustris*, which was only conferred on the highest-ranking senators who actually took part in the assembly.

It was less easy now for the senatorial class to leave Rome and go to the court of the Gothic king in Ravenna to take on high Palatine offices. Nonetheless the two main aristocratic clans—the Deci and the Anicii—frequently still held the most important offices, from the *caput Senatus* (leader of the senate) to the prefecture of the *Praetorium*. Alongside these families, a provincial Italian nobility had gradually evolved around the court in Ravenna which included many famous persons, notably Cassiodorus, the important minister from southern Italy, and many 'Liguri' from the Po valley. Amongst these was Faustus Niger (perhaps related to the Anicii family), *quaestor* of the Sacred Palace; Constantine, who later became the municipal prefect; and John, who was prefect of the *praetorium*. All were large landowners, but while the wealth of the great senatorial families had traditionally consisted in properties scattered across different provinces of the former empire which were now difficult to control, the property of the provincial aristocracy was by contrast concentrated in more limited areas and often within a single municipal territory. The big families who controlled the senate were as a result partly disadvantaged. Some of them, including members of the *gens Anicia*, had already moved to Constantinople to be close to the emperor. But although they came to form a new political oligarchy, their economic foundations were fragile.

The tendency for the senatorial elite to identify increasingly with the city of Rome while a quite distinct Palatine aristocracy was developing in Ravenna is evident from their efforts to block the papacy's attempts to assert its own power in the city. During the Laurentian schism, for example, Laurentius had the support of the majority in the senate and engaged in a lengthy struggle with his rival, Symmachus, who was supported by a group whose members included Cassiodorus and Liberius and the majority of the clergy. But Symmachus emerged as victor even over the senators who supported

Constantinople, and he consolidated his victory at the synod of 501, where he rejected the senate's claim, made twenty years earlier, that it had the power to ratify papal elections and to control ecclesiastical property, most of which originated in donations from the aristocracy. By abolishing this decree Symmachus brought to an end the senate's attempts to control the papacy, while the rapid decline of the Senate and its members in the following decades made this impossible. During the first crisis of the Gothic regime in the final years of the reign of Theoderic, it was significant that the king sent Pope John and a following of senators to Constantinople with a request for conciliation towards the Arians, even though this was impossible to achieve. But this was a clear illustration of the new power relations within the municipality of Rome. Only the death of Theoderic (526) saved the returning senators from meeting the same tragic fate as Symmachus and Boetius, both of whom belonged to the Anicii clan and were executed as traitors by the Gothic king.

The war between the Goths and the Byzantines that broke out a few years later marked the beginning of the end of the higher echelons of the Italic senatorial aristocracy. In addition to the severe economic impact on all social classes of the war which was fought by both sides in ways that did more damage to Italian territory and its population than to either enemies, during the reign of Totilia there was a deliberate attempt to displace and exterminate the aristocracy. Procopius of Cesarea, the historian who chronicled the war, described the deportation and murder of many senators. Those who managed to escape fled to Constantinople and did not return even after the end of the war and the issue of the Pragmatic Sanction in 554, which amongst other things attempted to restore to the senators properties that had been confiscated or lost during the war.

The arrival of the Lombards

In 569, fifteen years after the Pragmatic Sanction, Italy was invaded again, this time by the Lombards, and this proved to be an undoubted turning point in the history of the elites. Three famous passages from Paul the Deacon, the historian of Lombard Italy, vaguely described the forms of settlement imposed by the invaders, and gave some information on the elimination of both the senatorial and provincial Roman ruling class that took place in the early years after the invasion. The Lombard king Clephi 'put to death or drove from Italy many powerful Romans'. In the years that followed, 'many Roman nobles were killed for their greed' (572–84) by the Lombard *duces*. This had much to do with the circumstances of the Lombard invasion. Unlike the Goths, the Lombards were invaders and not allies of the empire, and as a result the Byzantines put up fierce resistance that included, more than frontal attacks, indirect tactics such as corrupting and poisoning their leaders—tactics that cost Alboin, the king who had led the invasion, his life, provoking the fury first of his successor Clephi and then of the dukes during the following decade in which the Lombards had no king.

But these descriptions cannot be taken too literally. The elimination of the senatorial class was not the result of physical elimination or banishment alone, although this did take place. A handful (it is not known how many, and there may only have been a few) of wealthy Roman property owners did manage to enter the ranks of the aristocracy of the new kingdom, which was open and had no rigid barriers as had been the case in all the former kingdoms that succeeded the empire. But the senatorial class *per se* disappeared, and with it went its values, way of life, culture, and administrative capacity. The senators, or the large Roman landowners, who managed to survive the storm of the first decades of the invasion did so in only one way: by becoming Lombards.

Paul the Deacon's information is confirmed by the sudden and total disappearance of references to figures identifiable with the senatorial type of Roman aristocracy in the Lombard territories. As well as the harshness of the Lombard conquest, the relative slowness (in comparison with what happened in Gaul, for example) with which the senatorial class had gained control over episcopal offices in the previous period also contributed to their demise. In Byzantine territories this occurred only after the Lombard conquest, but in the Lombard territories the failure of the large senatorial families to link their fortunes to the episcopal institution hastened their social demise. The weakening of the senatorial aristocracy was exacerbated further by the division of Italian territory into two separate political areas controlled respectively by the Lombards and the Byzantines: this meant that those who resided in the areas occupied by the new invaders now found themselves cut off from Rome, the ancient centre of senatorial power and the city in which all the powerful families had their roots.

The situation was different in the territories that had remained under Byzantine control. The letters of Gregory the Great demonstrated that many members of the old aristocratic families, even though technically resident in Rome, now lived permanently in Sicily or Constantinople and, like the patrician noblewoman Rusticiana, had no intention of returning to live, in Gregory's words, 'among the enemies' swords'. At most they sent gold to ransom prisoners. But on a smaller scale, a good part of the old ruling class—which for the sake of convenience we can still call senatorial even though its social composition was much broader—persisted within Byzantine Italy. Gregory the Great wrote letters to many of these patricians: one of the most important was addressed to the *ordo nobilium Neapolitanorum*, in which Gregory reminds them of their social duty as *domini* to care for the souls of the *rustici* in their service who were inclined to pagan superstitions. It is important to note that most of the nobles to whom Gregory wrote lived in southern Italy and Sicily, in other words as far away as possible from the areas that for decades had suffered the seemingly endless attacks of the Lombard invaders.

To avoid giving the impression that the senatorial class managed to survive in the Byzantine regions, it must be remembered that it was during the papacy of Gregory the Great that, as far as we know, the Roman senate met for the last time. The year was 603 and the occasion was the official acclamation of the images of Emperor Phocas and his wife by the senate itself and, importantly, by the clergy, the city's new aristocracy. Indeed, between 625 and 628 Pope Honorius I transformed the *curia Senatus* in the forum into the church of St Hadrian. Since the last person who can be identified with any certainty as a senator was Honorius' father, the consul Petronius, this episode (together with the transformation of the *curia* into a place of Christian worship and the rich donations the Pope made to the Roman Church from his own enormous family patrimony) suggests that in the twenty years after the end of the senate as an institution, Honorius was transforming the senatorial class into a class of clerics. In any case, the senatorial class was now diminishing rapidly and was unable to renew itself because imperial appointment and the title of 'vir illustris', obligatory for all new members of the assembly, could no longer be obtained. Neither imperial appointment nor the assembly existed any longer. The dominant feature of Byzantine Italy in the late sixth and early seventh centuries was determined, therefore, by the internal crisis of the traditional ruling class, which was accelerated by the contraction of the properties owned by the Roman-Italic aristocracy as a result of the Lombard invasions.

The scarcity of sources makes it very difficult to reconstruct the composition of the elites in the Lombard kingdom of Italy. There are clear signs, however, that the new ruling group was very heterogeneous: ethnic heterogeneity reflected the mixed ethnic composition of the invaders and there were distinctions between a small group drawn from the highest ranks of some particularly prestigious clans—the Beleos, Caupi, and Anawas—and others who after rising to high ranks of military command as dukes exercised power immediately below the king. Archaeological evidence from the first century after the invasion (the late sixth and early seventh centuries) shows that the elite of the kingdom had a strong military profile. This does not mean that they constituted a 'Lombard' aristocracy in ethnic terms, even in the tenuous way indicated above. The values typical of a warrior aristocracy now prevailed, and replaced the civil character of the former senatorial class. This is demonstrated by the objects that were placed in graves. In contrast to the objects associated with the Pannonic burials attributed to the *gens Langobardorum*, as well as older Italian evidence, these were remarkable for their militaristic nature and for the richness of the furnishings. The graves are those of the so-called 'knights' tombs' and the tombs of the wives of the 'knights' (seventh century) that have been found mainly in border areas of the Byzantine territory, an interesting example being the necropolis of Nocera Umbra.

From the seventh to the ninth century: Romans and Lombards compared

In 680 the first effective peace treaty was concluded between the Byzantines and Lombards, and this marks a symbolic starting point for studying the situation in Italy down to the Frankish conquest. A number of developments stand out quite clearly. First, the development of the elites in the Byzantine and Lombard lands had by this time produced two dominant social groups that had many features in common. If the Lombard aristocracy was traditionally a warrior aristocracy, the class of politically active freemen in Byzantine Italy was also called *militia* and its members *milites*. By the mid-seventh century the recruitment of the troops was gradually taking place at a local level in ways that made land ownership an indispensable economic basis for the new elites. Certain terms, such as *militia Neapolitanorum* or *Ravennensium*, or even *militia* or *exercitus Romanorum* or *Veneticorum*, indicate a social composition that went well beyond the aristocracy. The same was also true, for example, in the case of the *milites Comaclenses* who traded on the Po River, as a treaty dated 715 between Lombards and Byzantines illustrates. Nevertheless, these categories also included the *nobiles* or *nobiliores*, attributing to them a clear military function and identifying them as part of a military hierarchy that stretched from the dukes down to the tribunes. The tribunes, in particular, constituted a powerful group of landowners who by the beginning of the eighth century had already established strong roots in the *Venetiae* at a time when the territory around the lagoon was just beginning to acquire some regional autonomy. It might even be said that the tribunes represented the first aristocracy in Venetian history, flanking the *dux* or the *magister militium*.

The term *militia* had social, military, and political significance and was linked to the organization of the different Byzantine duchies and the exarchate. At the same time, the dukes and tribunes were members of an authentic landed aristocracy, and were also leaders of armed followers. One example was Toto, duke of Nepi, who with his brothers and 'many warriors and a croud of peasants' carried out a coup in Rome to claim the papal throne for his brother after the death of Pope Paul I in 768. His accomplices included people like the *secundicerius* Demetrius and the *chartularius*, later duke, Gratiosus: the former was an office-holder in the Lateran patriarchy, the latter had a military title. This pointed to two other features of the Italo-Byzantine ruling class. It included the clergy, the *primates ecclesiae*, as they were called in the *Liber pontificalis* of the Roman church; and while its wealth came from landed property, it was also an urban group that aspired to the highest urban offices. In the case of Rome, but not only in Rome, these were also ecclesiastical offices or were linked to ecclesiastical administration. Although it was explicitly said that he was an inhabitant of the small town of Nepi, even Toto is said to have possessed a *domus* in Rome in which the rebels, both leaders and troops, barricaded themselves for a year whilst controlling the city and the papacy. This suggests that the Toto family possessed a large aristocratic household in the city-capital which was the base for its political activity.

This warrior aristocracy consisted of landowners who also held important ecclesiastical offices and whose political activities were primarily urban. From the 720s onwards, these elites provided increasingly decisive leadership as the duchies of Byzantine Italy began to seek their independence from Byzantium.

Despite appearances, the social profile of the aristocracy in the Lombard territories was not radically different. The apparent differences derive in part from the sources, since the archival documents that are virtually nonexistent for the Byzantine areas are much more plentiful for the Lombard lands. The ideological representation of the two aristocracies was also different. In Rome, which by the mid eighth century was feeling the impact of the early expansion of the territorial domination of the Roman Church, the sources referred to the aristocracy by the ancient-sounding name *senatus*. This was not evidence of the impossible restoration of a vanished social order, but—in the same way that the leaders of the Neapolitan aristocracy regularly used the title *consul*—was an indication of the growing importance of the city elite attached to the papacy.

Militia, consul, senatus: the political-aristocratic vocabulary of the Byzantine territories seemed to differ radically from that of the Lombard kingdom, which by contrast identified the *gens Langobardorum*—the people-army of the Arimanni or *exercitales*—as the true holders of power, with a king and his *iudices*, that is his dukes and *gastaldi*, at its head. However, in reality the situation was quite different. The ruling class of the kingdom was made up of landowners who served in the army. In the Lombard world, the definition of *exercitus Senensium civitatis* (730), for example, is the precise equivalent of the Byzantine term *militia Romanorum* or *Neapolitanorum*. The Lombard aristocracy was also primarily urban, despite its considerable landed property. It is sufficient to cite the example of the city of Brescia, 'where there have always been a great number of Lombard nobles', according to a comment of Paul the Deacon referring to the end of the seventh century. In the early eighth century, Callistus, the patriarch of Aquileia—the source is again Paul the Deacon—deposed Arator, the bishop of Zuglio, from Cividale where he had taken office, and took his place because he was uneasy that a bishop under his authority might reside 'with the duke and the Lombards whilst he (who had his see at Cormons) spent his life in the sole company of common people'. Only lower-ranking people lived in the small semi-rural townships, it seems, while the aristocracy lived in the cities, especially politically important centres such as Cividale, the capital of the powerful Friuli duchy. This meant that the term 'Lombard' was never an ethnic concept: Paul drew on the political ideology referred to above to describe an aristocracy which was 'Lombard' by definition.

The two levels of the Lombard aristocracy

The available sources enable us to reconstruct the eighth-century-Lombard society in greater detail. References to members of the most prestigious families are very scarce in the charters, but they are more frequent in the pages of Paul the Deacon's *Historia Langobardorum*, although still somewhat sketchy, since the central protagonists are the Lombard kings. Almost the only records of the various dukes come from the same text, except for the dukes of Spoleto and Benevento. Since these dukes were sovereigns within their own territories for most of the Lombard period, a considerable number of their decrees have also survived. While we can find some references to the world of the highest Lombard aristocracy in northern Italy in the pages of Paul the Deacon, very few archival documents or records have survived. This poses major difficulties, not least because it is impossible to assess the scale or composition of the wealth of these leading families. The absence of use of written documentation might suggest that they lacked the self-confidence shown by families of more humble social conditions, or that their patrimonies were also less mobile. These more compact properties may reflect the concern of co-heirs to safeguard the destiny of a family's patrimony, and to ensure that the settlement of dowry portions, for example, did not result in the property being broken up.

Legislative documents tell their own story, which we should consider before turning to the charters. According to the military obligations set out in the Laws of Liutprand (chapter 83 of 726), freemen in Lombard society were divided into two main groups: those who owned a warhorse and those who did not and who were, in consequence, known as *minimi homines*. This subdivision corresponds in many ways to chapter 62 of the same Laws (724); when establishing the rank of persons obliged to pay the *wergeld*, the king identified two groups: one made up of the *exercitales*, who are *minimae personae* worth 150 *solidi*, and another group whose members were worth twice as much. The only complicating element derived from obligations for royal service: on this context even the lowest royal *gasindi* were estimated to be worth 200 *solidi*. A generation later, in 750, when Aistulf decreed his so-called 'military laws', in chapter 2 the basic division into two groups was replaced by a three-group classification, which might reflect either the development of military techniques or simply a more complex social division. However, the two richest groups were still identified by the possession of horses, while the third (the *homines minores*) did not. It may be, therefore, that the new classification was simply the result of greater legislative precision.

The most likely explanation is that all of these factors were in play. In any case, the next set of laws relating to military mobilization, the capitulary of Lothar of 825, which takes us into the Carolingian period, also divided the free population into two groups: the *bharigildi*, who were able to arm themselves completely, and the others who had to join with other low-ranking freemen to raise the means to arm and equip themselves. In the early decades of the ninth century, 'complete' arming clearly meant providing the arms and accoutrements of a knight, so it can be said that during the course of the century the basic social distinction in terms of military obligations remained the same: society was divided into those who were and were not knights. The development of military service for the king seems to have opened new opportunities of social ascendancy for the former.

The *potentes* referred to in Aistulf's chapter 2 are described as owners of seven *casae massariciae* (farmhouses). More will be said later of the landowning system, but this can be taken to indicate an average rather than a high level of landed wealth: members of the Lombard elite owned lands of much greater value. The legislator's principal concern, however, was to fix the basis for a general military mobilization: seven farmhouses constituted a patrimony sufficient to arm a knight with heavy equipment, and it was this, rather than the desire to register the wealth of the elite, that was exactly Aistulf's objective. But this source also points to the presence of a class of owners whose wealth consisted significantly of money. It was no accident that Aistulf's chapter 3 should have included *negotiantes*, or merchants, amongst those who could be mobilized like the landowners. The richest of them were described as the *maiores et potentes* and, as well as a second group described as 'those who come after', they were called to come armed on horseback, unlike a third group referred to as *minores*. Aistulf's chapters 2 and 3 therefore match perfectly, and constitute additional proof that the wealth of the Lombard aristocracy derived from money as well as land.

The Lombard kings made large gifts to their loyal followers, of whom the most important were the *gasindi*, who were bound to the king by an explicit and formalized relationship of patronage. Although there are very few references to these gifts in written sources, however, the twelve royal diplomas that in 762 were all granted to a single person who had no obvious title give an indication of the real number of donations. (The original documents have been lost, but a record of them survives in the inventory of Ghittia, an inhabitant of Pisa in 762.) The modest value of many of the gifts suggests that they constitute a capillary structure across the kingdom and its social fabric. We have more evidence of them in border areas, such as Spoleto and Tuscany, perhaps because the distance from the centre of power led the king's followers to request written documents to guarantee the concessions. This was less necessary for those who were physically closer to the court and who could be rewarded by the king in other ways, most obviously through the conferment of public office. This would explain why none of the *gasindi* of northern Italy that are known to us, such as Gisulf in Lodi and Taido in Bergamo, made any explicit reference to royal gifts. The family of Gisulf in particular was surrounded by many other *gasindi*, or *gastaldi*, or *viri magnifici*, a title usually held by high-ranking men close to the king, suggesting that the king's closest followers formed a relatively compact group.

To conclude, the aristocracy drew much of its influence from geographical proximity to royal power. Although the *gasindi* were paid, their relations with the king were based in ties of patronage, and it is significant that they were constantly described as persons of exceptional wealth in the documents of the period.

The family group of the woman named Ghittia from Pisa offers a good example of the profile of the 'middle' aristocracy in the kingdom. The inventory of her archive, which contains eighty-eight charters, shows that land was the basis of the family's wealth, while one of the most important members of the family seems to have been a high-ranking public official. Other charters refer to the acquisition of the *mundium* (juridical protection) of men and women; a precept by King Liutprand deals with the concessions of salt deposits, with indirect reference to some form of commercial activity. The inventory also lists the *mobilia* owned by the family. This included some money, but not much: two gold rings, a pair of earrings, a piece of gold, a belt with a gilt silver buckle, a silver bowl, some silver spoons, silver spurs. These costly luxury objects were for personal use, for banquets or war, or for the military parade. The male members of the Ghittia family were owners of land and servants, they were followers of the king and perhaps merchants as well; but they all shared the common social identity of the knight. The objects which had formerly been used to furnish tombs were now described in charters and handed down to heirs, indicating how the Lombard aristocracy now thought of themselves as a class of knights even if this did not mean that they were an effective warrior class in reality.

As we have said, references in the charters to the larger landed patrimonies are very scarce and the majority of these relate to the foundation of churches, hospices (*xenodochia*), or family monasteries. However, the large landowners possessed many *domocoltiles*, which were organized into different *casae massariciae* (farmhouses) with their respective servants or *aldi*, meaning that their estates were managed in two different ways: part of the estates were managed directly, while others were farmed by peasants on various forms of lease. The lands of the greatest *possessores* were not usually limited to the territory of their city: the possessions of the *gasindus* Taido, for example, stretched as far as the territories of Bergamo, Verona, and Pavia.

This was also true of the large patrimonies in the Lombard south, which had not been touched by the Frankish conquest and therefore showed greater continuity with the original Lombard period. Down to at least the middle of the ninth century the patrimonies of the aristocrats in the south (known as *Langobardia minor*) were spread out over the different territories attached to the two capital cities of Benevento and Salerno. For example, in 815 Alahis, the son of Arichis, donated to the monastery of S. Vincenzo al Volturno a patrimony whose origins can be traced back to the eighth century that included property in Venafro, Benevento, Salerno, Capua, and Telese.

The possessions of the highest class of the Lombard landowners were as a result spread across wide areas. But the essentially urban features of the aristocratic class that emerges from the charters is also evident: city residences were generally listed first in the possessions. Sometimes monasteries or *xenodochia* were also constructed in these houses: this was the case of Senatore and Teodelinda in Pavia in 714, and the two sisters Austreconda and Natalia in Verona in 745.

There is a document of considerable interest that dates from the time of Liutprand and records a commercial agreement between the Lombard kingdom and the merchants of Comacchio, the *milites* who sailed up the rivers on the Po plain transporting salt, spices, and probably precious cloths (715). The agreement provided clear evidence that the Lombard aristocracy had sufficient money to invest in new symbols of prestige and in luxury consumption goods. These included the *mantoras siricas* of Optileopa, the wife of the Sienese gastald Warnefrit (730) and the 'vestito vel ornamento . . . fabricato auro' ('a dress or ornament . . . made from gold') purchased for the marriage of Gradane, daughter of Rotpert of Agrate (745).

The possession of cash seems to have been reserved to the middle and upper classes of the kingdom. A certain Gaidoaldus *medicus* (doctor) was able to spend 100 *solidi* (726); Rotpert gave 300 *solidi* to his daughter Gradane 'in die votorum'. The monastery of S. Salvatore at Brescia, founded by the last Lombard King, Desiderius and his wife Ansa (757–74), also had considerable cash on hand. Their daughter, the abbess Anselperga, embarked on a dynamic policy of acquisitions, and paid 300 *solidi* to Stabilis, 200 to Duke John, 3,850 and then another 1,000 *solidi* to the family of Gisulf the equerry. In other words, money circulated quite freely amongst the higher social groups, and has to be taken into account as well as landed properties when evaluating the wealth of the higher strata of Lombard society.

Even when cash was not directly involved, wealth was often assessed in monetary terms. The *morgengabe* (the wedding gift that the husband use to give to his wife after their marriage) of the daughter of Orso of Lucca (739) consisted of objects, servants, and animals, whose value was estimated to be equivalent to about 800 *solidi*, while the numerous lands that the abbess Anselperga exchanged with the family of Gisulf, a royal equerry, for half the court of Alfiano on the Oglio River, was meticulously calculated in monetary values (3,850 *solidi*). The most remarkable case was again that of the court of Alfiano, the overall value of which was estimated at about 8,000 *solidi*.

These monetary estimates make us aware that the Gisulf family group was of the highest social rank. But many of the leading figures in this aristocratic society were even more wealthy. We get some glimpse of this from the Friulan families formed by the descendants of Duke Orso of Ceneda and Duke Peter of Friuli. Peter's sons Erfo, Mark, and Anto founded two monasteries, Sextus in Selvis and Saltus near Cividale. Erfo later founded S. Salvatore at Monte Amiata. All these monasteries were richly appointed, although we have details about only the two monasteries in Friuli that possessed three courtyards, a chestnut wood, mills, twenty farmhouses, a mountain in Carnia, woods, animals, and all the properties between Tagliamento and Livenza, as well as dwellings in Belluno near Verona. The children of Orso and his wife, *domna* Ariflada, were cousins of the three brothers mentioned above: John, who was possibly duke of Persiceta, and his sister Orsa sold 100 jugers of land to the monastery of S. Salvatore in Brescia (a royal donation), then donated seventeen farms to the monastery of Nonantola, as well as much other property (farmhouses, 100 jugers of land, other portions of land, etc.) belonging to them and to Orso, son of John, who was a monk at Nonantola. But that was not all, and Duke Orso founded and appointed the monastery of S. Benedetto in Adile, another monastery in Emilia.

This was truly the wealthiest aristocracy within the ruling elite at the time of the end of the kingdom in 774: it formed an *Austrian* aristocracy with its roots in north-eastern Italy, and was closely linked to the kings of Friulan descent. It was not by chance that the families of Orso and Peter can be traced across four generations, which is extremely rare for families of non-royal lineage in Lombard Italy, or that there was also information about them in the writings of Paul the Deacon. They constitute a unique example, since we have references to the family both in charters and in narrative sources. But they also left material evidence, especially the richly decorated evangeliary owned by Duke Orso that is today housed in Cividale. Even other wealthy Lombard families like that of Gisulf the equerry were by comparison clearly of lower rank.

The aristocracy of the peninsula between the Lombards and the Franks

The Frankish conquest of the Lombard kingdom in 774 did not lessen the prestige of the indigenous aristocracy, except for the nobles in the area of Lombard *Austria*. The unsuccessful revolt of 776 against the new Frankish rulers in the Veneto-Friulan area—maybe a part of a wider rebellion that never materialized—provoked a serious reaction from Charlemagne. The famous expression of the *Annales regni Francorum* in which the king 'disposuit eas omnes per Francos' ('had all of them replaced by Franks') refers precisely to the period following the revolt, and *eas* is the Veneto and Friulan *civitates*. This clearly means that the local ruling class was either replaced or weakened, interpretation that is borne out by the relatively abundant references to the confiscation of the properties of the local *possessores*. But as early as 799 we find that an influential Friulan aristocrat named Aio, who owned properties that stretched from Friuli to the area near Vicenza and Verona and who had previously rebelled against Charlemagne and then fled to the Avars, was pardoned, had his properties returned, and was given the title of count. It was precisely because Frankish law in Italy made Lombards counts (*langubardisci comites*) eligible to hold the highest public offices in the new Carolingian kingdom of Italy that the case of Aio was far from unique, although his involvement in an earlier rebellion makes this a particularly significant one.

The early years of the Frankish conquest were nonetheless harsh ones, even though the brunt was largely carried by the lower classes, and by the small and medium landowners whose plight can often be glimpsed from the wording of legal codes. But the former ruling class could not easily be substituted, since the early Frankish immigrants were few in number and rarely settled in the country. South of the Apennines, in the duchies of Spoleto and Tuscany, there is no mention of the Franks or other northern foreigners in written sources until the first decade of the ninth century. The first certain evidence of the spread of the vassalage system that was typical of the Frankish aristocracy also dates from the same period.

Prosopographic studies of the Frankish aristocratic families who settled in Italy during the age of Charlemagne and the subsequent years also reveal the fragility of their territorial settlements and the brevity of their genealogical lines. Amongst the counts it is often hard to find other members of their family who held office in Italy; nor is there evidence that the offices themselves provided a basis for establishing new family dynasties. It was also rare for Frankish aristocrats to serve as bishops in Italy in this period, although the situation changed significantly after 834, when Lothar made submission to his father, Louis the Pious, who had just been reinstated as emperor, and swore 'to go to Italy and stay there, and to not leave it again until his father commanded it'. Many supporters from leading Frankish families followed him to Italy and were for a long time cut off from their properties and benefices in the countries of origin (which were often even confiscated). Forced to settle in Italy, they were appointed to bishoprics, monasteries, and land that had been confiscated from their indigenous owners, so reducing the positions formerly occupied by the leading Lombard-Italic families. Frankish dominion in Italy was as a result intensified. The Frankish families who settled in Italy during this period included the Supponids, who settled in Brescia, Parma, Piacenza, Modena, and, for a brief time, in Spoleto, and became related to the Carolingians when the daughter of Adelchi, count of Parma, married the son of Lothar, Louis II. The Unruochings and the Widonians also acquired the duchies and marquisates of Friuli and Spoleto respectively, while the counts or marquises of Tuscany were descendants of a Boniface who lived in the 820s.

However, the sources offer clear information on only a very small number of high-ranking families, so that their presence in Italy, together with that of a few other lower-ranking families whose genealogical lines have survived, can only be dated approximately from the 820s and 830s.

Even though they were not of a very high level, we have some information on the Aldobrandeschi, a Lombard family originally from Lucca, which by about 850 had risen to the rank of count in various parts of southern Tuscany through ties of imperial vassalage.

But it is mainly the fact that this was a local family from the Lucca territory—an area which has an archival patrimony that is exceptional in terms of its age, abundance, and continuity—that explains why their origins can be traced back to the end of the eighth century and forward into the late Middle Ages. This remains, nevertheless, a very rare case.

The imperial nobility and the Italic aristocracy

We know little about the structure of aristocratic families in this period. The most significant feature was the importance of the female line, which constituted the connecting threads that held together different family agglomerates. Examples of this were the Supponids and Unruochings families on the one hand and the Tuscans and Spoletans on the other, both families that were united in pairs by marriage. The Unruochings were in addition related to the Carolingians because Eberhard, the companion of Lothar I and duke of Friuli from about 834, was the husband of Gisla, the daughter of Louis the Pious. In the latter case, the female line was the higher of the two, a fact that was acknowledged in an exceptionally important document: the will of Eberhard and Gisla dated 867. The Carolingian character of the family—which would reach its greatest ascendancy when their second son, Berengar, became first king of Italy and then, in 888, emperor—is evident from the fact that amongst the *mobilia* left to their first-born son, Unroch, was a 'corona aurea cum ligno Domini', in other words a crown containing a fragment of the relic of the True Cross, the possession of which was a distinguishing feature of members of the Carolingian family.

The will is interesting also because it contains many elements that help us to understand the culture of the family of Eberhard and how they perceived their public functions. From his father, the first-born son, Unroch, received the insignia of the highest level of public office: a sword with a gold hilt and point, a belt, a knife and gold spurs encrusted with jewels, a tunic woven in gold, a cloak and a fibula also made of gold, as well as other arms and various gold and silver objects. There were also luxurious vestments for the chapel, including an evangeliary 'de auro paratum', and the crown with the precious relic mentioned above. Berengar, the second-born, inherited a complete set of weapons, similar to that of Unroch, that were made of silver instead of gold, especially the sword, which had a hilt and point of silver, while the chapel objects were mainly made of ivory (including the cover of his evangeliary) as well as of gold and silver. The third-born, Adalard, received similar military and religious objects, but the former were made of ivory and gold (the sword in particular) while the latter were made of glass and crystal as well as gold and silver. The fourth son, Ralph, received fewer objects, and none for military parade; he did, however, receive the sum of 100 *mancusi*. This reveals a careful albeit not automatic, gradation of precious materials and the other objects that reflected the different ranks to which the sons were, at least in theory, destined and the public offices they were likely to hold during their lifetimes. They were also described as soldiers and also explicitly as knights, as the provision of sword, belt, spurs, coat of mail (*brunia*), helmet, and shield demonstrate. Finally, the will also illustrated the combination of the militaristic character of the aristocracy with its proclaimed religious devotion which added moral gravity to the public offices that the young Unruochings were to hold. This reflected very accurately the Carolingian concept of the *militia*, whose organization had from the time of Louis the Pious been reshaped under the influence of the bishops.

The role of women, which although subordinate was by no means unimportant within an aristocratic family that had not yet acquired a strong agnatic basis, is revealed by what was left to the three daughters, Engeltrud, Judith, and Eilwich, in the division of both the family's landed properties and of the *mobilia*, whose key role once again becomes evident. The *mobilia* included precious plates, *pallii*, and reliquaries decorated in gold, instead of the chapel vestments. But most importantly, the daughters received books from Eberhard's library, the size of which is also revealed. They received not only missals, hagiographic works, and sermons, but also (in the case of Judith) a codex containing the laws of the Lombards. Albeit on a more modest level, the division reflects the content of the part of the library that went to the sons, where religious works were accompanied by legal texts, the *liber rei militaris* (in other words, Vegetius), works on cosmography, and collections of imperial edicts. This means that Eberhard and Gisla saw their daughters' future in terms that were not entirely passive, although they would remain within the choice of their original or acquired family groups.

Eberhard's family estates were naturally landed properties, which were sometimes described in general terms such as 'all that is of our property in Langobardia and in Alamannia', referring to what was bequeathed to Unroch. On other occasions, however, there were references to single *curtis*, the agricultural holdings which even more than in the previous period were the principal sign of the landed wealth of the aristocracy and of their ability to support retinues of armed of *vassi*. The core of Eberhard's Italian properties was, for example, the *curtes* of Musestre at Sile, near Treviso. The reference to this aristocratic landed property raises a fundamental question, however. Not only Eberhard's family but all the other families of the high aristocracy of the Carolingian age—what German historians have called the *Reichsaristokratie*—had very weak roots in the cities, even though many of their members were counts or bishops. What counted much more, and constituted the essential base for political activities that extended across a multi-regional chequerboard, was their relationship with the Carolingian dynasty, which from the end of the ninth century in many cases also gave rise to future dynastic ambitions. The lesser aristocracy was by contrast necessarily more closely linked to the city—the *civitas*, consisting of a centre and its surrounding territory—where immigrants from across the Alps and natives lived together, forming a social class whose genealogical features in this period are almost completely unknown to us.

In that part of Italy that was not included (or only theoretically included) in the Lombard-Carolingian kingdom, the aristocracy remained more closely tied to the cities which continued to be the primary source of their political strength. In Rome, in the middle decades of the ninth century, the 'party of the nobles' almost always held power and controlled the papacy. Its leaders were the *Quiritum principes* who had used force to put Sergius II—one of the three popes of this century from the same family—on the throne of St Peter in 844, having taken control of the city after an impressive demonstration of military might. According to the official account of the *Liber pontificalis*, their rivals were not surprisingly described as 'rough people from the country', deemed to be quite foreign to those urban groups who through the exclusive organization of the Lateran patriarchy controlled the selection of the aristocratic clergy from which the popes were elected. Benevento, too, with its princely *pala-tium* and court, was another place where power was contested between families whose roots lay in many different parts of the southern territory. When after 849 the *Langobardia Minor* split into two principalities with their capitals at Benevento and Salerno, the competition doubled, as there were now two seats of power (and soon Capua would be a third), but the role of the aristocracy of the ancient capital remained unchanged. Indeed, the main branches of the two principal families in Benevento, the group of Dauferius *propheta* and of Dauferius Balbus or *mutus*, established links with various other princely dynasties until 861, when the former took power in Salerno with Guaiferius I and held it for 300 years. These families were urban in every respect and all owned houses in each of the three city-capitals, even though the bulk of their wealth derived from landed property: but their control of public offices and func-tions in the city-capitals, rather than of rural *domini*, was the key to their power. To argue, therefore, that the rise of the Capuan dynasty constituted the establishment of a new form of *Landesherrschaft* (Territorial lordship) in *Langobardia Minor* is seriously misleading, and greatly underestimates the urban character of this aristocracy both in the southern Lombard lands and in the Romanic territories.

The same can be said of Naples. As in the cases of Rome and Capua, not only were the links between urban political power and episcopal authority very close (to the extent that both Stephen I in 755 and Athanasius II in 877 were both dukes and bishops) but there was also from an early period a tendency for the ducal office to become a dynastic one. After Sergius I in 840 this became permanent, and continued down to the arrival of the Normans. The last example is Venice, or rather the Veneto duchy, as there was no real Venetian *civitas* before about 900. But despite the lack of developed urban structures, the aristocracies that settled in the different parts of the Venetian lagoon naturally focused on the urban centre that was emerging on the islands of Rialto. For almost a century after 811 the ducal office would be monopolized by a single family, the Particiaci, who became the first ducal dynasty in the history of Venice. Despite the unique location of the lagoon that gave rise to an aristocracy that was settled more on water than on land, Venice was in fact very similar to other examples discussed above, and reveals another aristocracy whose features were somewhat different from the one that dominated the Lombard-Carolingian lands of the Italic kingdom.

Crisis in the Italic kingdom and the new aristocratic families

The political crisis of Carolingian Italy accelerated after the death of Louis II in 875, and gave rise to important changes in the ruling class. The almost contemporaneous elections of Berengar I of Friuli and Wido of Spoleto to the Italic throne in 888 marked the start of a period of uninterrupted political instability. The conflicts between the Unruochings and the Widonians families, and the intervention of Louis of Provence and Ralph of Burgundy and, later, that of Hugh of Provence, who managed to reign for several years, from 926 to 946, all contributed to this process. The struggle between Hugh's son Lothar and Berengar II of Ivrea, who emerged the victor, then brought about the intervention of a third party, Otto I, king of Germany, whose victories between 951 and 962 resulted in the unification of the Italic and German kingdoms.

In this process the principal aristocratic families of the Carolingian age disappeared. The Supponids, the Adelberti marquises of Tuscany, descendants of the Boniface family, the Unruochings, and the Widonians (the last two lineages after a only brief period of royal power) were all replaced by other families, whose appearance on the political scene took place between the end of the ninth and the middle of the tenth century. The problems created by these substitutions are various. There is the initial question of the ethnic background of the new aristocracy: were the former families from north of the Alps now replaced by indigenous Lombard-Italic families? Were the new aristocratic families of a different origin to their Carolingian predecessors? What sort of changes were taking place in the structure of these families?

It is not easy to answer these questions, partly because up to the beginning of the period under discussion the genealogical information is still incomplete, so that we have no information on the background and origins of these families. This is particularly true of ethnic background, but even if it is not always possible to establish with certainty the Italic (i.e. Lombard) rather than Frankish or Burgundian origins of particular families, there is no sign that there were two different 'models' of aristocratic groups. A family like the Obertenghi, the descendents of Obert I of whom mention was made for the first time in 945 with reference to a count, then marquis and later count of the Sacred Palace, were also active as counts in Luni, Genoa, and Milan, and were considered to be of Lombard origin. But they did not differ in any respect from other families of undoubted Frankish extraction like the Anscarici, the Aleramici, and the Arduinici, active mainly in the area of Piedmont and Liguria. Anscar I originated from Burgundy and was a follower of Wido of Spoleto: he was referred to as *marchio* from 891 and ruled in the area around Ivrea. William was *comes* under King Rudolph at the beginning of the tenth century and a few decades later his son Aleram was *marchio* in the ill-defined *marca* of Ivrea, between Acqui, Savona, and Vercelli. The Arduinici came from over the Alps at the turn of the ninth and tenth centuries, and were first counts of Auriate (in the southern part of Piedmont) then, under Arduin 'the bald', rulers of the county and later *marca* of Turin. In the case of the Lombard aristocracy, we find that the career of Adalbert, known as Atto, the head of a family from Lucca later known as the Canossa, was no different. Adalbert-Atto was count of Modena and Reggio between 958 and 962, and was a vassal of the bishop of Reggio. His fortunes took a leap forward when he joined the party of Otto I when the latter overthrew Berengar II and took the Italic throne.

Although the family obtained the *marca* of Tuscany only at the beginning of the eleventh century, Adalbert-Atto was described earlier as *marchio* in the documentary sources. This shows that in the tenth century the title did not have an accurate territorial meaning, referring to a territory known as a *marca* because of its political and administrative configuration. For the Canossa family, as for others like the Obertenghi and the Aleramici, it reflected the fact that their political and social standing was superior to that of a simple count. Although public offices were connected to specific territorial areas and provided the starting point for the rise in the fortunes of these new families (even though the real key lay in the accumulation of landed property and in the services rendered as vassal to kings, churches, and monasteries), they did not confine the families' power to a specific locality. The ambition and the expansion of aristocratic families, articulated into different branches (the Aleramici were an especially precocious case) who rushed to call themselves count and marquis, first accentuated and then abandoned the specific links between title and territory. As the dynastic process strengthened, the titles were increasingly linked to the fortunes of the families that held them, while the areas in which those families exercised seigneurial power and owned property cut across administrative districts in ways that made the latter increasingly disarticulated.

This process, which led to the rise of forms of seigneurial powers linked in a variety of different ways to royal power, occurred not only because of the collapse of the unified political and administrative structures of the kingdom—of which it was at the same time both cause and consequence—but also because of the parallel phenomenon of castle building ('incastellamento'). The power of the ruling families in the tenth century was represented first and foremost by their castles, which were essentially autonomous fortifications even if they later received legitimation, with the public rights connected to them, by the rulers. But while the castles became increasingly the centres of seigneurial lordships and the centres of the power they exercised (*districtus*), this meant that aristocracies were now abandoning the cities. It was here, at the same time, that the bishops were establishing their own unchallenged power, which was greatly reinforced by royal grants which extended from the right to build and maintain city walls to responsibility for public administration (*publica functio*).

The role of public office in the rise of new families was in some cases critical, while in others the exercise of seigneurial lordship had older origins that may have been rooted in the processes of land clearance and cultivation that pushed the frontiers of agricultural land forward (this last element, combined with the need to resist the Magyar and Saracen raids, may also explain the origin and proliferation of castle building). It seems much less likely that these different origins were linked to any ethnic distinction between the Franks and the Lombards. Therefore, it is difficult to interpret the reconstitution of the ruling class after the fall of the Carolingian order in ethnic terms. The great change in the nature of the new aristocratic lineages, whose power derived from landed properties and vassal service, derived from the conditions of the Italic kingdom in the tenth century, which were profoundly different from the previous century, and not from any attempt by the Lombard aristocracy to reclaim the power it had lost during the century of Carolingian rule. The very different political character of the post-Carolingian world made possible the rise and expansion of an aristocracy through the development of castle lordship and the consolidation of the family monasteries which constituted the essential means for the consolidation of family-based patrimonies. This also explains why so many of the families that rose to power during the tenth century would continue to exercise that power long afterwards. These families of counts and marquises proved long-lived, and over time played important roles in different regional and urban contexts. The Este and Malaspina families, who originated from the Obertenghi, were in this respect typical. It is for that reason that the late tenth and the eleventh centuries have rightly been seen as the breeding ground for aristocratic dynasties that were more strongly organized than in the past on the basis of agnatic succession and were destined to continue throughout the high and late Middle Ages in Italy.

The aristocracy and the cities

It may be possible to trace some elements of a Lombard identity within the aristocracy, but to do this we must move down to more middling social levels, for example to the small and medium rural aristocracy which in Tuscany was long known as the *Lambardi*. But in fact this was a reference not to ethnic or national features, but to the fact that these groups continued by ancient family tradition to use Lombard law. The fact that references to these *Lambardi* appear only in sources of a relatively late date—not before the eleventh century, although the roots of these family groups are certainly much older— also warns against any ethnic explanation of its origins.

But if the *Lambardi* cannot be contrasted with a 'Frankish' aristocracy, they did stand in contrast to the cities; and in this their situation was similar to that of the other families of the *principes Italiae*, the much more important dynasties of counts and marquises. During the course of the tenth century, the increasingly effective consolidation of episcopal power in the cities accentuated the essentially rural character of aristocratic power in the territories of the kingdom of Italy. Even the largest and most powerful aristocratic families would only become involved in urban politics much later and then on very different terms. But the lack of involvement of the aristocracy of counts and marquises in the urban world deeply conditioned their own evolution, since the vitality and political influence of the cities did not permit the formation of regional or sub-regional territorial political systems. Throughout the former Italic kingdom, the basic political unit largely remained the city and its surrounding territory. Only in the south was the situation somewhat different, but even here the ninth and tenth centuries were a period of instability that had weakened the principalities of Benevento, Salerno, and Capua from within long before the arrival of the Normans.

As the year 1000 approached, it was the cities that emerged from the extreme territorial and institutional fragmentation of the ancient Italic kingdom as the central axes of political life. It was therefore entirely logical, given the separation from the higher aristocracy, that the cities should have given rise to a new aristocracy that was linked directly to the dominant urban political power, the bishop. From the late tenth century onwards evidence proliferated of episcopal vassalage, which enabled the bishops to recruit followers from families of high social rank (known as *capitanei*) many of whom, even though gravitating towards the cities, had landed properties and lordship rights in the country. Episcopal vassals of lower rank were instead firmly settled in the cities. From Tuscany to Lombardy, the episcopal *milites* constituted the basis of a new aristocracy: to the traditional combination of landed property in the surrounding territories and urban residence, they added the bond of vassalage to the bishop's see, which was the source of benefices and concessions that in turn strengthened their power and social rank. To resist demands from the citizens (*cives*) the Milanese archbishop Landulf in 983 'distributed the riches of the church and many benefices of the clergy to the *milites*'. This was a symbolic date, because it heralded the appearance of urban factions that were determined to contest control of the cities in the most important urban centre in northern Italy. These conflicts would grow in the period that followed, even though the origins of the formation of a new body of client—the bishop's vassals—was certainly of earlier origin.

There were at least two central features of the aristocracy in Italy in the early Middle Ages. The first was the mobility of the aristocratic groups, which almost until the end of the period in question never formed a closed or hereditary social category (which is also why we have avoided using the term 'nobility' in this essay). An initial move towards a more exclusive structure did occur in the late tenth century, but it was uncertain and was never consolidated. The second feature was that the cities were the principal centres of political life, and it was here that the aristocracy, although with many vicissitudes, came to focus their activities: even at the moment of the maximum 'ruralization' of the aristocracy in the tenth century, new aristocratic groups were forming within the cities that were destined to influence their development from within. While it is true that the genesis of this new urban aristocratic class was closely linked to the episcopate, however, many members came from the aristocracy that originated in royal vassal service and held the title of count. An example comes from two Veronese families who held the rank of counts, the San Bonifacio family of Milo (documented from 906) and the Gandolfingi family of Gandulf (recorded from 930) from Piacenza, both originally vassals to Berengar I. Both families entered the orbit of the Canossa family and then of the Veronese commune at different periods. The paths followed by the Italian aristocracy towards the close of the first millennium were complex; but that complexity should not deceive us. Despite their castle strongholds, even the most important aristocratic families soon found themselves once more irresistibly drawn towards the cities.

4

Ecclesiastical institutions

Claudio Azzara

Ecclesiastical institutions in late Roman Italy, and the role of the bishops

Early Christianization of the Roman world took place mainly in the cities in ways that reflected the peculiarly urban character of the empire. Following the Edict of Theodosius of 380 that made Christianity the sole state religion, ecclesiastical institutions that had previously developed slowly and with little unity now began to be organized in more stable and permanent ways.

Each local Christian community was headed by an *episcopus* (bishop, 'overseer') who acted as ruler, teacher, and administrator of the sacraments, starting from the ordination of priests and confirmation. The care of souls instead was the task of the *presbyter* (priest, 'elder') who was also responsible for the day-to-day administration of the sacraments. The bishops and priests were in turn assisted by deacons. The mass of lay believers retained some influence in the election of their bishops and in the management of the affairs of the community, but their role in liturgical celebrations was greatly reduced.

The gradual separation of the church into what later became distinct and well-defined groups of clergy and laity was accelerated by the diminishing importance of the eucharistic sacrifice, a ritual that after the sixth century had become formalized to the point that it could be celebrated even without the presence of the people. Many social groups were now also excluded from the clergy, and in the period of the late empire slaves, colonials, and those who had been freed by pagan masters were all barred from entering the clergy. In addition, priests had now to provide proof of good moral conduct and education, qualifications that were not available to all. As a result the *ordo clericorum* became a separate group within the community of believers, and acquired exclusive functions in worship and the management of church property. The exclusion of the laity from the administration of ecclesiastical property was reiterated on many occasions and notably during the synod held in Rome in 502.

A clearly defined leadership structure would develop only later with the domination of the Roman papacy, and in the meantime individual Christian churches remained largely independent and continued to differ on both theological and disciplinary issues as well as in their political and social orientation. The bishops met in the synods that were convoked from the second century onwards. Originally these were local meetings that only later took on an 'ecumenical' character with the aim, at least in theory, of bringing together all the bishops of the Christian world.

The diversity of institutions and doctrines was so great that many historians prefer to use the terms 'churches' and even 'Christianities'.[1] Nevertheless, the different Christian communities did have some features in common, and in particular an increasingly well-defined territorial organization. As early as the time of Pope Gelasius I (492–6) the diocese referred to a congregation of believers ruled by a bishop, but this soon came to describe the territorial district surrounding the city where the bishop resided. In most cases the diocesan districts followed the boundaries of the earlier Roman *civitates*, that is to say the existing territorial organization dominated by the towns, but there were many exceptions. In southern Italy, for example, the diocesan network seems to have been tighter as a result of the higher density of towns compared to northern Italy. In addition to the episcopal sees there was also the metropolis, an ecclesiastical territory made up of a number of dioceses and headed by a

---

[1] See e.g. the debate in recent manuals: C. La Rocca, 'Cristianesimi', in *Storia medievale* (Rome, 1998); and A. Rigon, 'Le istituzioni ecclesiastiche della cristianità', in S. Collodo and G. Pinto (eds.), *La società medievale* (Bologna, 1999), who uses the term 'Christianities'.

metropolitan, or archbishop, who presided over all the bishops in his ecclesiastical province.

The gradual decline of the political and administrative structures of the late Roman empire meant that the western bishops often took responsibility for a range of administrative tasks in their own cities. As a result they took over responsibility from the civil magistrates for the welfare as well as the pastoral care of townspeople. Since the bishops were generally recruited from aristocratic families, they had considerable political experience and were familiar with the traditions of communal government. Now they took responsibility for provisioning the cities with food and maintaining the city walls to protect the population from the increasingly frequent barbarian raids. The new role of the bishops was soon reflected in the literature of the time. They were depicted confronting the invading barbarian chiefs and their warriors armed only with their spiritual authority and the protection of God and persuading the invaders to spare the defenceless inhabitants of their cities. A good example of this is Paul the Deacon's account of the meeting that supposedly took place on the Piave River between Felix, the bishop of Treviso, and Alboin, the Lombard king, who as a result agreed not to attack the city and even allowed the bishop to remain in possession of his church intact.[2]

Acceptance by the bishops of duties previously performed by the civil magistracies was not only a consequence of the decline of imperial institutions but meant that the bishops were the last representatives of the former urban ruling class who were still trusted by the Roman-Christian people. But this was also because the Roman state had recognized the bishops' right to exercise certain civil authority since the time of Constantine. An example of this was the *episcopalis audientia*, the civil jurisdiction that had been conferred on the bishops in the Roman empire in the fourth century and which was subsequently reconfirmed in many kingdoms of the barbarian west (from the Visigothic kingdom in Toulouse to the Ostrogothic kingdom in Italy), as well as in Byzantium. This civil jurisdiction has recently been the subject of a number of studies[3] which show that it

---

[2] Pauli, *Historia Langobardorum*, ii. 12.

[3] See G. Vismara, 'La giurisdizione civile dei vescovi nel mondo antico', in *La giustizia nell'alto medioevo (secoli V–VIII)*, Sett. CISAM 41 (Spoleto, 1995). The authoritative text by the same author on the same topic is *Episcopalis audientia* (Milan, 1937).

was integrated with the state jurisdiction in ways that conferred powers not only of arbitration but also of control.

In Italy in late antiquity and in the early Middle Ages, as in the Roman west as a whole, therefore, the bishop came to play the key role in urban government and defence. The beatification of bishops after their deaths was intended to perpetuate the shepherd's earthly protection of his flock, while recent prosopographic studies have shown how the higher clergy was 'Germanized' in the Lombard and Carolingian periods. Modern studies have also shown how many of the older written sources deliberately distorted and exaggerated the importance of local dioceses in ways that enable us to understand how the identity of each episcopal see was constructed and consolidated in collective memory. Similar approaches have been applied to the study of the formation of city and regional identities, and their relations with other sees, especially with the episcopacy in Rome. Recent study of the documents relating to the schism of the Three Chapters, for example, which brought a number of bishoprics in north-eastern Italy and Rome into conflict between the sixth and eighth century, has shown that the implications were never simply theological. Similar conclusions have been drawn from studies on the *Liber pontificalis Ecclesiae Ravennatis* by Agnellus, a ninth-century narrative source which provides fundamental information about the bishoprics in Ravenna and their antagonism towards the Roman papacy.

The collapse of the episcopal networks in the Italian peninsula following the barbarian invasions and especially after the Lombard invasion that began in 569 has been another major subject of research. This suggests that the bishoprics experienced profound disruption in the second half of the sixth century. Many sees were deserted as their prelates fled before the violence of the Lombards, their functions were transferred to other places, and the population of many diocesan territories fell, particularly in the Apennine regions of central Italy. Further research is needed to establish what happened to individual sees, why some were deserted and their powers transferred, as well as when these changes occurred, since in some cases these caused radical changes in the landscape and in the population following not just the immediate impact of the Lombard invasion but also the twenty-year war between the Goths and the empire (535–53).

Ecclesiastical institutions in the countryside

The structures of ecclesiastical organization in the countryside are harder to reconstruct than those in the cities of late antiquity and the early Middle Ages. In recent decades historical research on the organization of the provincial churches and rural parishes has focused exclusively on the late medieval period, for which the sources are much more plentiful.[4] Our knowledge of institutional structures for the earlier period is much more limited because of the restricted numbers and the geographical distribution of the available documents. For the crucial sixth and seventh centuries of the Lombard period, for example, most research is based on documents relating to Tuscany, which in both political and geographical terms differed greatly from most of the territories in the kingdom located north of the Po River. There are also major chronological gaps in the sources for this period. For the sixth–early seventh century the extensive correspondence of Pope Gregory the Great provides an important source for reconstructing the organization of ecclesiastical institutions, as do the imperial precepts or *capitolari* from the Carolingian period, whereas the earlier Lombard laws by contrast contained nothing of relevance. In short, while we have information for a limited number of areas and periods, the shortage of information makes it impossible to attempt a more general interpretation, and new archaeological research is needed to show how the development of rural parishes and rural society were linked in this period.

Nevertheless, the period between the conversion of the Lombard king and aristocracy to Catholicism and the establishment of the Carolingian order was very important for the development of ecclesiastical institutions in Italy because, while demarcations of responsibilities were extremely confused, lay and ecclesiastical institutions were also closely interdependent. There was a significant increase in

---

[4] Studies on ecclesiastical organizations in the Italian countryside in the early Middle Ages remain centred on the essays by C. Violante, 'Le strutture organizzative della cura d'anime nella campagne dell'Italia centrosettentrionale (secoli V–X)', and A. A. Settia, 'Pievi e capelle nella dinamica del popolamento rurale' in *Sett. CISAM* 28 (Spoleto, 1982). A recent overview is L. Pellegrini, '"Plebs" e "populus" in ambito rurale nell'Italia altomedioevale', in *Società, instituzioni, spiritualità. Studi in onore di Cinzio Violante* (Spoleto, 1994).

the number of rural churches during the seventh and especially the eighth centuries, however, that reflected changes in the devotional behaviour and the use of property by the Lombard aristocracy in this period. A 'saturation point' was reached during the ninth century, after which new foundations became much rarer, while there were even cases of the decay and abandonment of existing churches. Reliable sources indicate that in Lucca, in northern Tuscany, forty-three new churches were built during the eighth century, in contrast to only twenty-one in the following century. Even in southern Lombard Italy, where the dioceses were smaller and more compact because of the greater number of urban centres, there was a similar increase in the foundation of churches by powerful laymen in the second half of the eighth century.

Evidence from laws issued by the Carolingian kings suggests, on the other hand, that from the late eighth century many rural ecclesiastical buildings were being abandoned, and that this process accelerated during the ninth century. These laws frequently reminded congregations that they were responsible for the maintenance or restoration of their church, an obligation that if necessary could be enforced by local public officials. There is clear evidence that the abandonment of many churches and chapels in this period was caused by the collapse of their revenues, meaning that they were no longer profitable for the families that had founded them. The principal cause for this was the increase in the number of foundations.

The reason for the proliferation of religious buildings in the seventh and eighth centuries had less to do with the religious needs of the population resident in a particular place than with the desire of the richest and most socially prestigious members of the community to construct religious buildings on their properties without taking account of whether or not there was a large community of potential believers. They were motivated by reasons of private devotion as well as the desire to display their status, and by the prospect of income through attracting new donations for each individual church. This also means that the proliferation of privately built churches cannot be taken as evidence of new patterns of rural settlements in this period.

Nor does archaeological evidence in this case offer clear information about the changing demographic density and social structures of the population that gravitated around a particular church. And such information cannot be gained from cemeteries either. In Italy the right to burial was reserved exclusively to baptismal churches from the ninth century onwards; before that time burials took place either in the open countryside or in private churches. Even after the ninth century, however, members of wealthy families were still buried in private chapels or in monasteries and abbeys, whilst the lower classes were buried in the parish cemeteries. This does confirm the traditional picture of the parish church as the church of the poor, in contrast with the private chapels that were the typical churches of the wealthy.

The scant documentation that exists suggests that the connections between church building and rural settlements were highly heterogeneous. Houses were sometimes built around churches constructed in isolated locations, especially if the church had some particular attraction such as the possession of important holy relics. Alternatively, new churches might be located within an already established community to meet its spiritual needs. The charters from the Lombard and Carolingian era make the reconstruction of patterns of rural settlement even more difficult, however, because the meaning of the different terms used (*locus, casale, curtis, castrum*) is no longer clear. We can only say that rural churches could be located both within villages or close by or even at some distance, indicating a variety of different patterns which may have reflected regional differences which, however, remain impossible to reconstruct.

The study of relations between the parish churches and the ancient Roman settlements is also extremely complex and relies on equally uncertain information. There is a vast literature on the continuity between the Roman *pagus* and the medieval church, but historians have disagreed strongly over this. In juridical terms the element of continuity has generally been accepted, although this too might well have derived from continuity of settlement, since the early churches were established in centres sited along the principal Roman roads, quite independently of the territorial jurisdiction of the *pagus*. The founding of a church may even have brought the revival of a declining Roman centre. Only archaeologists can tell us whether in any particular locality there was real continuity of settlement between the Roman age and the early medieval period, or whether the appearance of continuity simply derives from some later recovery.

The growing number of new rural ecclesiastical foundations in Lombard Italy reflected the gradual but difficult Christianization of the *gens Langobardorum*, and seems to have encouraged the gradual formation of more clearly defined territorial boundaries around each parish church (to some degree repeating the model that had already been established for the dioceses) and the creation of new geographical districts. It was between the end of the seventh and the beginning of the eighth century that the term *plebs* first began to appear in documents with the double meaning of 'baptismal church' and 'community of souls', especially in central and northern Italy starting from Tuscany. When referring to a territory, the word *plebs* seems to be of popular origin, but in official ecclesiastical documents by contrast it is used with this meaning only from the ninth century to replace the older terms *parochia* or *diocesis*. It was in this period, therefore, that *plebs* began to refer to a specific area that did not have precise geographical boundaries but nevertheless defined a congregation of believers attached to a particular baptismal church for reasons of worship.

The documents also reveal that the territory of each parish church was anything but stable or well defined. The frequent vacancy of the episcopal sees made the dependency of the various parish churches on the dioceses somewhat uncertain, while the growth in the numbers of the churches brought constant changes to the organization of church districts. The definition of the church's boundaries remained particularly unclear for the faithful, and in many regions (for example, the Tuscan Apennines) individual believers were uncertain about the boundaries of ecclesiastical districts. Evidence of this kind suggests that it would be premature to identify the parish church with a clearly defined territorial space that defined a community's identity. This was also true for the church hierarchy. The sources indicate that in the eighth century in particular the territories of the baptismal churches were consolidated while the smaller churches within the same district (called variously *oratoria, oraculi, tituli,* and *monasteria*) came to accept their common dependency on the larger church in a relatively hierarchical system. The functioning of the baptismal churches and the minor churches, and the pastoral work of the clergy attached to them, can also be documented reasonably well. The oratories tended to have permanent officers under the direction of the rector of the local baptismal church. In the baptismal churches priests were chosen by the *populus*, in the private churches by the founder. Priests were consecrated by the bishop, who established them in the churches in their care and instructed them in the administration of the parochial property. They remained attached to the bishop by bonds of devotion and submission (*oboedientia* and *salutatio*), which were represented in material terms by the payment of a tax.

In contrast to these indications of reorganization and discipline there are others, however, that suggest confusion and inconsistency in bonds of jurisdictional dependence, as well as enormous sacramental and liturgical variations between individual churches, baptismal fonts, oratories, altars, and even priests. This reflected the absence of clear definitions of dependency and responsibility. A priest might, for example, have been consecrated by a bishop different from the one in whose diocese the church in his care was located; or a single altar in his church might have been consecrated by a bishop other than the ordinary of his diocese; and so on. Powerful laymen who founded oratories tried to reserve for themselves and their heirs the right to choose the rectors of the oratories, although there is also some evidence to suggest that the link between the rectors and the founders of private churches was a less direct one. Several baptismal churches even risked being 'privatized' and falling under the authority of a powerful lay figure. Signs of other irregularities such as dishonesty in the collection of tithes, the actions taken by many bishops to the detriment of the parish clergy, the lack of discipline amongst the rectors of the minor *tituli*, and the inappropriate criteria often followed in the choice of the rectors became even more evident in the ninth century, when Lombard Italy had already been part of the Carolingian empire for some time. In all probability this was the result of the intensification of practices arising in earlier periods.

These contradictory situations seem also to have prevailed in southern Italy, where written sources reveal that the attempts to regulate the smaller churches under the authority of the parish church were anything but consistent, and it frequently happened that private churches evaded the control of the bishops and the parish churches altogether. As in the north, further research on specific cases is needed before any more general hypotheses can be attempted. But it must also be remembered that as well as the Lombard-Frankish kingdom in the centre and north and the Lombard kingdom in the south, many other regions of the Italian peninsula were also part of the imperial-Byzantine world which had its own distinctive ecclesiastical institutions. In each region there were also important local changes

and developments that cannot be overlooked; for example, the growing numbers of immigrants from over the Alps in the different
ecclesiastical sees of Lombard Italy who accepted Carolingian
principles of authority but brought with them different customs as
well.

Monasticism

Monasticism is a spiritual way of life that is found in many different
religious faiths. In the Christian religion it first developed from the
deserts of Egypt in the third century, and later spread to the west
from the fourth century onwards, more often in the communal and
coenobite than in the solitary eremitic form. Monasticism took root
mainly in Italy, in Provence, and outside the empire in Ireland, where
it developed separately. After the end of persecutions against the new
religion, the various monastic communities became more permanent
and established rules to guide their life and work. Between 530 and
550, Benedict, the founder of the monastery of Montecassino, drew
up a written Rule on the basis of an earlier text (the so-called *Regula
magistri*) that thereafter played a pivotal role in the west alongside the
Rules drawn up by Colomba and Caesarius of Arles.

The Benedictine Rule moderated the mainly contemplative nature
of more radical monasticism by assigning specific manual tasks to the
monks and placing the monastic community under the authority of
an abbot. It quickly came to prevail over all others, and in the ninth
century, as part of the wider Carolingian effort to establish uniformity and more centralized control, the Benedictine Rule became the
only form of monastic regulation permitted in the territories under
Frankish rule. The adoption of the Benedictine Rule was encouraged
by the initiatives of Louis the Pious (816 and 819), but by this period it
had already spread spontaneously throughout most of Lombard-
Carolingian Italy. It was slower to reach some areas of southern Italy,
where it was not adopted until the period between the end of the
ninth and the eleventh centuries because the influence of eastern
Greek models and of Rome remained strong.

Monasticism found considerable success in Italy from its initial
introduction, which was followed by the founding of many religious

houses, including convents, that attracted members from the highest social classes of society. Many influential religious figures emerged from this movement and were often raised from the cloister to assume episcopal functions. The best known of these was Gregory the Great. Born into a wealthy patrician family, he renounced his promising political and administrative career and retired to a monastery that he had founded himself, where he gathered around him fellow monks willing to follow him. He was later forced to abandon the monastic life to become the bishop of Rome, an office to which he had been called by virtue of his great administrative capacities and spiritual gifts. Gregory the Great was not only the most important example of the figure of pope/monk, who combined practical pastoral capacities and ascetic qualities, but also the greatest promoter of the example of St Benedict, to whom he dedicated a biography in his *Dialogues*.[5]

Monks sent by Gregory the Great travelled from Italy as far as the kingdom of Kent to begin the Christianization of the Anglo-Saxons. Some time later, however, the direction of the missionary work was reversed, and it was the monks from the British Isles who carried out new conversion activity in Italy and on the Continent. Towards the end of 612, the Irish abbot Colomba, who had spent years in Frankish territory promoting the founding of new monasteries, went to the court of Agilulf, king of the Lombards. A few years later, with the approval of the king, he founded the abbey of Bobbio in a remote area of the Emilian Apennines that was also close to the principal thoroughfares.

The foundation of Bobbio was destined to play an important role in the development of Italian monasticism, and marked the beginning of the establishment of a long series of monasteries in Italy by Lombard kings and aristocrats. In the seventh century, King Grimoald founded the convent of S. Agata in Pavia and in the following century monasteries such as S. Pietro in Ciel d'Oro in Pavia, S. Salvatore (which later became S. Benedetto) at Leno near Brescia, and S. Salvatore (later S. Giulia) in Brescia were founded by the kings Liutprand, Aistulf, and Desiderius respectively. Monasteries of different sizes and affluence were built in both urban and rural areas in other parts of the peninsula, from the Veneto to Tuscany, from Friuli

[5] Grégoire le Grand, *Dialogues*, ed. A. de Vogué (Paris, 1978–80) (Sources chrétiennes, 251, 260, 265), ii.

(for example, S. Maria in Sylvis at Sesto al Reghena) to the duchy of Benevento (the large nunnery of S. Sofia at Benevento). Many of the monasteries created during the eighth century were sited in strategically important localities: this was the case of Nonantola, near Modena and hence close to the border with the exarchate; of Farfa, near Rieti, built by the duke of Spoleto at the gates of Rome; and of S. Vicenzo al Volturno in Sannio, built with the assistance of the dukes of Benevento, in a border area that separated their own lands from the potentially threatening presence of the northern kingdom and of Rome.

Many different factors contributed to the varied yet constant and influential process of founding new monasteries by the Lombard aristocracy. The motives came from the zeal of new converts to gain merit for life in the next world, but also from the religious policies adopted by the rulers who, especially in the early phases, wanted to establish links with their Roman Catholic subjects to enable them to compete better with the Catholicism of Rome and the empire. However, the creation of a monastery also and most importantly meant the construction of a centre that was capable of organizing the territory in which it was located, making it an important centre of economic activity that would also attract new wealth in the form of the donations that from the time of Liutprand (713–44) were greatly encouraged and regulated by the secular authorities. The expansion of monasteries founded by rulers and aristocrats, as well as private churches, offers clear evidence of the adoption of strategies designed to increase the wealth and strength of certain families, as well as of the aristocracy's desire to exercise and display political and social hegemony. This is supported by recent studies on S. Salvatore di Brescia and S. Vincenzo al Volturno, which have also made possible comparisons with tendencies in the Merovingian world and with the developments in Italy during the Carolingian age.

Archaeological research has made a crucial contribution to our knowledge about the Lombard monasteries, and new information on the development of material structures has enabled us to reconstruct how ecclesiastical properties expanded. New excavations have been carried out most recently at Sesto al Reghena and work may soon begin to correlate the different surveys already carried out at sites like Bobbio. A new project is also about to start on the abbey at Leno in the territory of Brescia.[6] The southern monastery of S. Vincenzo al Volturno remains unique because of the length of time it has been examined and the extraordinary wealth of the archaeological site. Successive archaeological digs have revealed the enormous size of what was in reality a monastic city around which complex economic activities developed, as well as properties that extended to distant territories, enabling the monastery to exercise economic, political, and cultural influence over a very wide area.[7]

Archaeologists have also helped us understand the criteria that guided the choice of the locations in which the new monasteries were founded, but since these were determined by specific local needs and circumstances they did not conform to any single generalized pattern or strategy. Nevertheless, an important starting point was often the presence of earlier structures such as the remains of a Roman *villa*, which often provided the base for new religious buildings in the countryside.

With the establishment of Carolingian power throughout most of Italy, new ties were established between the great monasteries, political power, and aristocratic interests. Almost everywhere existing foundations were enriched, while many new institutions were founded both in the cities (such as the church of S. Ambrogio in Milan, built in 789) and in the countryside (for example Pomposa, near Ravenna, and Santissima Trinità, later S. Clemente di Casauria, in Abruzzo). In this period many Franks also began to hold high offices in the abbeys and the massive increase in ecclesiatical property was accompanied by the granting of fiscal and juridical immunities, so that the protection (*tuitio*) offered by kings and emperors underlined the fundamental role played by the leading monasteries as political supporters of the Carolingian rulers. But when central power declined in the ninth century this also had important effects on the monasteries. Those ecclesiastical bodies that had been granted immunities (and these were not only monasteries) now had the

---

[6] See, for Sesto al Reghena, C. G. Menis and A. Tilatti (eds.), *L'abbazia di Santa Maria di Sesto fra archeologia e storia* (Udine, 1999); for Bobbio, the most recent study using written sources is A. Piazza, *Monastero e vescovado di Bobbio (dalla fine del X agli inizi del XII secolo)* (Spoleto, 1997); for Leno, an excavation that will continue over the next few years has been organized by the Università Cattolica of Milan.

[7] On S. Vincenzo al Volturno, see P. Delogu, F. De Rubeis, F. Marazzi, A. Sennis, and C. Wickham, *San Vincenzo al Volturno. Cultura, istituzioni, economia* (Montecassino, 1996).

opportunity to develop independent power similar to that of the lords, even to the extent of developing their own systems of vassalage. But many older foundations now had to face the competition of the newer foundations that had been granted many privileges by the secular powers and in some cases had developed as family monasteries. The nascent seigneurial dynasties that were becoming established used the newly founded monasteries as centres around which to reinforce family ties, strengthen their economic and patrimonial position, and assert and legitimize their newly found power. One of the most interesting examples of this was the monastery of S. Benedetto di Polirone (today, S. Benedetto Po) near Mantua, founded in 1007 by Thedald of Canossa. Finally, the monasteries were also engaged in warding off attacks from those attempting to establish their power in the neighbourhood, which included both secular lords and bishops. The extensive patrimony of the abbey of Nonantola was the object, for example, of the ambitions of the count of Piacenza and of other powerful figures including the bishops of Piacenza, Tortona, Parma, and Modena. The Saxon emperors could offer some protection, and like the Carolingians before them they also looked to the monasteries to maintain their authority in the complex Italian world.

The great wealth of the leading monasteries also made them inviting prey for the various raiders that roamed through Italy between the end of the ninth and the beginning of the eleventh centuries. As well as raids by Magyars, the Saracens made devastating attacks on S. Vincenzo al Volturno in 881, on Montecassino in 883, on Farfa in 898, and on Novalesa in 906. At S. Vincenzo al Volturno, the Saracen assault on the monks was strongly supported by the peasants seeking revenge for the harsh economic exploitation to which they had been subjected by the monastery.

Certain unusual forms of monastic life evolved in southern Italy, which was politically fragmented and which, because it had remained outside the Carolingian kingdom, provided opportunites for different cultural traditions to take root. In southern *Langobardia* the Lombard-Carolingian models that prevailed in central and northern Italy were also influential, but the eastern Greek imprint remained strong in Ravenna, Rome, and the Byzantine south. Greek monasticism took forms in southern Italy that were not simple imitations of the eastern models, however. Although this still remains a difficult area to study, there are signs that the eremitic life was widespread, and in the case of Nilo di Rossano stretched as far north as Lazio. In Apulia both Greek and Latin forms of monasticism co-existed, but after the arrival of the Normans, who also sought to use the existing institutions to consolidate their power, the organized communities were privileged over the anchorites and hermits. Centres like Cava dei Tirenni henceforth became a model for new foundations, including Monreale in Sicily which was built by the Norman king William II. But Greek monasticism was not eclipsed until the thirteenth century, when Latin culture finally prevailed in southern Italy.

Reform of the Church and ecclesiastical institutions in Italy

With the collapse of the public administrative districts during the tenth century, those bishops and abbots who held some form of immunity quickly consolidated their political authority over the populations living on ecclesiastical land. After the Saxon dynasty took the imperial throne, the bishops again enjoyed fiscal and juris-dictional privileges within the cities and on the lands owned by the Church or by the bishops, and took on wider administrative func-tions so that effectively they came fully to represent the *cives*. But while the bishops secured new civil power in cities, their ability to govern in ecclesiastical affairs remained weak because many privil-eges and patrimonies in their dioceses continued to be controlled by private churches whose rectors depended on the lay lords who owned the churches. Many of the private churches were sited close to the rapidly increasing number of castles, and often succeeded in taking over the religious functions of the parish churches. But if this was certainly disruptive in organizational terms, the private churches did nonetheless play a positive role in pastoral terms, and in particular were able to care for souls in isolated rural communities and for those living on newly colonized lands.

The institutional and ideological interdependence of ecclesiastical and lay institutions that went back to the Carolingian age now gave rise to intolerable strain. On the one hand, resistance increased to the powers exercised by the laity over the Church's offices, rights, and property, while on the other attempts were made to curb the excessive involvement of churchmen in worldly affairs. Proposals were made for the reform of the Church and of the clergy, whose highest ranks carried out duties that were no longer distinguishable from those of the lay lords and whose lower orders lacked training and were associated with ignorance, since many priests were unable to read the holy Bible. Various reform initiatives originated from different sources within the Church: some came from bishops such as Attone in Vercelli or Raterio in Verona, but the most important came from the monasteries. The part played by the Burgundian abbey of Cluny is well known, and more generally it was the monasteries that played the most important part in the reform movement and especially the new reformed Vallombrosan, Cistercian, Calmaldolese, and Carthusian orders that were founded between the tenth and eleventh centuries.

Popular religious movements, especially in Tuscany and Lombardy, also made a distinctive contribution to church reform in the eleventh century, although this was opposed by both the lay aristocracy and by bishops in central and northern Italy. Of these popular movements, the most important, and the subject of many classic studies,[8] was the Pataria movement that began in Milan in opposition to the archbishop and the ruling classes of the city and drew its support from artisans and merchants. Supporters of the Pataria movement called for a more highly educated and moral clergy, and for greater involvement of the laity in ecclesiastical life, at its most radical even demanding public trials for immoral clergy and direct recourse to the Bible when authoritative priests were not available.

The various reform programmes and their impact on the Italian Church and society have been quite fully studied, although further research may add more details about local case studies and specific individuals to demonstrate the complex, varied, and often contradictory nature of the movements that developed around the question of church reform. But to realize these broad-based, varied, and often quite extreme demands for reform, some guiding force able to coordinate and channel the different currents and movements towards clearly defined objectives was needed. It was the papacy that came to assume precisely this role, and in so doing modified the more

[8] See C. Violante, *La pataria milanese e la riforma ecclesiastica*, i: *Le premesse (1045– 1057)* (Rome, 1955), together with the fundamental work by the same author, *La società milanese nell'età precommunale* (Rome, 1953).

radical positions and avoided the danger of overturning the whole structure of the Church. The struggle against the lay investitures for ecclesiastical offices, simony, and concubinage (which also involved the problems of loss of ecclesiastical property as a consequence of claims from concubines and children) that was designed to protect the *libertas ecclesiae* helped establish a revived church that was free from lay interference, hierarchically organized under the pope, equipped with more refined ideological and juridical instruments, aware of its role in the world, and ready to present itself as a single and all-embracing institution, as the *societas christiana*, with its own claims to the political leadership of the west.

5

The papacy

Claudio Azzara

The papacy in the late Roman empire

After the Roman emperors adopted Christianity as the official state religion with Theodosius in 380, the new creed and its institutional structures were inevitably faced by the need to redefine the theoretical role of the *princeps*, who was already described as *pontifex maximus* and venerated in the pagan tradition. The resulting construct was based on a model of imperial authority that was distinctively Christian-Hellenistic, weaving together doctrinal arguments drawn from ancient political culture in ways that were most coherently set out in the life of Constantine compiled by Bishop Eusebius of Caesarea (*c.*260–339). On the basis of the concept of *speculum principis*, the *respublica* was ruled by an emperor who was one and only, an exact earthly reflection of the one God, the ruler of the universe, who held divinely granted power and very specific authority with regard to religious and ecclesiastical matters. Entrusted with safeguarding the *pax* and *unitas* of the Church, he was above all called on to defend orthodoxy from any possible deviation.

The definition of religious orthodoxy was delegated to the councils which were convened from the second century, first on a local scale and then with an 'ecumenical' nature, that is, aimed—at least in theory—at bringing together the bishops of all Christendom. From the first of the great ecumenical councils, held in Nicaea in 325 to dispute the theory of Arius on the nature of Christ, the emperor played a primary role in these assemblies of priests, which he convoked and presided over. It was also he who undertook the concrete application of the decisions made by the councils, using all the coercive power of the state. In short, from the early Christianizing of the Roman empire, a link was formed between imperial power and the ecclesiastical institutions in which reciprocal roles were not clearly distinguished but presupposed a close collaboration that was necessarily overlapping and often ambiguous. For their part, the ecclesiastical institutions had nowhere near the degree of organization, unity, and consolidation they would later attain through a process of slow evolution, and in particular lacked any clearly defined supreme authority capable of imposing order with any degree of continuity through the still heterogeneous lower levels.

In the church of the late Roman empire, the bishop of Rome did not enjoy any particularly high status. First and foremost he was the prelate of his own city, and any more general honorific superiority he was granted over the other bishops derived from the fact that his city was the *caput orbis*. In the absence of institutional links between the various local churches, the unity—which was already called 'Catholic'—of the Church lay in the uniformity of the faith professed by all its members. But it was not long before the conviction spread that the protection of this unity and uniformity in questions of faith was to be found in 'communion' with Rome, which became the guardian of orthodoxy as the absolute and undisputed custodian of the precepts of the councils.

From the papacies of Callistus I (217–22) and Stephen I (254–7), the bishops of Rome began to define themselves as the successors of the apostle Peter, who—according to a tradition founded on rather late sources—had established and occupied the first episcopal throne in Rome. As the successors of Peter in Rome, the popes laid claim to apostolic supremacy, just as Peter had been given primacy over the apostles in the mother community in Jerusalem after the Resurrection of Christ. Moreover, interpreting the famous passage from Matt. 16: 18–19, it was Christ himself who had invested Peter with a special role: *tu es Petrus et super hanc petram aedificabo ecclesiam meam* (Thou art Peter; and upon this rock I will build my church).

Using the Petrine tradition to its best advantage, the bishop of Rome continued to lay claim to a primacy—although not yet a supremacy—over the whole Christian Church, which still lacked a clearly defined hierarchy. The benefits of this initiative would not be enjoyed until a much later date, and although gradual, change met with considerable resistance. The rivalry of other prestigious episcopal sees, and above all Constantinople, the new capital of the empire, gave rise to persistently ambiguous formulations: as late as the time of Emperor Justinian (527–65), Rome continued to be one of the five sees that retained the apostolic title (the others being Constantinople, Alexandria, Antioch, and Jerusalem), even though the emperor himself was prepared to recognize that the Roman pope was *caput omnium sanctarum ecclesiarum* (supreme head of the Holy Church).

From the time of the papacy of Gelasius I (492–6), the honorific title of *papa* (father) previously used by all bishops began to be reserved exclusively for the bishop of Rome, who, as well as the pastoral duties relating to his own diocese, now took on greater responsibility in three separate but interrelated spheres. First, he governed a widespread ecclesiastical province that initially included the whole of Italy, but later was reduced to the central-southern area of the peninsula and the islands of Sicily and Sardinia after the creation of a new ecclesiastical province to the north around the city of Milan, which became the imperial residence from the mid-fourth century. Secondly, the pope was head of all the bishops of the Western dioceses, including those of Africa, with regard to questions of discipline and faith. Finally, the claim to descent from Peter ensured the bishop of Rome a special role within the Church as a whole, which was defined by Gelasius I as that of *principatus*. But although recognized in theory, the authority of the *principatus* was not always upheld in practice and the Eastern Churches, especially the great sees of Alexandria and Constantinople, tended to take independent action on matters that regarded them directly.

While its role within the Church was taking form, the papacy also had to face the difficult question of relations with the empire, which from the time of Constantine continued to be ambiguous. In response to the emperor Zeno's *Henotikon*, or Law of Union (482) that was considered contrary to the prescriptions of the Council of Chalcedon in 451, Pope Gelasius I produced a formula that was to have enormous future success (and misuse). Gelasius devised an 'equal' collaboration in the government of the world, which was equated with Christendom, between the *regalis potestas* (regal power) and the *auctoritas sacrata pontificum* (the holy power of the priests).[1]

---

[1] This principle is illustrated in a letter to Emperor Anastasius that can be dated Jan. 494: *Epistolae Romanorun Pontificum genuinae et quae ad eos scriptae sunt a S. Hilaro usque ad Pelagium II*, ed. A. Thiel (Brunsbergae, 1868), i. 349, ep. 12.

Only Christ could legitimately be king and priest at the same time. After Him, the two prerogatives had to be divided between two separate figures, even though they were called on to maintain a close and continuous collaboration as the *ecclesia* was undividedly part of the *res pubblica*. It was a formula that sought to achieve a balance but remained ambiguous, since it implied the primacy of sacred over political authority by stating that the representatives of the former would have much greater authority because they would be held accountable even for the kings of men at the Last Judgment.

The papacy in the barbarian kingdoms of the west

After the fall of the western Roman empire in 476, the popes were forced to handle a political situation that was without precedent, since they found themselves now in an Italy that was ruled by barbarian chiefs: first the transitory experience of Odoacer and then, from 493, the more stable and long-lasting reign of Theoderic the Goth and his successors. Even before this period, the intensification of the barbarian invasions of the increasingly less effectively defended Italian territory had forced the bishops of Rome—like many prelates in other cities—to confront the invaders to protect their own flock of believers. One well-known episode is the legendary account of the meeting on the Mincio River between Pope Leo I (440–61) and Attila the Hun, who, it was claimed, was persuaded to turn back by the pope's personal admonition.

Between the end of the fifth and the beginning of the sixth centuries, the unified imperial domination had been irreversibly replaced by a great number of barbarian kingdoms, both in Italy and throughout the west, where the papal *principatus* reigned. In these kingdoms, the Roman or Romanized peoples of the Catholic faith were forced to live alongside a newly arrived barbarian minority that was Arian, when not still pagan, and were now governed by barbarian rulers. The relations among the various local churches, and between each of the churches and Rome, became increasingly problematic. With the progressive conversion to Catholicism of the barbarian kings, the churches in the various regions began to organize themselves around the political authorities of the kingdom in which they existed, and hence to refer to those powers rather than look to Rome, as occurred, for example, in the Frankish or Visigoth kingdoms. In other cases, however, such as northern Africa, which was conquered by the Vandals, the new arrivals were persecutors of the Catholic Church. In Italy itself, the pope found himself under the rule of an Arian Gothic king, Theoderic, who, after having sought a peaceful coexistence with the ecclesiastical institutions (he was even called upon to intervene to resolve the dispute between Pope Symmachus and the anti-pope Laurentius between 498 and 505), ended up as their oppressor and was responsible for the incarceration and subsequent death of Pope John I (523–6).

The situation for the popes worsened following the Lombard invasion of the Italian peninsula in 569 and the rise of the Lombard kingdom in the central-northern regions and two other powerful Lombard duchies were established in Spoleto and Benevento: they were hostile to the rest of the territory, which remained loyal to imperial rule. The violent invasion of Italy by the Lombards did not spare churches and monasteries, whose properties and weak defences made them tempting prey. The flight of the inhabitants and of many bishops from the more heavily besieged areas led to the disintegration of the diocesan network and forced the popes (in particular Pope Gregory the Great, 590–604) to make repeated attempts to ensure the functioning of the episcopal sees by nominating *visitatores* for the vacant posts in their metropolis until new canonically correct elections could be held.

Gregory the Great played an active role in negotiations with the king of the Lombards, and with the dukes of Spoleto and Benevento, to safeguard the Roman people from greater dangers, compensating for the inertia of the imperial authorities and often taking decisions that differed from those pursued by the empire. This was the case, for example, with the negotiations conducted with King Agilulf which met with the displeasure of Romanus the exarch in Ravenna, the senior representative of imperial power in Italy. In such dramatic circumstances, as well as maintaining full political, ideological, and cultural adherence of the papacy to the Catholic empire, the main concern of the popes was the government of the Roman people, the flock for which the bishop of Rome had direct pastoral responsibility. But besides their spiritual obligations the popes now also had to take on numerous additional duties to replace the imperial institutions that had abandoned these tasks. These included guaranteeing the supply of provisions necessary for the city's military defence, maintenance of the city walls, and even the organization of the watch guards, to the point of paying the enemy to avoid attacks or to ransom prisoners.

In short, from the end of the fifth century, in the diocese of Rome in particular, but also throughout the whole metropolis of central and southern Italy, the popes increasingly became the main point of reference for the people living in imperial territory, not only for spiritual functions but also with regard to numerous political and administrative questions. The popes' growing awareness of their increased role was revealed in various contexts and specific initiatives, and the archaeological evidence now available has thrown fresh light on these developments.

First, there is ample documentation to show that the popes were responsible for increased building activities in Rome: recent archaeological excavations have added extensive additional information to what was already known from the papal biographies in *Liber Pontificalis* regarding the architectural work commissioned by the popes, both new construction work and the restoration of existing buildings.[2] These initiatives, of course, related primarily to sacred buildings (churches, monasteries, baptisteries, graveyards), but from the eighth century they also included public buildings such as aqueducts, hospices, and even the city walls which provides evidence of the development of more general plans for modernizing the organization of urban space in Rome. Even in matters involving civic architecture, therefore, the popes gradually took over roles previously held by civil magistracies and by the emperor himself. Ongoing archaeological exploration will undoubtedly continue to add to our knowledge in this field.

To meet the growing expenses they were obliged to assume, the popes also tried to rationalize the use of the Roman church's territorial possessions, which in that period were concentrated in large complexes known as the *patrimonia sancti Petri* located in various

---

[2] For a recent formulation, see P. Delogu, 'Solium imperii-urbs ecclesiae. Roma fra la tarda antichità e l'alto medioevo', in G. Ripoll and J. M. Gurt (eds.), *Sedes regiae (ann. 400–800)* (Barcelona, 2000).

Mediterranean areas, and above all in Sicily. These issues had been studied since the eighteenth century before becoming the specific subject of research in the nineteenth and the early twentieth centuries, but our understanding of them has also benefited greatly from new inquiries based on archaeological evidence.[3]

In order to manage its landed properties the papacy had to improve its administrative structures, and this resulted in the creation of a large network that was directed by officials known as *rectores*, making use of written documentation in the best tradition of the Roman empire, despite the fact that this had fallen into disuse in the barbarian west in the same period. The papal chancery, the *scrinium*, which produced and archived the enormous documentation produced by the Roman see, gradually provided the basis around which a learned and expert bureaucracy developed to deal with everyday affairs, ensuring procedural continuity and an understanding of the rudimentary principles of management. This third aspect has recently attracted particular attention.[4]

The conservation of documentation in the archives of the Roman *scrinium* (conciliar acts, papal letters, the biographies of popes compiled in the so-called *Liber Pontificalis*, as well as the first collections of decrees dating from the late fifth to the early sixth centuries which, with the conciliary canons, would form the basis for canonic law) meant that the local churches increasingly looked to Rome for authoritative guidance on questions that arose from time to time on the most varied doctrinal and disciplinary issues. This further strengthened the authority and prestige of the Roman see with regard to the western churches, which nonetheless continued to govern themselves and to fiercely defend their autonomy.

Developing in this fashion, the relations between Rome and the churches in the various western kingdoms in this period were not based on the assumption that the papacy had either a true governing capacity or the explicit intention (and opportunity) to promote an organic and planned missionary operation in the non-Catholic world, for which the prerequisites were missing. This attitude

---

[3] The most recent outline is F. Marazzi, *I 'patrimonia sancata Romanae ecclesiae' nel Lazio (secoli IV–X). Struttura amministrativa e prassi gestionali* (Rome, 1998).

[4] The most recent specific survey is by E. Pitz, *Papstskripte im frühen Mittelalter. Diplomatische und rechsgeschichtliche Studien zum Brief-Corpus Gregors des Grossen* (Sigmaringen, 1990).

prevailed even after a new awareness of the opportunities for the evangelization of the barbarian tribes replaced the traditional aversion for the barbarian enemies of Christendom that derived from the largely ecclesiastical culture of the late Roman world. The fact that the popes could not rely with any certainty on the political power (and the ecclesiastical hierarchies) within the individual kingdoms made missions of conversion impracticable, as they could not succeed without the support of the kings, and in the case of both the Franks and the Visigoths tended to be left to the local clergy. The situation would change significantly, however, when papal authority was strengthened when the Carolingians provided military and political support to impose conversion on the Saxons at the end of the eighth century.

In the pre-Carolingian era, the only missionary movement that could legitimately be ascribed to the Roman popes was the initiative advanced by Pope Gregory the Great for the evangelization of the Angles, resulting in the expedition from Rome to the distant kingdom of Kent in 596. This was, however, a relatively isolated event, explained with difficulty even by the ancient sources and for which they invented an extraordinary motivation, namely the profound impression that the blond beauty of certain slaves from the British Isles had made on the pope so that he could no longer leave in paganism these Angles who so greatly resembled 'angels'.[5]

The papacy from Byzantine-Lombard Italy to the Carolingian empire

There were no missionary initiatives from Rome even with the Lombards, although an initial religious dialogue had been started between Gregory the Great and King Agilulf, whose wife, Theodelinda, was Catholic, albeit a follower of the schismatic faith known as the Three Chapters. The Lombards came round to a gradual acceptance of Catholicism during the seventh century after a long cohabitation

---

[5] The first documentation of this episode is in a biography of Gregory the Great dating from 680–704: *The Earliest Life of Gregory the Great by an Anonymous Monk of Whitby*, ed. B. Colgrave (Cambridge, 1985), p. 91.

within the kingdom—which slowly stabilized politically and territorially—with a majority of Catholic Romans, until the old ethnic groups fused into a new society. This forced the Lombard kings to find a model of power that was acceptable to all their subjects. Nevertheless, the papacy never fully converged with the Lombard kingdom in Italy. The *modus vivendi* that was reached did not allay the popes' fears of the territorial expansion of the kingdom that might take over Rome itself. Moreover, the Catholicism of the Lombard kings by no means neutralized the popes' political and ideological alliance to the empire, even though occasional, and sometimes serious, crises continued to take place. One such crisis exploded in 726 around the worship of sacred images, which had been forbidden by the iconoclastic order of Emperor Leo III the Isaurian. In this circumstance, the pope and the imperial powers in Italy, which supported him, bitterly opposed the emperor and his specific line, but did not seek to overturn the imperial institution as such, nor question its role in this sphere.

The Lombard threat became a dramatically urgent issue for Rome starting from the reign of Liutprand (713–44), the king who had most explicitly and deliberately set himself up as *christianus Langobardorum rex* and protector of the Church. As the imperial positions in the peninsula weakened due to the iconoclastic crisis and the military emergency in the Balkans and the East, the internal unity of the kingdom encouraged more aggressive pressure by the Lombards against the exarchate, culminating in the definitive capitulation of Ravenna in 750/51 following an offensive led by Aistulf, a successor of Liutprand. The collapse of the exarchate opened the way to even more radical solutions, making possible, although not necessarily feasible, the extension of Lombard occupation to the whole Italian peninsula. Aware that it could no longer count on the protection of imperial arms, the papacy now decided to turn to the Franks as the only practicable alternative. In 751 Pippin had been proclaimed king of the Franks, and the new dynasty in turn needed a stronger legitimization. In 754 Pope Stephen II personally went to Ponthion to consecrate his power through the highly symbolical act of ceremonially anointing Pippin as king. In return, Stephen requested that Pippin intervene in Italy against the Lombards to restore the lands taken from the exarchate and hand them over to the *patrimonium beati Petri*, namely to the Roman Church, and not to the empire.

This petition, which implied a completely new political structure in Italy, was similar to others that had been made by the predecessors of Stephen II to Carloman, Pippin's father, and then repeated by Popes Paul I (757–67) and Stephen III (768–72), who extended their claims beyond the exarchate to include *Venetia* and *Histria*. Historians have debated at length down to recent times the true contents of these agreements that were documented by sources that naturally supported the papal position. But the fact remains that the papacy was now claiming to take the place of the empire in central and northern Italy, and with the assistance of the Franks was seeking to create a new territorial structure under the leadership of Rome. The papacy also claimed responsibility for the *grex* of believers resident in those areas which were no longer protected by the imperial army.

The papal appeals to the Franks became even more pressing after Desiderius came to the Lombard throne in 756. Desiderius strengthened his authority in central and southern Italy and took control of the duchies of Spoleto and Benevento, even intervening in the contest between the Roman factions over the election of the pope in an attempt to place his own candidate, Philip, on the throne of Peter after the death of Pope Paul I in 767. It was the real danger that papal power and even the city of Rome might fall under the dominion of the Lombard kings that persuaded Charlemagne to accept the appeal that on this occasion came from Pope Adrian I. He advanced into Italy and defeated Desiderius in 774, so ending the independent kingdom of the Lombards and establishing Frankish rule in its place as Lombard Italy became a part of the Carolingian kingdom, with the exception of Benevento which managed to retain its political independence.

Charlemagne did not keep the promise that, according to the *Liber Pontificalis*, he made to the Pope in 774[6] (in the wake of the agreements between his predecessors and Rome) to transfer to the sovereignty of the papacy all the regions that once had belonged to the exarchate of Ravenna as well as the provinces of *Venetia* and *Histria*, following a hypothetical line that runs from east to west joining Luni and Monselice, and the duchies of Spoleto and Benevento taken from the Lombards. The popes continued to exercise sovereign rights only over a territory that corresponded roughly to modern Lazio, which

---

[6] *Le Liber Pontificalis*, ed. L. Duchesne (Paris, 1955), i., p. 498.

formed the basis for their 'temporal dominion' in the Middle Ages. This was seen by contemporaries as a simple political reality, without any perception of the contradiction between the spiritual and the temporal aspects of the papal authority, which would only come in later times.

The new political structure forged by Charlemagne brought into being an empire in the west led by the Franks that mirrored the empire in the east, and called for a redefinition of the traditional relationship between papal authority and imperial power. Rome's break with Constantinople, which was the result of a sudden escalation of events rather than of a longer linear process of separation, definitively overturned the political structures of late antiquity. The pope was the instrument through which the *translatio imperii* transferred authority from the *princeps* of Constantinople to the king of the Franks, who in his turn became the new Roman emperor. All this was the result of a specific contingency in which the popes had to make rapid decisions in response to the unfolding political scenario. There seems little to support the once popular theory that the Franks' decision to join forces with the papacy in the eighth century was simply the inevitable consequence of consistent strategy that had been deliberately followed by the popes since the time of Gregory the Great (or even that of Gelasius), which sought to resolve the ancient dualism with the emperor in favour of the Roman papacy with the aid of the Catholic barbarian kings of the west.[7] The coronation of Charlemagne as emperor by Pope Leo III (who had been protected by the king against the attacks of the Roman aristocracy) took place in 800 on Christmas Day in Rome, thus permitting the city to further claim its role as *urbs regia*.

As a result, the conditions were established in the Carolingian west for re-establishing the traditional model of an imperial Church, with Charlemagne as *princeps* in place of the Byzantine *basileus*. The resulting equilibrium achieved in a system characterized by a symbiosis between the lay and ecclesiastical institutions at all levels was not without persisting ambiguity, however. Despite the fact that in his preface to the *Libri Carolini* Charlemagne claimed that, as the Church was under his protection, it should also be under his command and

---

[7] An example of this school of interpretation can be found in W. Ullmann, *The Growth of Papal Government in the Middle Ages: A Study in the Relation of Clerical to Lay Power* (3rd edn., London, 1970).

not under that of the pope, in the end it was the pope who in fact assumed control of the Church in the west. Moreover, it was on this same principle that the medieval popes would later lay claim for the extension of their own role from the western Church to the west as a whole, even though their plans were then thwarted not by the empire, which entered an irreversible decline from the middle of the thirteenth century, but by the nascent national states. During the Carolingian age, the papacy's theoretical position on this question was also revealed in a famous forgery—later widely exploited—known as *Constitutum Constantini* (Donation of Constantine), by which Emperor Constantine I was alleged to have donated the Lateran palace, together with the city of Rome and the whole *pars occidentis* of Europe, to Pope Sylvester.

The actual consolidation of the role of the papacy within the universal Church in this period was the consequence of several different tendencies, in which the political powers of the Franks played a major role. Missionary work in Hessen, Thuringia, Alamannia, and Friesland, which were gradually conquered by the Pippin dynasty, had taken place under the auspices of Rome. Charles Martel and his sons had supported the evangelizing work of the Anglo-Saxon monk Wynfrid-Boniface (c.675–754), who had deliberately sought to legitimize his mission in Rome by claiming to subordinate to the Roman Church the churches founded beyond the Rhine. At the same time, Wynfrid-Boniface had also worked to reorganize not only the new churches created by the mission but also the Frankish Church, on the basis of a model in which the bishops of each province were subject to the metropolitan archbishop, who in his turn received the *pallium* from the pope. This undertaking was fiercely opposed by the Frankish Church which defended its independence.

The plan for the 'Romanization' of the various local churches, including the Frankish Church, was taken up again with greater determination and energy by Charlemagne, who was responsible for the adoption of the Roman model of rites and regulations in all the churches throughout his extensive domain. Charlemagne encouraged the general adoption of the liturgical books used in Rome, as well as the so-called *Dionisyo-Hadriana*, the main Roman collection of conciliary canons and papal decrees. Likewise, he advocated the observance of the Benedictine Rule in monasteries, which gradually replaced all others. The aim of the Frankish king was to standardize the faith, pastoral activities, and internal organization of the churches and monasteries in all his territories in order to achieve more uniform institutional organization and more effective political control. The popes played an entirely marginal role in this restructuring, but benefited from the outcome, as it was done in the name of Rome. By now the whole western Church was coordinated around the Petrine see, with the partial exception of the Celtic Irish Church, which maintained its own separate organization and practices. At the same time, the great patriarchates which had competed with Rome in late antiquity—Alexandria, Antioch, Jerusalem—had all declined in the face of Islamic expansion in Asia Minor and northern Africa, as well as in the Iberian peninsula. From the 960s, the Slav areas also opened up to Roman influence, which was in fierce competition with the Greek Church. Latin-Catholic evangelization of Bohemia, Moravia, Pannonia, Poland, and, in the Balkans, of the Croats and Slovenes took place in different stages, thanks to the joint initiatives of the papacy, the Germanic clergy, and the imperial authorities.

This situation favoured the increasing importance of the role of the Roman papacy in the affairs of the universal Church in unprecedented ways, especially in the second half of the ninth century, despite an evident cultural deficit that had rendered weak, and even contradictory, the papal position in theological and doctrinal debates in the eighth and ninth centuries. This backwardness with respect to the churches of the continental and insular west was nevertheless overcome by means of a form of cultural evolution which has recently been the subject of several important studies.[8] Amongst other things, this took the form of a vigorous rediscovery of texts of theology, hagiography, and church history from the tradition of late antiquity (often through new translations from the Greek), and a reappraisal of the eminent figure of Gregory the Great and his work. Moreover, the greater power the Carolingians gave to the archbishops over their bishops had led the latter to seek to safeguard their threatened independence by placing themselves under the direct protection of Rome. To this end, a collection of documents was forged, the so-called *Decretales Pseudoisidorianae* (the authenticity of which was not

---

[8] Essential reading on this specific theme, and more generally on the whole question of the early medieval papacy, are the volumes by Girolamo Arnaldi listed in the section on this chapter in Further Reading.

doubted until the fifteenth century), which removed the bishops from the discipline of the metropolites and the provincial synods and placed them instead under the authority of the pope. Although the canonical collections did not acknowledge the *Pseudoisidorianae* until the eleventh century, there is no doubt that the documents provided the pope with a weapon with which to intervene in the affairs of the local churches.

From post-Carolingian crisis to eleventh-century consolidation

The strength of the papacy in the second half of the ninth century stemmed in part from the personal charisma of popes such as Nicholas I (858–67) and John VIII (872–82), although the crisis of the imperial power during the reigns of the last of the Carolingians does not seem to have reinforced papal authority through a kind of mutual compensation, but rather to have weakened it. The dissolution of the Carolingian political structure and the disordered distribution of power within the society halted the process of ecclesiastical centralization and made it impossible for the Roman see to continue improving its administrative structures. The throne of Peter, on the other hand, from the end of the ninth century until almost the mid-eleventh century, fell prey to the factions of the Roman aristocracy which during this period managed to influence the choice of popes, even to the point of nominating men of doubtful morality and little religious learning. The ethical dissolution and decline of the bishops of Rome was quickly perceived by contemporaries, and it reached its most outrageous point in the scandal provoked by the macabre episode of the trial of the corpse of Pope Formosus by his successor, Stephen VI, in 897.

In 1046, Emperor Henry III intervened in the dispute between the factions of the Roman aristocracy over the control of the papal office, imposing a German bishop, Suidger of Bamberg, who took the name Clement II. For a decade, the throne of Peter was occupied by German prelates, nominated by the emperor and therefore not involved in local affairs. With their stronger authority, and supported from the time of the papacy of Leo IX (1049–54) by the newly established college of cardinals, these popes gradually managed to become a reference point for the many different interest groups and forces (ranging from the various new or re-created monastic orders to popular movements such as the Milanese *Pataria*) which supported the urgent need for a profound moral and institutional restoration of the post-Carolingian Church. It was a Church that in the west had become enmeshed with the roles and lifestyles of the lay aristocracy in ways that were increasingly less acceptable and provided tangible evidence of declining standards of culture and spirituality.

The papacy managed to coordinate and channel reform currents into a single coherent initiative designed to free papal authority from lay influence so that it could be recognized to represent and lead the whole Church. The Lateran Council held in 1059 during the papacy of Nicholas II (1059–61) which reserved the election of future popes to the cardinals—excluding the control by laymen, including the emperor—was in this respect decisive. Another fundamental step in the progressive consolidation of the authority of the Roman papacy over the Church was the document known as *Dictatus papae*, produced in 1075 by Gregory VII (1073–85), which declared the total and exclusive dependence of the episcopate on the pope.

In short, together with the more general evolution of the institutions and society of western Christendom, this period saw the gradual completion of the centuries-long process by which the office of the bishop of Rome was transformed from an initial honorary primacy to a real jurisdictional supremacy over an increasingly hierarchical church. Obedience to Rome came to be synonymous with orthodoxy, so that anyone who opposed the Roman see was liable to be condemned as a heretic. Moreover, the hegemony now exercised by the pope over the Church gave rise to another question of extreme importance: the claim to exert supreme authority over the entire *societas christiana*, which would have settled the historical struggle with imperial power to the advantage of the pope. The papacy that emerged from the changes that had taken place in the eleventh century was now backed by the new military support of the Norman kingdom in southern Italy and hence was ready to take up this further challenge. It first took shape in the long dispute over episcopal elections known as the investiture struggles which resulted in the compromise formulated at Worms in 1122. It would reach its climax in the following century, however, in the struggles between the popes and the Swabian emperors. Although these struggles ended in an apparent victory for the Roman papacy, they actually increased the papacy's efforts to seek to extend its temporal powers, which would remain thereafter a constant source of trouble for the institution.

Rural economy and society

Chris Wickham

Economic geography

Italy is not a coherent whole in socio-economic terms, and never has been. Its historical disunity reflects the extreme difficulty involved in even travelling from north to south along a long peninsula that is essentially created by a set of mountain ranges, the Apennines. Until the railways were built, by far the easiest way to travel long distances was by sea, with land routes only imposing themselves because the network of Italian cities was so important to most travellers that intermediate stops were as significant as final destinations. Land routes therefore shifted in importance as cities did; so, for instance, the Via Flaminia, the Roman consular road to Rome from the Adriatic (and thus Ravenna), declined in importance across the early Middle Ages, as did the Rome–Ravenna axis, whereas the new Via Francigena, from the cities of northern Tuscany, Lombardy, and, eventually, France, a pilgrim road to Rome and, increasingly, a commercial route, developed fast from the ninth century onwards. These roads, and others, show that, across the mountain systems of the peninsula, communications were always possible, and indeed were never interrupted. But they were seldom, until the last century, so universal and organic that they made a single political system easy in Italy—and, between 568 and 1871, there was not one, even nominally; and they were never so organic that they made Italy a single economic unit, before the 1960s at the earliest—not even the Romans had managed that.

Italy was therefore a territory of separate economic regions in our period, onto which were mapped its major political units. Let us look at the most important ones in turn. In the north, the valleys of the Po and Adige, which create the great alluvial plain between the Alps to the north and the beginning of the Apennine barrier to the south, make up Italy's largest single economic unit, across which travel is easy both by land and by river. This is the least Mediterranean part of Italy, for winters are cold, rye was in our period a more common cereal crop than wheat, and olives do not easily grow at all except in the thin line of south-facing Alpine foothills, the area of the Italian lakes. The Po plain, *Italia annonaria*, was in the late Roman empire the land of government (it housed successive administrative capitals at Milan and Ravenna) and of army supply for the imperial frontiers beyond the Alps. But it was not fully integrated with the rest of the peninsula, *Italia suburbicaria*; its aristocracies were separate from those of Rome and the South, and even its material culture was distinct, with, for example, different kinds of fine table wares being produced—the South produced pottery painted with red stripes if it could not import the best plates and bowls from Africa; the North preferred glazed wares. Under the Lombards and Byzantines, the North remained the land of government, with the rival capitals of Pavia and Ravenna, but the localization of the period made effective control outside the region almost impossible, and most of the peninsula went its separate ways.

The Apennines largely fill the peninsula, but their twists create four main low-lying regions, three on the western Tyrrhenian side and one on the east, on the Adriatic. These are classic foci of the Mediterranean agricultural triad of wheat, vines, and olives, and all of them have been fully part of whatever wider maritime economy has existed in any given period. Northern Tuscany is the first of these, the Arno valley and its outliers, a region that has in general shared its political and economic history with the North. Lazio, focused on Rome, is the second, and Campania, focused on a number of rival cities which have since the late empire always included Naples, is the third, both of them volcanic and potentially prosperous agriculturally. Under the empire, these two were a single economic region, for the senatorial aristocracy of Rome owned on a large scale in Campania and often summered (i.e. spent money) on the coast of the bay of Naples. Even at the low point for long-distance exchange, the eighth and ninth centuries, Rome and Naples, the largest cities in Italy, maintained some commercial links, as archaeology shows; but their regional economies, and their political systems, were by now separate—Campania was indeed by 900 divided politically between five or six independent states, although their economies were more internally integrated. The fourth region, Puglia, in the heel of Italy, is more geographically separate from the others, and its closest economic links have often been with Greece, a short hop over the sea; it was a major olive region under the empire, and was again (or still) from the eleventh century.[1] Puglia was an important political centre only after the Byzantine reconquest of the South in the late ninth century, but its economic resources were sought after by the Campanian powers before that. Between these peninsular regions, we are in the mountains: narrow valleys separated by oak-dominated woodland and *macchia* (Mediterranean scrubland), with poor communications. The autonomous Lombard duchies of Spoleto and Benevento were mountain polities above all, with at most small inland and coastal plains to give them a certain prosperity (these included most of Puglia and half of Campania for the powerful Benevento of the mid-seventh to mid-ninth centuries, however); the mountains preserved their effective independence, but also prevented either duchy from establishing a lasting political coherence.

Finally, Sicily, and Sardinia (and Corsica, French since the eighteenth century) provide a set of separate regions in themselves. Sardinia and Corsica were relatively isolated in our period. Although the Romans valued and exploited the former's grain potential, little is heard of it from the seventh century to the eleventh; the latter was conquered by the Lombards in the early eighth century, but again hardly exploited. Sicily was, however, one of the major grain reserves of the Mediterranean, and in the centre of the sea lanes; the eastern empire kept firm control of it and its produce until the Arab conquest of the ninth century, and then in the tenth and eleventh centuries it was a rich and developing Arab emirate in its own right, with more irrigation and new crops: citrus, sugar, and cotton. It is not well

---

[1] Naples–Rome exchange: P. Arthur, 'Early medieval amphorae, the duchy of Naples and the food supply of Rome', *Papers of the British School of Rome* 61 (1993), pp. 231–44. Puglia and Greece: G. Volpe, *Contadini, pastori e mercanti nell'Apulia tardoantica* (Bari, 1996), pp. 323–35; and olives: ibid. 271–4; J.-M. Martin, *La Pouille du VIe au XIIe siècle* (Rome, 1993), pp. 362–6.

documented after 600 either, but seems to have maintained a Roman rural lifestyle (including a villa economy) rather longer than was common elsewhere, perhaps into the eighth century.[2]

In the period of the Roman empire, the peninsular and insular regions of Italy (i.e. excepting the Po plain) had a greater economic unity, focused on the huge city of Rome, than they were to have again until at least the thirteenth century, and arguably the twentieth. Senatorial landowning structured the Centre–South, and so did Roman markets. We hear of some specialized agrarian productions, such as the transhumant pastoralism of sheep that underpinned large-scale wool production in the central Apennines and northern Puglia, or the pitch and timber export of central Calabria, or the pigs of Lucania, or the oil specialisms of several parts of the South.[3] Such 'cash cropping' never meant that peasants did not practise subsistence agriculture as well, but it did mean that their surplus was relatively specialized, whether it was given in rent to landlords or sold in markets. If we find in our post-Roman documentation reference to specialized rents of this kind, then we can postulate some economic integration between different areas, an area with a grain surplus linked to another with a wine surplus, and so on. If, conversely, we find relative homogeneities in rents across areas of different ecologies, we must postulate much more localized patterns of exchange, with each area producing the same products and consuming them on the spot. Broadly, in the early Middle Ages, we find the second pattern. Once our runs of early medieval documents start, in the eighth century and later, mountain and plain areas alike produced the same sorts of rents, with at most relative tendencies towards more animals in the mountains, wine and oil in hill country, grain on the plains. If there were structural economic relationships here, it was at the level of the single city and its hinterland, rather than any wider economic region. Larger-scale agricultural systems are hardly documented again before the late eleventh century and the twelfth.

---

[2] A. Molinari, 'Il popolamento rurale in Sicilia tra V e XIII secolo', in R. Francovich and G. Noyé (eds.), *La storia dell'alto medioevo italiano alla luce dell'archeologia* (Florence, 1994), pp. 361–77.

[3] E. Gabba and M. Pasquinucci, *Strutture agrarie e allevamento transumante nell' Italia romana III-I s. a.C.* (Pisa, 1980); A. Giardina, 'Allevamento ed economia della selva in Italia meridionale', in A. Giardina and A. Schiavone (eds.), *Società romana e produzione schiavistica*, i (Bari, 1981), pp. 87–113; S. J. B. Barnish, 'Pigs, plebeians and potentes', *Papers of the British School at Rome* 55 (1987), pp. 157–85.

If the early Middle Ages displayed this relative agricultural homo-geneity, the economic localization it implied equally represents the fact that each micro-region had its own economic and indeed social history. These different histories cannot easily be discussed in a sur-vey chapter such as this: in northern Tuscany alone, the territories of Lucca, Pisa, Florence, Arezzo, and Siena would have to be discussed separately, and the mountains to their north and the two or three sectors of more or less unurbanized hill country to their south separ-ately again. All one can say is that the parameters that caused such differences are fairly similar from one micro-region to another: eco-logical differences first, of course, but also different patterns of land-owning, the differing importance of urban society for each, different rural settlement patterns, and the wide variety of political systems that each fitted into. The last three of these will be discussed in other chapters; landowning will be characterized here. On the basis of these parameters, I shall briefly set out three case studies, so as to give a certain minimum specificity to my generalizations; we shall then move into more synthetic surveys of, respectively, the rural economy, aristocratic power structures in the countryside, and peasant society.

Patterns of landowning

Late Roman landowners could be enormously rich, the richest of them perhaps the largest private owners there have ever been, with estates in Italy and Africa and often half of the other provinces of the western empire too. There is no sign that this scale of ownership outlasted the political fragmentation of the Roman empire, which began in the Mediterranean when the Vandals took Carthage in 439 and reached its culmination for Italy in the crisis decades of the Gothic Wars and Lombard invasion. From 600 at the latest, what we find is sets of aristocracies which, with few exceptions, were based on a single city-territory or, at the most, one central territory and its immediate neighbours. Such owners varied greatly in wealth, but their estates tended to consist of fragmented properties scattered around the city where they lived; such landowning contributed to the unity of that city and its countryside rather than to any wider economic or political patterns. There are so many of these in our documents, from every period, that they hardly need illustration. They tend to be found as donors to urban churches (in the eighth and early ninth centuries or, again, in the eleventh) or as lessors of the estates of cathedrals or important monasteries (in the tenth century and onwards above all). Their leaders were the backbone of city politics in every period, including city autonomies when these were possible: in the ninth century in Campania, in the late eleventh in much of the peninsula.

The upper and lower limits of the urban aristocracy need some attention, however. Major political leaders were of course much richer in land than was this relatively modest stratum. In 750, say, the Lombard king, the pope, and the duke of Benevento were huge and wide-ranging owners; the king owned perhaps a tenth of north-west Italy, the only region for which a calculation has been attempted.[4] Their principal dependents, the leading dukes of the North and the central figures in court entourages, were also richer than average as well, in part precisely as a result of the generosity of kings and princes. But, conversely, specific signs of this generosity, documented royal gifts of land, are not often visible until the tenth century; even royal associates were not necessarily hugely wealthy. Gaidoald, doctor to the Lombard kings for over forty years, gave in 767 to his own monastery, S. Bartolomeo just outside Pistoia, what may have been half his property; it amounted to six estates, all in the territory of Pistoia and its immediate neighbours, plus a church in the royal capital of Pavia, the latter being the only sign of his royal link. Taido of Bergamo, a *gasindio regis* or royal retainer, made his will in 774; his eight estates and ten tenant houses all lay between Bergamo and Verona, a span of some 100 km, except for a house near the capital. Only some Beneventan aristocrats owned more widely, from Campania to Puglia.[5] Overall, there were few lay landowners in Italy before Charlemagne's conquest who could match the great owners of Francia. After that conquest there were more, for the Franks themselves took land in Italy; in the ninth century the leading Frankish stratum,

[4] P. Darmstädter, *Das Reichsgut in der Lombardei und Piemont 568–1250* (Strasbourg, 1896), p. 5.
[5] *CDL* 2, nn. 203 (cf. 1, n. 38 for Gaidoald in 726), 293; for Beneventans, see e.g. *Chronicon vulturnense*, i, ed. V. Federici (Rome, 1925), nn. 34, 36, 38, 41, 47. For aristocratic scale, see C. Wickham, 'Aristocratic power in eighth-century Lombard Italy', in A. C. Murray (ed.), *After Rome's Fall* (Toronto, 1998), pp. 153–70.

men like Eberhard of Friuli (d. 866) or Wido III of Spoleto (d. 895, by then king of Italy and emperor), owned land from the North Sea to the Adriatic. But the fragmentation of the Carolingian empire ended this again, and the main international Frankish families either died out or adjusted to power on the regional and local level. By the late tenth century once more, only a handful of families, mostly marquisal families, owned much land outside single city-territories in the Italian kingdom; in the states of the South, for their part, all private landowning was restricted by the small size of each political territory. To the largest lay owners, we must add the lands of the great eighth-century monasteries, S. Ambrogio in Milan, Bobbio, Nonantola, S. Giulia in Brescia, Farfa, Monte Cassino, S. Vincenzo al Volturno, S. Sofia in Benevento and a handful of others, who became as rich and wide-ranging in their ownership as any great Frankish aristocrat, and who—with some difficulty, it has to be admitted—held onto their lands better too. Their episcopal counterparts were sometimes as rich, but their lands were, unsurprisingly, mostly restricted to single dioceses; the next wave of monastic foundations, these of the decades around 1000, seldom matched them in scale.

No word translated our word 'aristocrat' until after 1000; exactly what made someone aristocratic was at best a package of attributes, including wealth and official position. There was throughout our period a grey area of informal status difference stretching from the city elites to the peasantry, with a wide variety of small and medium owners making up the strata between them. The relatively restricted scale of aristocratic landowning in fact made a relatively independent peasantry possible. There were certainly some cities—such as Milan, as we shall see, or Rome—where the total weight of urban land-owning was so great that it dominated the countryside already (or still) in the early Middle Ages. But these were exceptions, and even there the individual owners had, as a rule, very scattered lands which, even cumulatively, rarely included whole villages as single units (the exceptions were mostly in the hands of kings and the southern princes, or, subsequently, in the hands of royal monasteries such as S. Giulia in Brescia). Seen from the standpoint of peasants, the lands and powers of outside owners were an important element in social action, but they only circumscribed, rather than determined, the activities of peasant owners and the rural elites, who dominated what village politics there was and usually also controlled the local church when there was one. Every time we have enough documentation, we find local-level political networks of this type in the majority of rural areas. I shall return to the point later.

Some case studies

The territory of Milan had one of Italy's major cities at its centre, and Milan had a wider hinterland than just its diocese, stretching north-wards into the diocese of Como and the valleys of the Lombard Alps. Toto of Campione, a childless owner living in the Alpine foothills near Lugano, gave his lands to the archbishop of Milan in 777, for example; Toto was only a medium owner, dominating his village and perhaps the villages around it at the most, but it was Milan, not his own diocesan centre of Como, which attracted him. Generosity by other such owners, and by Carolingian rulers on a larger scale, allowed the archbishop, through his great urban monastery of S. Ambrogio, to accumulate much land in the dioceses of Milan and Como, as the documents of the monastery make clear, in the ninth century in particular. The archbishop's own land is less clearly visible, but his feudal dependents, *capitanei* and *valvassores*, were numerous in every part of the same area by the eleventh century—some were old families which by now numbered themselves among the arch-bishop's entourage (archbishops tended to be from capitaneal fam-ilies themselves), others were newer families whose lands were largely church leases. Most of the city landed elite was part of this ecclesi-astical political network, for the archbishop was particularly powerful in Milan until a set of revolts against him in the 1030s–1070s (and, indeed, even afterwards); the city could be seen as a compact network of owners, with considerable landed wealth. Urban hegemony was further developed when leading rural owners moved into the city from the late tenth century onwards. Throughout the Milanese, the impact of urban power could not easily be avoided. All the same, rural landowners continued to exist in most villages. Furthermore, when local signorial lordships, with localized judicial powers, developed in the eleventh and twelfth centuries in Italy, the Milanese was an area in which they are particularly clearly documented. Many of the controllers of local justice were city-dwelling, but signorial courts were local, and were non-urban foci of political power, no matter who their ultimate lords were.[6]

This mixture of urban political supremacy and a multiplicity of levels of local social autonomy is visible in the territory of Lucca in Tuscany as well. We see Lucca through the eyes of its bishops and their huge archive, as we see Milan through S. Ambrogio, but we can at least say that episcopal wealth built up quickly, above all between the 720s and the 820s through the gifts of both urban aristocrats and of village-level elites, and that as a result the bishop's property extended throughout the lands in the city's territory, although much less beyond. It is clear that city and country leaders alike wanted to be part of the bishop's political network (major urban families once again regularly provided bishops). Once they had reached this position, however, they used that network for their own purposes, leasing episcopal land—often the same land that they had given—on long-term leases. Some country dwellers dominated their localities simply by taking such land in lease, in fact. The bishop of Lucca did not have nearly as much political power as his Milanese counterpart, for Lucca was also the centre of the marquis of Tuscany; one result of that was, in fact, that he did not have as much control over his tenurial dependents. In the late tenth and eleventh centuries, the bishop's leases steadily became the stable patrimonies of urban and rural families. Very few villages indeed were completely controlled by urban owners, even those closest to the city; it was not until the late twelfth century that the urbanization of rural elites reduced the effective autonomy of village societies. In the Lucchesia, signorial powers were never an important element of local political structures, and urban judicial rights remained hegemonic. The territory was almost as focused on the city as was Milan, indeed. But there was always a substantial independent space for rural-level social action.[7]

Not all of Italy was as urban-focused as these two. In some areas, rural political circumscriptions were an alternative social focus to the city even in the Lombard-Carolingian period (an example is

[6] For Toto in 777, Ch.L.A., XXVIII, n. 855; for the Milanese in general, C. Violante, *La società milanese nell'età precomunale* (Bari, 1953); G. Rossetti, *Società e istituzioni nel contado lombardo durante il medioevo* (Milan, 1968); H. Keller, *Adelsherrschaft und städtische Gesellschaft in Oberitalien (9.–12. Jahrhundert)* (Tübingen, 1979); R. Balzaretti, *The lands of Saint Ambrose* (Turnhout, 2002).

[7] H. M. Schwarzmaier, *Lucca und das Reich bis zum Ende des 11. Jahrhunderts* (Tübingen, 1972); C. Wickham, *The mountains and the city* (Oxford, 1988).

Sirmione, a *castrum* on Lake Garda); in others, there were rival rural power centres, such as the competition posed by the monastery of Nonantola to the city of Modena, 10 km away; in others again, the signorialization of the countryside in the eleventh century led to the temporary eclipse of urban hegemony, for example around Florence. And there were whole regions which were rather less urban from the start.

One example is the Abruzzo, a region of high mountains with a narrow coastal strip in Adriatic central Italy, documented for us in the cartularies of S. Vincenzo al Volturno and of S. Clemente di Casauria, a monastery founded by Louis II in 873. The cities of the Abruzzo, such as Corfinio and Penne, and even the largest, Chieti, were not significant urban centres, and local political and social life had no obvious foci until Casauria was founded. The Adriatic coast was an area of large-scale public landowning, and many of the mountain valleys of the hinterland were blocks of public land as well, although in the mountains their inhabitants sometimes consisted of isolated and autonomous peasantries with nothing except personal links to the king or the duke of Spoleto. When lay families or monasteries got their hands on these large blocks of lands, they were given a rather more secure territorial basis than was normal in the North. In the hill country between these blocks, however, land was more fragmented, and there was space for peasant owners as well as richer, aristocratic landowning. The peasantry prospered by clearing land until the mid-ninth century, when it began to lose ground to its aristocratic neighbours, as land sales show. The foundation and land acquisitions of Casauria extended that process. In the late tenth century, Casauria and other local powers began the process of *incastellamento*, castle-building, which in south-central Italy involved the rapid, planned concentration of most rural settlement inside the walls of the new fortifications. This further developed the patterns of aristocratic and monastic dominance in the zone.[8] This steady move towards a structured dominance by large owners, through the political and demographic aggregations of the new castles, is typical of the southern mountains.[9] One major reason for it was precisely the

[8] L. Feller, *Les Abruzzes médiévales* (Rome, 1998).
[9] For parallels, see P. Toubert, *Les structures du Latium médiéval. Le Latium méridional et la Sabine du IXe siècle à la fin du XIIe siècle* (Rome, 1973); C. Wickham, *Il problema dell'incastellamento nell'Italia centrale* (Florence, 1985).

weakness of cities, which were elsewhere the foci for so many landowners that they prevented any single one of them from being hegemonic, even at the village level. Conversely, the scale of these powerful lordships was much smaller, that of a single village or at most a group of villages—the nominal territories of each of the Abruzzo's cities was thus split up into many pieces. This is a pattern that was typical in eleventh-century France, in fact; it was much less typical in Italy, at least in the lowland regions, where urban-focused societies were in a majority. It would nonetheless be mistaken to cut rural areas like the Abruzzo out of our image of Italy; the peninsula had plenty of them too.

Rural economies

Early medieval Italy was more forested than it was either during the Roman empire or after 1000. We can conclude, as a result, that its population must have been lower as well; although we can put no precise figures to demographic fluctuations, or timings for that matter, it is likely that the population had begun to increase again by 800 at the latest. The silvo-pastoral background to most village territories ensured a variety of diet, and peasants ate more meat than they did before or after the early Middle Ages. Conversely, as soon as we have documents, we find signs of land clearance; in the early ninth century we can see it along the Po, in the Sabina near Farfa, and in the Abruzzo.[10] But the world of the agrarian pioneer was fairly restricted; the wide lands around the cities had been settled without a break from Roman times and before. It would be wrong, in fact, to look for a non-humanized landscape anywhere in early medieval Italy; only the most barren mountains and the marshland of the lowest river plains were not inhabited at all, and by the eleventh century some places were inhabited more densely than they were in the nineteenth.[11]

---

[10] M. Montanari, *L'alimentazione contadina nell'alto medioevo* (Naples, 1979); for clearance, V. Fumagalli, *Coloni e signori nell'Italia settentrionale, secc. VI–XI* (Bologna, 1978), pp. 51–62, 90–2, 113–18; G. Tabacco, *I liberi del re nell'Italia carolingia e post-carolingia* (Spoleto, 1966), pp. 113–22; Feller, *Les Abruzzes*, pp. 323–54.

[11] E. Conti, *La formazione della struttura agraria moderna nel contado fiorentino*, i (Rome, 1965), pp. 120–4.

Rural estate structures were inherited from the Roman period as well. Already by the late empire the Romans had abandoned the slave plantation, the estate cultivated by slave gangs who were wholly directed and supplied by their master or his agents. Instead, late Roman estates were cultivated by families of tenants, whether free or unfree in status, who were responsible for the cultivation of their own plots of land, and who simply owed rent to their landlords.[12] This economic pattern, that of dependent peasant agriculture, has dominated most of human history, and was nearly universal in our period. In a pattern of this kind, landlords are largely cut out of the productive process, for peasants make their own choices about agricultural planning and its rhythms. Almost all that changes is the type of rent, as well (of course) as its weight. In the early Middle Ages, most rents from peasants were in kind, and reflected the range of agricultural products available on any given tenant plot: the simplest type of rent structure, one that does not require any wider economic relationships to work. This began to change in the tenth century, when rents in money became increasingly often required by lords from peasants, at least in the most urbanized parts of Italy, much earlier than in the rest of Europe. Such a development entails the existence of markets in which such peasants could get coins in return for produce—such markets did indeed exist, above all in cities. The expansion of cities at the end of our period made possible, that is to say, the expansion of the sale of produce by peasants, and the expansion of the role of money in economic transactions.

Landlords, as has already been implied, do not do much more than collect the rent in this system; the practice of subletting, which was typical of the Roman empire (it can be seen very clearly on Gregory the Great's Sicilian estates in the 590s), and which became steadily more common again after 850, also meant that there could be several layers of leaseholders between the landowner and the peasant, which further decreased the direct involvement of any of them. But there were also ways in which lords could intervene more directly in agriculture. We find leases, in tenth-century central Italy in particular, that provided explicitly for the planting of vineyards; we also find

[12] D. Vera, 'Le forme del lavoro rurale', in *Sett. CISAM* 45 (Spoleto, 1998), pp. 293–342.

clearance leases, aimed at deforestation, with, typically, a five-year gap before rent was due. Here, landowners were determining the direction of agricultural practices, albeit not the practices themselves. And they could go further, in the framework of the bipartite estate, the 'manorial system' (in Italian, the *sistema curtense*, for *curtis* is the standard word for 'estate' in our period), a pattern which characterized much of northern and central Italy—though not the South, where simple rent-paying was always dominant—in particular in the eighth to tenth centuries.

Bipartite estates were divided between a central demesne and an array of tenant plots. The demesne was cultivated directly under the supervision of the landlord or his agents, by the tenants, who owed labour-service as part of their rent. This pattern of estate management is hardly known in the Roman period at all; it is only documented once in Roman Italy, in the territory of Padua in, probably, the 560s. When our early medieval documents begin again in the eighth century, however, bipartite divisions are commonly referred to, and labour service is often cited in leases as part of 'custom' (*consuetudo*). From our first leases in the 730s, labour could be a heavy requirement: as much as three days per week, or one week in three, in some cases.[13] This obligation represented a considerable degree of control over peasant labour on the part of landowners. How it had developed is a matter of considerable debate. It is striking, however, that in the eighth century many demesnes were fairly small, or fragmented, or not fully cultivated; they were not obvious economic powerhouses. It is most likely that labour-service had more of a social than an economic purpose: it represented the rural power of lords, their ability to coerce their dependants.

Italian peasants were of diverse social status. The free/unfree dividing line, inherited from the Roman world, was crucial: it separated a peasantry with full legal rights, and obligations to participate in the public activity of the kingdom (defined in a court case of 864 as army service, bridge-building, and attendance at court), from one with no

---

[13] J. O. Tjäder (ed.), *Die nichtliterarischen lateinischen Papyri Italiens aus der Zeit 445–700* (Lund, 1955–82), n. 3; *CDL* 1, n. 57 (735–6), 2, nn. 192 (765), 263–4 (772), are the first specified labour-rents in the Lombard period, mostly for one week in three. See in general B. Andreolli, 'Contratti agrari e patti colonici nella Lucchesia nei secoli VIII e IX', *Studi medievali* 19 (1978), pp. 69–158.

public standing at all.[14] The unfree could not make legal contracts and could not go to court (except to claim that they were really free), and were under the unlimited power of their lords. There was a steady association between labour-service and unfreedom, in fact; although many free tenants owed labour as well, it was seen as part of rural subjection, and the most prosperous free tenants did not do it. It is in this framework that it may be most useful to understand the popularity of the bipartite estate, then: as a representation of the authority of landowners over peasants.

In the ninth century, the bipartite estate reached its height; this is seen above all in the estate surveys of monasteries and other major churches of the period 850–920, of which the largest are from Bobbio (two surveys, from 862 and 883) and S. Salvatore–S. Giulia in Brescia (c.900). On their lands, estate division had become very elaborate, with large groups of tenants owing standardized services, and some quite careful accounting of that service (for example, the diet of tenants on service days is sometimes listed); there is some reference to artisanal labour as well, including female workshops (*genitia*), probably for textiles. S. Giulia even had a permanent slave workforce on some demesnes, probably agricultural specialists (they were fed better than were the tenants). This developed manorial organization may have been influenced by Frankish example, for manorial surveys began in northern Europe at the start of the ninth century, apparently under royal encouragement; Bobbio and S. Giulia were, indeed, particularly close to the Carolingians.[15] It is also probable that such estates became more organized to cope with a steady growth in urban demand; this runs against an older view that manors are a marker of an economy without exchange, but that view is no longer held by most historians of the ninth century, who instead point to references to merchants and markets in our sources—S. Giulia went so far as to get an exemption from

[14] Manaresi, *Placiti*, n. 66. In Lombard areas of Italy, *aldii*, half-free, also existed in law, but they are substantially less visible in our documents. For the free/unfree distinction and its changes, see F. Panero, *Servi e rustici* (Vercelli, 1990).

[15] For estate surveys, see the collection edited by A. Castagnetti *et al.*, *Inventari altomedievali di terre, coloni e redditi* (Rome, 1979); for diet, Montanari, *L'alimentazione*, pp. 168–9, 184–6, 215–18; for bipartite estates in general, B. Andreolli and M. Montanari, *L'azienda curtense in Italia* (Bologna, 1983); P. Toubert, *Dalla terra ai castelli* (Turin, 1995), pp. 115–250.

tolls for one of its merchants, Ianuarius, from the emperor Louis II in 861.[16]

The manorial system declined quickly in the tenth century in Italy, centuries earlier than it did north of the Alps. It is not entirely clear why. One reason was that Italian estate structures were too fragmented and changeable (as land was given, leased, or bought and sold, often in quite small units) for the complex organizational structures of labour service to survive. Another was that, as exchange developed and generalized money rents became possible, landlords could leave the agricultural market to the peasantry rather than engage with it themselves (a development that would be reversed in its turn after 1100, when cities were expanding still faster, and many lords found that playing the urban grain market on a large scale brought its own rewards). Servile status was also in rapid decline in the century and a half after 900 in Italy; by 1100 there were few unfree peasants, and the servile underpinning of obligations was that much weaker as a result. Lords did not stop wanting to coerce and dominate peasants in the tenth century, of course; it is just that they sought less to do so through the work process. The tenth century was, on the other hand, a period in which the *political* powers of lords in the countryside were beginning to crystallize, as we shall see.

Underpinning both the development of the bipartite estate and its decline was an expansion of rural exchange, which seems to have been continuous from the eighth century onwards. Urban markets expanded and diversified; rural markets, too, begin to be documented. The new castles of the tenth century and later, whether or not they were major settlement centres, were characteristically associated with markets, which thus spread across the countryside as these new political foci did. Rural exchange networks were as yet mostly restricted to single city territories; only seldom can we see longer-distance commerce for anything except luxury items before the eleventh century. By the eleventh century, however, it is clear that the river Po and the Via Francigena were significant channels for internal traffic, and in later centuries there would be many others.

---

[16] MGH, *Diplomata Karolinorum*, iv, ed. K. Wanner (Munich, 1994), n. 32.

Rural society: the patterns of power

The two major points of change in the structures of rural power in early medieval Italy were the sixth century and the tenth–eleventh; they frame our period. The sixth century, of course, saw the ruin of the Roman political system and its replacement by a network of local polities, many of them with a new Lombard (or Lombardized) ruling class. I have already stressed that aristocratic landowning became more small-scale as a result, and that there was more space for peasant landowning. In the eighth century, when our documents return, rural power structures seem as a result to be fairly loose by medieval European standards. Major landowners had considerable control over their tenants, in ways that we have just seen, especially but not only if they were unfree. But they were surrounded by medium and small landowning neighbours, who had their own autonomous social roles. In Lombard areas these were often called *exercitales* or *arimanni*, 'army-men' (so called even if, as is likely, they rarely actually saw military service), and even maintained titles inherited from the traditions of the Roman army, *vir devotus* and *vir honestus*. The practical autonomy of this rural stratum is well illustrated in a royal inquiry from 715 into the diocesan boundary between Arezzo and Siena, which had since the Lombard conquest come to include large sections of the secular territory of Siena inside the diocese of Arezzo. The bishop and gastald (secular ruler) of Siena protested this, unsuccessfully, in 714–15 as did most of their successors in the next 500 years. One reason for their failure in 715 was that the local inhabitants, however loyal in secular terms to Siena, were perfectly happy to be part of the diocese of Arezzo, and witnessed to that effect. They resisted the arm-twisting of the gastald of Siena:

Warnefrit the gastald said to me: 'Here is the [king's] messenger come to enquire about this case, and, if you are interrogated, what do you have to say?' I told him: 'You must watch out that he does not interrogate me, for if I am, I have to tell the truth.' He said in reply: 'So be silent before the king's messenger'. But now I am here, and I cannot dispute that I know the truth, by God's witness . . . [that this is the land of the diocese of Arezzo].

Interestingly, even a tenant of one of the gastalds of Siena so testified: he identified more with his neighbours than with his landlord.[17]

In the urbanized regions of Italy in the eighth and ninth centuries, instead of direct rural control by the powerful, what we find is links of clientship. Smaller owners associated themselves with locally powerful lay owners, for example, either village-level elites or aristocrats, by giving land to the latter's church; cathedrals and major monasteries also accumulated land from owners who intended to remain independent, but who found an ecclesiastical patron useful. It is quite possible that such gifts were the result of coercion, at least sometimes, and we can occasionally show it, as with a court case of 845 in which a monastery in Verona took eight peasants from the diocese of Trento to court, claiming they were its servile dependants; the peasants argued that they were free owners, performing services through a patronage agreement; the monastery conceded that freedom but, arguing now that those services were rents, successfully claimed their land in court. Here, a patronage agreement led directly to the expropriation of peasant land, with the legal freedom of the peasants itself at risk. Court cases of this kind are not uncommon in ninth-century Italy, and show the free peasantry on the defensive.[18] But in other cases it is much less clear that gifts to the powerful were in themselves dangerous; in our ecclesiastical archives, small and medium owners generally only give portions of their property, and when we can study localities for several generations, it seems clear that most such donors maintained their tenurial autonomy—indeed, in most parts of urban Italy, peasant landowning survived into the twelfth and thirteenth centuries.

Aristocratic power in the countryside had advanced by then, however. The political autonomy of Lombard-Carolingian *arimanni* was linked to the commitment that kings had to their direct links to the free, an inheritance from both the public role of the Roman state and the image of the community of free warriors that underpinned Lombard political legitimacy. This weakened slightly in the ninth century,

[17] *CDL* 1, n. 19 (pp. 74, 76); see S. Gasparri, 'Il regno longobardo in Italia', in S. Gasparri and P. Cammarosano (eds.), *Langobardia* (Udine, 1990), pp. 241–9; J.-P. Delumeau, *Arezzo. Espace et sociétés, 715–1230* (Rome, 1996), pp. 475–85. For military activity, see S. Gasparri, 'Strutture militari e legami di dipendenza in Italia in età longobarda e carolingia', *Rivista storica italiana* 98 (1986), pp. 664–726.
[18] Manaresi, *Placiti*, n. 49; also nn. 36, 110, 112.

as it became increasingly clear that not all the free were actually necessary for public duties: when Louis II called up the largest army of the century, for the Beneventan war of 866, he excluded men with property worth less than 10 *solidi* from all obligations; the slightly more prosperous poor had duties of home defence rather than front-line army service. Military activity was more and more the responsibility—and soon the privilege—of the powerful and their personal dependants. Both the Lombards and the Carolingians worried that the poor free were at risk from the oppression of the powerful, and legislated to protect them; usually ineffectively, however, for royal agents such as dukes and counts were themselves the major oppressors.[19] Under these circumstances, the safest place for many rural owners was in the clientele of a more powerful figure; this would doubtless come at a price but, as we have seen, it did not necessarily always mean that such owners actually lost their land.

As the state became weaker in the tenth and eleventh centuries, these trends became ever clearer. The state could protect its inhabitants less effectively, and local *potentes*, powerful men, imposed themselves ever more authoritatively. Two elements stand out in these developments: the founding of private castles and the crystallization of signorial rights. Private castles are rare before 900, but in the first decades of the tenth century they become common in northern Italy; after 950, they can be found everywhere in the peninsula except in the Byzantine territories of the South. Berengar I and other kings conceded castle-building rights as part of a defence in depth across the country, initially in the period of the Hungarian invasions (899–937); later castles seem to have been entirely the work of private initiatives. Their varying impact on settlement will be discussed later, but their importance for rural power was great, no matter what settlement forms they were associated with. Castles were frequently, in north–central Italy, nothing other than the estate centres, *curtes*, of the past, with fairly simple defences around them; even then they were the representation of a new form of rural activity, local and private military defence.[20] Sometimes the local peasantry was persuaded to man

[19] MGH, *Capitularia*, ii, ed. A. Boretius and V. Krause (Hanover, 1897), n. 218, c. 1; see in general Tabacco, *I liberi del re*.

[20] See in general Toubert, *Les structures*; A. A. Settia, *Castelli e villaggi nell'Italia padana* (Naples, 1984); B. Rosenwein, 'The family politics of Berengar I, king of Italy (888–924)', *Speculum*, 71 (1996), pp. 247–89; and below, Chapter 7.

their defences, in return for protection; sometimes it was the task of the lord's military entourage. Either way, castles became recognized, concrete, foci of local power, in a way that estate centres before 900 had never had to be.

It is now recognized that castles and signorial rights did not automatically go together; in many places, the former pre-existed the latter by as much as a century. Signorial rights is our term for a parcel of private political powers, which were increasingly in the eleventh century held by local lords: rights of justice above all, but also rights to hospitality, to military service (especially guard duty), to tolls on roads and rivers, to dues for the use of common land, and—in the case of the strongest *signorie*—rights to dues when grain is ground in mills, when land is bought and sold, or when land is inherited. These rights had several different origins: some were former royal prerogatives, conceded to or usurped by lords; some were rights that landlords had always had over their tenants, which were increasingly often extended to their small landowning neighbours; some were ad hoc inventions. In the eleventh century, it became more common for lords to gain these rights over whole territories, over owners and tenants alike, in what modern authors often call the 'territorial *signoria*'—by 1100, in northern Italy, a common term was *dominatus loci*, 'domination over a locality'. Although castle-building did not automatically generate *signorie*, there can be no doubt that the two processes, both of which involved the development of nodes of political control in the countryside, were related, and indeed most *signorie* had a castle in the centre.[21]

The way these developments took place was regionally diverse. In Lombardy, castles began in the early tenth century, and the whole countryside was divided up into *signorie* by the late twelfth. In northern Tuscany, where the marquises of the Canossa dynasty maintained public authority until the civil wars of the 1080s and even later, up to the death of Matilda in 1115, although castles certainly came in in the mid and late tenth century, signorial rights are hardly documented until the late eleventh. In the central–southern mountains, where landlordship was often more large-scale, castles become the main

---

[21] See in general G. Tabacco, *The struggle for power in medieval Italy* (Cambridge, 1989), pp. 191–9; Keller, *Adelsherrschaft*, pp. 147–96; C. Violante, 'La signoria rurale nel secolo X', in Sett. CISAM 38 (Spoleto, 1991), pp. 329–85; L. Provero, *L'Italia dei poteri locali* (Rome, 1998).

focus of landed power by 1000, without much reference to signorial rights at all, probably because they were taken for granted—this is certainly true of the lands around Farfa in the Sabina, where by the early eleventh century the monastery can be seen with extensive judicial powers. In the plains of Lazio and Campania, however, where castles were common and land was as fragmented as in the North, signorial rights are still seldom referred to before the middle of the eleventh century: here, in the small polities of these regions, Rome, Gaeta, Naples, Amalfi, Salerno, local rulers maintained their own courts as important political foci, and rural power in Campania did not fragment and become privatized until the political crisis of the expansion of Norman power in the second half of the century.[22] The trend was, all the same, one of ever greater and ever more formalized and legalized private power, everywhere in Italy; even the Byzantine South (and, later, Arab Sicily) would experience the same process once the Normans conquered them. The period 900–1100 saw these trends establish themselves throughout Italy; in the end, a half-century more or less would not make much difference. The crisis was generalized: of the concept of public power, inherited from the Roman world. City autonomies themselves, at least in the kingdom of Italy, were products of the same process.

The result of these trends was that by 1100, local lords, i.e. substantial landowners, often called *milites* in our texts, had much more authority over their poorer neighbours, *rustici*, than they had had in 800 or 900. The *milites/rustici* opposition could, for the first time, be seen as distinguishing an aristocratic from a non-aristocratic stratum. Such lords were often themselves from new families; in particular, most of the texts we have from the eleventh century which lament and describe the local domineering of lords have as their targets lords of relatively recent origin, whose rights were less fully recognized by others. Here are the peasants of Casciavola near Pisa, complaining about the violent claims to signorial rights by the lords of nearby San Casciano around 1100:

After their castle was destroyed, we should have been free of any service, but, before the destruction, they began to do rapine against our property, not by custom or by our will. [So, around 1070, the peasants complained to the

[22] See e.g. for Salerno V. Loré, 'L'aristocrazia salernitana nell'XI secolo', in *Salerno nel XII secolo* (in press).

Marquise Beatrice, and the lords of San Casciano backed off.] Afterwards, when all power lost its strength, and justice was dead and perished in our land, they began to do us evil, as if they were pagans or Saracens. They began to attack our houses, to assault our wives as they lay in bed and beat them, to take all our goods from our houses, to strike our children and roll them in water and mire, to take all our animals, to devastate our fields, to despoil our gardens of all their fruits, and to take all our possibilities of life.

By comparison with this, gastald Warnefrit of Siena was pretty mild-mannered, 350 years earlier, even though he was rather more powerful a figure, controlling a whole city territory as he did—the lords of San Casciano, by contrast, were only one out of a large group of leading Pisan families.[23] But the new local domination of lords like these tended to be focused on the arena of local political and judicial rights. The landowning peasants and village elites who were subjected to signorial lordship normally remained landowners, and still were when signorial powers faded again in the thirteenth century. The political power of military figures was much more clear-cut by 1100, but the parameters of village society were not greatly changed. In a final section of this chapter, we shall look at how these were structured.

Village society

Not all of Italy was divided into clearly defined villages in our period. Most of Italy's settlement was dispersed under the Roman empire, and some of it remained so until the *incastellamento* period and beyond. Furthermore, Mediterranean non-irrigated agriculture tends to be fairly individualistic, with peasant families working independently on their networks of fields, and no role for the village community in choices about, for example, when to harvest, unlike in the open fields of northern Europe. Only in mountain areas, where communities might control common pasture lands, would one expect villages to be economically active, and even this is hardly documented before the eleventh century, when a developing woollen cloth industry began to stimulate the specialized rearing of sheep—in the eleventh century, too, iron-mining and silver-mining expanded,

[23] See the edition and commentary by G. Garzella in M. Pasquinucci, G. Garzella and M. L. Ceccarelli Lemut, *Cascina*, ii (Pisa, 1986), pp. 73–5, 161–2.

which tended to be managed by villages as well. Before that century, however, the village community was not an essential part of local economic life in most of Italy; and, in the Byzantine areas of Italy, such as around Ravenna and Rome, no territorial structures of a village type existed at all before the period of *incastellamento*. In Lombard areas, village identities did develop, however, quite quickly. Rothari in his *Edictum* of 643 envisaged that rural violence might consist of groups of peasants (*rustici* or *servi*) going into a village (*vicus*) to attack others, and burn down houses—indeed, such groups of *rusticani* might revolt against lords in some cases; villagers (*vicini*) could also swear oaths to each other; villages had territories (*viciniae*), and horse theft was more serious if the thief removed the horse from one of them.[24] Such territories were sufficiently significant by the eighth century that most references to estates, tenant houses, and land parcels in our documents are explicitly attached to a village.

Until the tenth–eleventh centuries, however, villages were probably not very coherent social units. Their restricted economic role was one obvious reason for this. Community identity was also not helped by social divisions, most notably between free and unfree peasants; it was not unknown in the Carolingian period for a *servus* to claim in court that he was rightfully free, but to lose because his free neighbours testified against him. The fragmented patterns of tenure that were normal in Italy themselves undermined village solidarities, for even among the free the interests of owner-cultivators and of the tenants of different lords were not always the same. Only on the largest estates might a common experience of subjection have aided collective identity: examples would have been the single-village properties that are visible in S. Giulia in Brescia's estate survey or, certainly, the oil-producing village of Limonta on Lake Como, given by the emperor Lothar to S. Ambrogio in 835, whose peasants claimed their freedom as a collective group in a sequence of court cases lasting from 882 to 957.[25] At the end of our period, the situation changed.

[24] *Rothari* 19, 279–80 (cf. *Liutprand* 134, 141), 340, 346.

[25] See Manaresi, *Placiti*, n. 9, for the free testifying against their neighbours; for Limonta, see A. Castagnetti, 'Dominico e massaricio a Limonta nei secoli nono e decimo', *Rivista di storia dell'agricoltura* 7 (1968), pp. 3–20; R. Balzaretti, 'The monastery of Sant'Ambrogio and dispute settlement in early medieval Milan', *Early Medieval Europe* 3 (1994), pp. 1–18.

Unfreedom faded away in most of Italy, as noted earlier; *incastellamento* in many places generated new nucleated settlements, which had much more group identity; rural churches, which had always been the foci for collective action, gradually became more numerous everywhere; and the territorialization of the *signoria* created a new framework for the united action of the peasantry. In the late eleventh and twelfth centuries, villages across Italy developed communal structures, which were indeed increasingly called 'communes', on the model of cities. Village identity and collective action was much stronger in 1100 than it had been in 700, mirroring the rise in aristocratic power in the countryside.

The relative weakness of early medieval villages did not, of course, mean that peasants were socially isolated. Rather, they acted in informal groups of friends and neighbours, sought the help of patrons, and, above all, operated in webs of kinship. It is clear from the laws of the seventh and eighth centuries, and from later documentary examples, that individuals could rely on their kin for much practical support, for help in times of crisis (as with the *consanguinei* and *amici* who helped Paul the Deacon's great-grandfather Lopichis rebuild his abandoned house in Friuli after escaping from captivity among the Avars in the mid seventh century), or for the offering of supportive oaths in court cases, which is the subject of some careful legislation, and which also worked in practice—people regularly appeared in court with their kin in our court-case documents. If one engaged in feud (*faida*), too, one sought the support of one's kin as a matter of course.[26] Above all, kin cooperated economically. There were many instances in which kinsmen, most often brothers, though occasionally cousins, shared undivided land after the death of their fathers, and even more in which they divided land field by field, so creating interlocking networks of properties that could only with difficulty have been cultivated separately. It is these networks of relatives, supplemented by friends as with Lopichis' house, that mattered most for the peasantries of the early medieval Italian countryside in the organization of their daily lives; patronage by the powerful (including local elites) came next; the village

[26] Pauli, *Historia Langobardorum* iv. 37; *Rothari* 359–64, *Liutprand* 61 for oath-helping; *Rothari* 74, *Liutprand* 13, 135 for *faida*.

collectivity, in most of the peninsula, only after that, until close to the end of the period.

The core of peasant social action was the household, which seems to have been in most cases restricted to a married couple and their children, with only occasional reference to one or more grandparents or unmarried relatives. The household was male-dominated; in the Lombard parts of Italy, exceptionally so, for the Lombards regarded women as permanently subject to men—in turn, to their father, their brothers at their father's death, their husband at marriage, and their sons at their husband's death—and as incapable of taking legal action or having any public role except through the mediation of their guardian (*mundoaldus*). In the Byzantine parts of the peninsula, women had a little more independence, for they could appear in court in their own right, and widows could have custody over their children rather than vice versa; but a general male dominance was assumed everywhere. Lombard law displays a concern for the protection of women that is so exacting that it makes the social marginality of the gender peculiarly clear—there are laws of Liutprand that specify what constitutes mistreatment of a woman by her guardian, or which state that if a man steals a woman's clothes while she is bathing in a river, so that she had to return home naked, he is to pay her a remarkably high fine. Both Rothari and Liutprand expatiate upon the inconceivability that women might bear arms, and its immorality if they did; Liutprand in 734 discovered with horror that this inconceivability meant that female violent attacks on a house or village had become excluded from legislation, and that, as a result, 'perfidious men, astute in their malice' were setting up women to attack in their place, 'more cruelly than men'. He enacted that the women should be shaved and publicly beaten, and that their husbands should pay for their damage. Even here, however, the king, at least, assumed that the real perpetrators were men.[27]

These examples have been taken from the Lombard laws, and are thus representations of normative theory rather than practice—though Liutprand's later laws are often generalizations from specific cases, and so for the most part the events they describe probably happened at least once. What sorts of negotiation actually went on

[27] Respectively, *Liutprand* 120, 135 (cf. 125), *Rothari* 378, *Liutprand* 141. See in general R. Balzaretti, ' "These are things that men do, not women" ', in G. Halsall (ed.), *Violence and Society in the Early Medieval West* (Woodbridge, Suffolk, 1998), pp. 175–92.

inside peasant households are invisible to us for the most part in this period. We do have some anecdotal evidence for the practical situation of women in the countryside, however. In the years 765–71 a widow called Alitroda—not a peasant, but no more than a medium landowner—was in effective control of a private church just outside Lucca, nominally held by her infant son Atripert; she put clerics into the church to run it. Her autonomy here was not less great because her son was legally her guardian. When, however, she made the mistake of sleeping with one of the clerics, her brother-in-law Peter, she was denounced to the bishop for incest by, significantly, her kin and neighbours (*proximi et vicini*), and the bishop expelled her for it; here, the kin acted to police immorality inside the family. Kin were not always so keen to moralize, though, as shown by the case of Gundi of Monactiano in the Abruzzo, a Frankish aristocrat in the countryside near Casauria: widowed, she became a nun, but her son and *mundoaldus*, Amelfred, subsequently married her off illegally to another aristocrat, Sisenand. Sisenand and Amelfred were fined for this illegality in 873, but Gundi, unlike Alitroda apparently a passive figure in these events, lost her property and her freedom for it. The players here were again not peasants, hence the fact that the case is well-documented, but the constraints involved would have been the same at any social level.[28]

Women could own land. In Byzantine Italy, they inherited equally with men, in theory; in Lombard Italy, they inherited if they had no brother. In addition, they had dowries, which were predominantly given by the husband to the wife in all parts of Italy in this period; in Lombard Italy, the main marriage gift, the *morgincap*, amounted to a quarter of the husband's property (for Franks, it was a third), which would support a widow after her husband's death. These procedures could result in quite a lot of land being female-owned. But this ownership, too, was normally controlled by men; charters for land sales by wives in Lombard regions always include the husband as co-vendor, and also two of the wife's male kin to testify that the woman has not been coerced to sell by her husband, as a law of Liutprand enacted. Laurent Feller has also shown that in the ninth-century Abruzzo a husband and wife in financial difficulties would pledge or

---

[28] *CDL* 2, n. 255 (cf. 186) for Alitroda; Manaresi, *Placiti*, n. 76, 82, with Feller, *Les Abruzzes*, pp. 463–6, 670–5, for Gundi.

even sell off the *morgincap* before any other of their properties.[29] Female-owned land was less extensive than male-owned land; it was mostly run by men; and it was also held to be more expendable. All of this confirms the (male) presumption of the period, that women needed no real autonomy under any circumstances.

The solidarities and the constraints of household and kinship relationships in the countryside did not change much in our period— indeed, they remained among the basic patterns of Italian rural society, changing only in detail, into the twentieth century. When rural aristocratic power became more explicit and more territorialized, in the half-century or so each side of 1000, and when village solidarities developed to match that power, wider social relationships became available, both vertical and horizontal, to add to those of the family. Rarely would they have been in competition, though; they would have involved additional opportunities and coercive constraints, but the closest family bonds, inside the household and between brothers, would have come first. The peasantries of Italy in the eleventh century were moving towards effective village-level collectivities, without in any way sacrificing the family bonds that had been their major safeguard in the past.

[29] D. Herlihy, 'Land, family and women in continental Europe, 701–1200', *Traditio* 18 (1962), pp. 89–120; Feller, *Les Abruzzes*, pp. 468–72; *Liutprand* 22 for the law; see further, for female property-owning, B. Pohl Resl, 'Quod me legibus contanget avere', *Mitteilungen des Instituts für Österreichische Geschichtsforschung* 101 (1993), pp. 201–27; C. La Rocca, 'Segni di distinzione', in L. Paroli (ed.), *L'Italia centro-settentrionale in età longobarda* (Florence, 1997), pp. 31–54.

7

Changing structures of settlements

Riccardo Francovich

The end of the ancient world: decline and revival of the villa system

The transformation of rural settlement patterns in Italy in the period from late antiquity to the Middle Ages can now be reconstructed in the light of new archaeological evidence. This has focused attention on a number of important developments. The first is that the disintegration of the late Roman settlements and organization of production, in other words the gradual decline of the ancient world, started in the middle of the imperial age and continued down to the Gothic War, lasting from the third to mid-sixth century. Classical and medieval archaeologists studying the formation of early medieval landscapes have focused primarily on the collapse of the villa system in different regions or, in the case of those regions where this phenomenon had not developed significantly, on the decline of the Roman settlement patterns and of the networks of economic and social relations that had supported them. But there is also clear evidence that many forms of political and administrative organization remained in place and continued to shape the landscape even after the Gothic War. Recent research on early medieval castles has been of particular interest in this respect and has provided an 'archaeology of power' on which to chart the rise of lordship. The complex dynamics that transformed the countryside between the seventh and eighth centuries and gave birth to the early medieval village has been another major subject of research.

An outline of the changes at work in the Italian countryside between the fifth and tenth centuries is now beginning to take shape, even though vast areas still remain to be explored. In fact, despite the considerable scale of recent research carried out in Italy, a complete account can still only be attempted for a limited number of areas (part of northern Italy, Tuscany, Lazio, Abruzzo, and Apulia), whereas other regions, such as Umbria and Basilicata, have not as yet been the subject of any extensive archaeological study. In addition to this uneven geographical distribution, there is also a critical lack of methodological unformity in the research methods adopted in different studies. This means that it is still not possible to propose a single uniform, albeit complex, model of the transformation of the countryside which is valid for Italy as a whole. However, the information collected does allow us to identify certain general as well as many particular regional features, in proportions that vary according to the area studied.

Following the long and fierce debates of the 1980s and 1990s, historians are now less interested in demonstrating the discontinuities between the ancient world and the Middle Ages than with developing improved analytical tools to enable us to understand better the underlying forces and regional peculiarities of this process of long and profound transformation.

Scholars now generally accept that the ancient landscape, or landscapes, began to disintegrate at a certain point. Research carried out on different regions throughout Italy has revealed that, while there were many regional differences, there were also certain common features in this process. First, the system of slave villas existed only on the Tyrrhenian coast of central Italy; absent in the Po region, in the Apennine regions it coexisted with other forms of settlement. Secondly, although the crisis of the third century affected all regions, it was felt most strongly precisely where the villa system had been most fully developed, and was much less drastic in those areas where the villa coexisted with pre-Roman systems organized around villages or with more dispersed settlements. Nevertheless, this first phase of decline did not bring radical changes to the economic and settlement structures of the countryside. Thirdly, the partial revival experienced during the age of Constantine (fourth century) was experienced in every region, even though this did not reverse the overall tendency of decline. There is evidence of replanning that extended even to architectural structures in order to redistribute internal space in the residential areas, in many villas from the Valdarno to the Po regions, and this was linked to more general changes in the use of the land that included a return to pastoralism and the cultivation of cereals in vast areas that had previously been dedicated to more specialized forms of farming. A final common feature was the gradual decline that resulted, in the period between the beginning of the fifth and the end of the sixth centuries, in the end of the villas, a transformation rooted in changes in their functions, in building materials, and in prevailing economic systems. All the villas that have been excavated (from Calabria to Romagna) reveal a considerable reduction of the inhabited area resulting from the subdivision of rooms, earth floors, and the construction of wooden huts over the mosaics. Cemeteries were established both inside and outside the perimeters of the buildings; simple stone buildings, perhaps makeshift shelters, suggest a sometimes temporary occupation of ruined buildings. In fact, most of the villas that had thrived in the second century had become dilapidated complexes by the fifth and sixth centuries, and the retrieval of pottery dating from this period near villas that had been active in the second and third centuries offers no real proof of any functional continuity.

Generalizations of this kind inevitably level out regional differences which deserve further consideration. In some areas there were already signs of decline in the third century, while in others they appeared only as late as the fourth century. Although the crisis led to desertion and deterioration, its impact was lessened by the expansion of the population into new areas and even by changes in forms of production. In northern Italy, the transformation started in the third century. Studies carried out in the Trentino lowland, in the area around Lake Garda near Verona, and in Emilia have shown that villas and farms were being deserted or suffered severe structural deterioration, while there are clear signs that the countryside was also being abandoned. An initial phase of decline was followed by a partial recovery that lasted until the Theodosian age (mid-fourth century), sometimes leading to expansion towards previously uncultivated areas. This was probably due to the renewal of links with the urban centres. The period in which Milan was imperial capital (286–402) may have affected the area between Lombardy and lowland Trentino, but we still do not know how the reorganization of the countryside shaped the process of concentration and restructuring of properties and management systems. Nor is it clear whether this was a productive phenomenon in economical terms.

The excavation of some settlements in Lombardy (such as Angera, Calvatone and Muralto[1] has revealed how the smaller settlements played a mediating role between the cities and the countryside in the Roman age. The data available show that the decline of the third century was not immediately continued, and indeed that there was a degree of prosperity in the fourth century. The fact that these inter-mediary centres in the distribution chain of goods were hardly affected by the first wave of recession means that the greatest reper-cussions were felt by the weaker complexes, and that recovery was only made possible by a general reorganization of the population and networks of production. Of the seventy known sites in Lombardy (fifty villas and twenty rural buildings), ten were expanded during the fourth and fifth centuries as a result of important and in some cases even monumental transformations. The inhabited areas and the intensive cultivation of the land were converted into a complex net-work of villas, farms, and simple houses in the area around Brescia and the Verona area of Lake Garda.[2]

From the fourth century, the trend towards partial demographic expansion and the farming of new lands also affected the lowland Trentino region, where housing structures were being built in the hill areas. It is unclear whether the inhabitants moved up to the higher land to escape some instability or whether they were seeking new areas to cultivate. Nevertheless, the continuity of the burial grounds linked to the various *fundi* show that this process did not involve the desertion of the older countryside. Emilia, too, was affected by the Constantinian revival, partly as a result of the new links that

[1] G. Cantino Wataghin, 'Il territorio', in R. Francovich and G. Noyé (eds.), *La storia dell'alto medioevo italiano alla luce dell'archeologia* (Florence, 1994), pp. 142–50; G. Sena Chiesa (ed.), *Angera Romana. Scavi nella necropoli 1970–1979* (Rome, 1985); M. T. Grassi, 'Rinvenimenti monetali da Angera (Varese). Scavi 1980–1984', *Bollettino di numismatica* 11 (1988), pp. 7–151.
[2] E. Roffia (ed.), *Ville romane sul lago di Garda* (Brescia 1997); N. Mancassola and F. Saggioro, 'Ricerche sul territorio tra tardoantico e altomedioevo. Il caso di studio del Garda orientale', in G. P. Brogiolo (ed.), *II congresso nazionale di archeologia medievale* (Florence, 2000), pp. 127–31.

developed with the cities when Milan became the imperial capital.[3] Whereas the third-century crisis had divided up and modified the space within the sites to accommodate new functional roles, the revival had various different effects: where new crops successfully replaced the old, no significant modifications took place, while those areas that enjoyed preferential relations with the city or adopted specialized farming techniques underwent a period of development.

Moving to central Italy, only southern Tuscany has been the subject of research and excavations to enable us to explore these complex patterns. The absence of polarizing urban centres and the progressive decline of many cities of the early imperial period make it difficult to reconstruct the changing relationship between city and the countryside. The crisis of the third and fourth centuries did not lead to a generalized shift of cultivated areas to previously peripheral zones, however, but rather made possible the survival of a certain number of more efficient farmsteads. The processes of transformation in the countryside also encouraged the development of both private and public latifundist estates whose centre were located in ancient villas, some of which were maritime, or else in villages. The re-emergence of the village as a focus of aggregation is a feature found in many different and widely separated areas, and raises the question of the extent to which the 'villas' had already become small villages in this period. There is evidence that many *mansiones* situated along the consular roads, as well as *thermae* and sentry posts, had been transformed into villages, many of which played an important role before becoming episcopal sees. The function of these nucleated settlements is, however, still far from being fully defined, and their influence and density throughout the territory has yet to be established.

In various parts of Tuscany, settlements began to develop alongside the *latifundium*: caves, makeshift dwellings, and small groups of houses were inhabited by people who made a living from the Apennine woods. Although in central Tuscany there was a similar decline in the number of sites with respect to the early empire (up to 90 per cent in some cases), settlement patterns based on medium to large farmsteads seem to have developed which, in the area around Siena, might have had close relations with the urban centres. Similarly, in

---

[3] J. Ortalli et al. (eds.), *Antiche genti di pianura. Tra Reno e Lavino. Ricerche archeologiche a Calderara di Reno* (Bologna, 2000).

the more distant hills (such as the Valle dell'Ombrone and the Valdorcia), estates at the centre of medium-sized properties that were divided up into farmsteads suggest a system of surplus farming destined for the city. Patterns in the area around Grosseto were also comparable to those found in the Siena region: the villas remained the dominant feature in the countryside, both close to the cities (which were in heavy decline, if not already abandoned, as had occurred at *Cosa, Heba, Statonia*) and in more distant hill areas, and were linked to nearby villages. It is precisely in the peripheral areas that evidence of the presence of small and medium-sized farmsteads has been found. On the coast, the maritime villas that exploited the fishing resources of the lagoons and ponds still played a central role. However, the internal transformations introduced in the villas during the fifth century are indicative of profound functional changes which lead us to suppose that these production systems were being replaced by smaller sites occupied by small communities that engaged in coastal navigation.

To complete the picture of developments in Tuscany, we must also briefly mention the northern part of the region around Lucca and the *ager Pisanus*, about which little information is available. Here the fourth-century revival was the result of the combined presence of a series of villas that had survived the previous crisis and of family-run agricultural and pastoral activities that used the woods for lumber production.

There was a similarly varied picture in the centre and south of the peninsula. In Lazio, the villa of Mola at Monte Gelato was deserted in the third century and reoccupied between the fourth and sixth centuries, resulting in the reorganization of the ancient structures, and in particular the subdivision of the rooms and their functions following patterns similar to those identified in northern Italy. Studies of sites in Abruzzo, Apulia, and Sicily offer further indications of the ways in which ancient landscapes were being changed. Inland, along the Apennines, the village had remained the main settlement pattern probably throughout the entire Roman period. In Abruzzo, the decline of the third and fourth centuries left the territorial organization of late antiquity virtually intact, at least until the time of the Gothic War. There was also continuity in the large coastal valleys as well as in numerous small villages. To the south, in the Biferno valley in Molise, the period of late antiquity saw the number of sites reduced by a half with clear signs of functional changes.[4] The smaller localities were worse hit by the crisis, while the larger complexes managed to survive until the fifth century.

Apulia and Sicily seem to have experienced a different tendency. In Apulia, settlement patterns encouraged the development of certain centres of production which grew to the detriment of others, which were deserted. This was accompanied by the concentration of property: the village re-emerged with a central role in the management of water resources and cereal production, which had expanded from the end of the fourth and fifth centuries in response to the new needs for provisions and the decline of transhumant animal farming. In Sicily, on the other hand, from around the fifth century the population was concentrated in sites on the plain and hill areas (medium and large villas and *vici*) that had been established in the Roman age. The discovery of tenth-century pottery in many of these inhabited areas suggests that these sites may have been used continuously from the Byzantine period until the Arab invasion and beyond. Many of these localities were situated on rivers or along the main communicating roads, although there were no hilltop settlements at least until the seventh century.

The decline of the villa system and the rise of the early medieval castle

Let us now turn to the definitive dissolution of the villa system between the fifth and sixth centuries, whose causes lay mainly in the slow death of an entire cultural system. This was no sudden phenomenon, however, but the result of contingent events. Although the Gothic War (535–54) represented the climax of the process, the decline had quite separate causes, which included the inability to prevent the provincialization of Italy, the drain of wealth towards the provinces, the dependence on foreign markets, and the marginalization of the Italic aristocracy in the imperial context. The

[4] G. Barker, *A Mediterranean Valley: Landscape Archaeology and the* Annales. *History in the Biferno Valley* (London, 1995).

fourth-century revival was only an isolated episode, derived from the illusion that a period of political stability might solve deep-rooted problems which the ruling classes seemed unable to perceive at all clearly.

Even in this final phase, there was no process of complete desertion of settlements or of systematic shifts towards new areas, while the areas that had previously been inhabited continued to be populated, albeit less densely. However, functions, structures, and productive activities did change. In the sixth century, subsistence farming became widespread, the links between the cities and the countryside weakened, and only a few areas (the Byzantine part of Abruzzo, Lazio, and perhaps also Sicily) were still involved in Mediterranean trade. Generally, forms of parasitic occupation of old rural centres using the ruins of former settlements evolved together with new features, the early medieval castles and small churches, often built using the ruins of deserted villas. Intensive surveys in southern Tuscany have revealed the existence of small, dispersed, and generally poor settlements that indicate the total collapse of the forms of control exercised by the elite in the Gothic age. This pattern is described as 'chaotic' precisely to underline the profound differences from the landscape that had preceded it. It was the product of a period of severe recession which resulted in irrational use of the territory and in intermittent and unplanned occupation of the old countryside. Signs of close inter-dependence among the settlements, and between the cities and the countryside, now disappeared, as did those of a territorial hierarchy that had still existed in the first half of the fifth century.

This might suggest a kind of anarchy that reigned for a certain period in the countryside, freeing the peasants from all forms of subordination. But here some qualification is required. Although it is evident that this was a period of progressive and irreversible simplifi-cation in social structures, in processes of production and building, the idea that all hierarchies collapsed does not tally either with the documentary records or with the admittedly scarce archaeological evidence. In northern Italy the *castra* system, albeit in a looser form, replaced the complex late Roman settlement structures.[5] The red-slip

---

[5] G. P. Brogiolo, 'Towns, forts and countryside: archaeological models for northern Italy in the early Lombard period (AD 568–650)', in G. P. Brogiolo et al. (eds.), *Towns and their Territories between Late Antiquity and the Early Middle Ages* (Leiden, 2000), pp. 299–324.

pottery, which continued to circulate until at least the early decades of the seventh century in central Italy, was made using a production cycle that involved firing kilns, sub-regional markets, and distribution systems which had reacted to the collapse of the Mediterranean trade by converting to other forms of agriculture and production (glass and metal). The fragmentation of settlements with the expansion of widespread small nuclei is evidence of the transformation of the complex system of social and economic relations that had emerged again during the fourth century. Further evidence for this has come from the discovery of grave-goods which provide information about funeral rituals suggesting that the social order had not been levelled out during the sixth and seventh centuries.

The early medieval castle was an important aspect of the changes occurring in the sixth and seventh centuries. The profound transformation of the Italian countryside was already well advanced when the Gothic War broke out in 535. Although underestimated in the past by historians, this proved to be a genuine watershed. The end of the old settlement system was not a result of the devastation brought by the armies, which was generally quite minimal but was caused by the acceleration of the militarization of society and of the countryside. This became a central feature of the sixth and seventh centuries. Fortifications had nearly always existed along the borders, but what made this period different was that internal boundaries were now constantly shifting, giving rise to the need for fortified settlements in strategic locations to control the territory. The castles built or restructured by the Goths, Byzantines, and Lombards were always seats of public power and were designed for defensive purposes; they were never the product of private initiatives to control resources and the population, as would be the case instead in the later Middle Ages. But this placed important limitations on many new settlements: once the urgent need for defence had been removed, many of these locations were quickly deserted and never subsequently reoccupied. Only those centres that managed to take on other functions that had formerly been delegated to the cities survived.

How did the foundation of these fortified sites affect the wider changes in settlement patterns? For the moment we do not know the answer to this question, because there is insufficient information available. Research is at an advanced stage only in a few regions (including Lombardy, Trentino, Liguria, and Abruzzo); for other regions (Tuscany, Lazio) there are only some preliminary studies, while most of southern Italy has yet to receive adequate attention from archaeologists. It seems certain, however, that successful fortified sites like Castelseprio (Varese) or Monselice (Padua) became centres capable of coordinating economic and administrative activities in the surrounding areas. The *castrum* in Monte Barro (Lecco), by contrast, was quickly deserted, as were hundreds of other small and medium-sized sites that had been fortified often by re-utilizing the pre-Roman city walls.

It is in this context that the new forms of settlement introduced by the Lombards have to be considered. These have been studied primarily on the basis of the ways in which cemeteries were sited, but systematic research on the settlements to which the cemeteries were linked has not yet been carried out. It is therefore difficult as yet to outline any more general patterns, because it is clear that the different phases of the invasion and the different environments in which the Lombards settled were key factors in triggering reciprocal cultural interactions. Some scholars have argued that the pattern of the Lombard settlements was determined by considerations of defence: their relatively small numbers and strong military organization, combined with the more or less open state of war, made the defence of strategic roads, cities, fords and mountain passes the primary functions of their settlements.[6] This hypothesis has still to be proved, however.

Certain areas illustrate very clearly this final chapter in the history of the landscapes of late antiquity. Throughout northern Italy, the settlement pattern centred on the villa began to decline during the fifth century, but down to the middle of the sixth century some settlement complexes were partially and selectively replanned. In lowland Trentino, for example, stone buildings were replaced by wooden constructions; at Varone, the interior of a villa was used as a burial ground. Nevertheless, there does not seem to have been a dramatic abandonment of the countryside. In Lombardy, only twelve of the seventy villas and farms registered in the first century still existed in the fifth century, and seventeen were reused until the sixth century. The villa at Sirmione was deserted around the end of the century; in about the same period the villa in Desenzano was destroyed by fire.

---

[6] C. Citter, 'I doni funebri nella Toscana longobarda ed il loro inquadramento nelle vicende storico-archeologiche del popolamento', in L. Paroli (ed.), *L'Italia centro settentrionale in età longobarda* (Florence, 1997), pp. 185–211.

At Pontevico, continuing inhabitation from the fourth and sixth centuries is suggested by the presence of buildings with a stone base and a wooden upper structure. At Nuvoleto, after the demolition of the thermal establishment around the end of the sixth century, small spaces with wooden upper structures predominated. In the area around Lake Garda near Verona the true moment of crisis seems to have occurred in the fifth century, although some areas continued to be inhabited throughout the sixth century. Here, too, there was a tendency to remodel ruined buildings and convert them into more modest structures, often using perishable materials. Recent excavations have revealed, moreover, that the clustering of the rural population around religious buildings was a phenomenon that dated from the fifth century.

Piedmont remained relatively prosperous down to the beginning of the fifth century, as the villas of Ticineto and Centallo demonstrate. During the century, religious buildings began to appear within the villas, in both the Novara and Cuneo regions, while other areas that continued to be used for residential purposes became smaller and had a different distribution of the spaces.[7] In Emilia, the final crisis of the villa system occurred between the fifth and sixth centuries, and was accompanied by marked environmental decay and the collapse of many buildings.

Systems of fortification were constructed both in the Alpine passes and near the cities throughout northern Italy during the fifth century. At Monte Barro, the Gothic rulers built the *castrum* on a series of natural terraces; the built-up area covered about eight of the fifty hectares enclosed by the city walls. The distinctive feature of this settlement was its regularly spaced buildings with courtyards, the largest of which was the seat of public power. The social structure of the inhabitants was very hierarchical and the settlement had many different functions: a refuge for the valley population, a military garrison, a gathering place for livestock.

Castelseprio was built at about the end of the fifth century as an important and extremely complex fortified centre: the walls enclosed an area of over six hectares, including public buildings, dwellings and a road network. In the Lombard era, Castelseprio played a key role for

[7] E. Micheletto, 'Forme di insediamento tra V e XIII secolo. Il contributo dell' archeologia', in L. Mercando and E. Micheletto (eds.), *Archeologia in Piemonte iii* (Turin, 1998).

a large surrounding area and became the headquarters of a civil and ecclesiastical district. The lavish frescoes of the church of S. Maria *foris Portas*, dating from the Carolingian age, are a further testimony to the lasting centrality and importance of the settlement.

At Monselice, the early medieval settlement was established on a hill towards the end of the sixth century as a Byzantine fortress that was later conquered by the Lombards. During the Lombard occupation, the importance of the centre grew until it came to play a leading role in the region of the Euganean hills. The *castrum* was surrounded by walls that enclosed an area of three hectares. Within the walls a group of Lombard tombs has been found to contain rich grave-goods dating from the first half of the seventh century.

Between the end of the fifth century and the early decades of the sixth century, the Tuscan countryside also shows unequivocal signs of selective changes that gave rise to new forms of settlement. Although the communities of the inland areas were typically sparse, the coastal areas saw the transformation of the maritime villas into protected maritime settlements. The phenomenon is most visible in the *Cosa/Ansedonia* (Grosseto) area, where both the geographical position and the presence of ancient city walls provided a natural place of shelter. The entire border area between Tuscany and Lazio was also affected by the changing boundaries of the episcopal sees, and by the creation of networks of fortifications that stretched inland along the main roads and rivers as far as Lake Bolsena. In the middle of the sixth century throughout most of Tuscany there was a low density of population, and the landscape contained many open and uninhabited areas that alternated with others where a close-knit network of new houses and buildings had been constructed from the ruins of deserted villas. There is nothing to indicate whether the complex social and economic hierarchies that still existed in the fourth century had survived, and it is not possible to establish whether close links still existed between the cities and the countryside. In fact, little else is known of the Tuscan cities between the sixth and seventh centuries.

There are signs that settlements along the main medieval roads were becoming polarized, however. This is the case with the Via Francigena as it traversed the Valdorcia, where there were settlements based on artisan and commercial activities relying on contacts within a limited area. At Torrita di Siena the village of late antiquity was radically modified, becoming an aggregate of huts and shelters built with materials from the ancient ruins and inhabited by a population engaged in agriculture, cattle-breeding, and artisan activities such as ironworking and livestock slaughter.[8] A network of rural churches, often parish churches, formed part of this new settlement pattern, with the dual function of organizing religious activities in the countryside and providing a place of congregation for the scattered population. At S. Marcellino in the Chianti region, the parish church was built on the location of a villa that had been used until late antiquity, and some sparse settlements have been found nearby. At S. Cristina (Buonconvento), a recent excavation has demonstrated that the present parish church existed in this period, built on a previous Roman complex partly inhabited and partly used as a burial ground with tombs dating from late antiquity to the seventh century.

Between the end of the fifth and the middle of the sixth century, production and circulation of pottery at a regional level was diversified, with some zones operating in Mediterranean markets while others were already oriented towards sub-regional production using a system of kilns which mass-produced earthenware goods that were distributed over short and medium distances. In the Siena district, the major centres seem to have been still directed towards wider markets, while the poorer ones were limited to local and cheaper products. The coastal sector of the Albegna valley received Mediterranean goods until the end of the sixth century, while inland this trade ended during the fifth century. In the Lucca district, there was a sudden drop in imported pottery, and at the same time an important increase in imitation products.

By the middle of the sixth century the urban market had definitively declined, and Mediterranean imports continued only in the form of military supplies organized by the Byzantine government. The presence of *sigillata* pottery and amphorae was no longer a sign of economic vitality and trade, but merely of the total dependence of *castra* and cities on imperial provisions, divorced from the hinterland. The farms that supplied agricultural products to the cities ceased to exist; the cities themselves came to resemble rural settlements rather than the urban centres of the fourth century. The circulation of goods was reduced to local products, while peasant families

[8] F. Cambi and C. Mascione, 'Ceramiche tardoantiche da Torrita di Siena', in L. Saguì (ed.), *Ceramica in Italia. VI–VII secolo. Atti del convegno in onore di J. W. Hayes* (Florence, 1998), pp. 629–34.

increasingly moved towards subsistence farming. There was even greater fragmentation in the production and distribution of pottery during the sixth century, and from the early decades of the seventh century industrial production ceased altogether. The remains of the previous complex system were limited to the products of a few kilns with a restricted number of purchasers.

In Lazio, the continuity of the settlement network of late antiquity may have been stronger than elsewhere. There are, however, discrepancies between what has emerged from the south Etruria survey[9] and what has been observed regarding the number of churches (approximately thirty) and cemeteries of late antiquity and the early Middle Ages (twenty-six), which seem to indicate a higher population. The cemetery areas are large, which implies that they were used by a considerable number of settlements: for example, between the sixth and seventh centuries the cemetery of Rignano Flaminio contained about 500–600 graves, but still has to be linked with some major settlement that has not yet come to light. Most churches continued to be used until the seventh century and later.[10] The thermal complex at Poggio Smerdarolo in the Tolfa mountains was occupied between the sixth and seventh centuries by a cemetery. Further north, the villa of La Selvicciola was inhabited until the seventh century, when a small church with a Lombard cemetery was erected on its ruins.[11]

Both the Gothic War and the Lombard invasion considerably influenced forms of settlement in the Teramo area in Abruzzo. The buildings of late antiquity were reused as dwellings or cemeteries. In the lower Pescara valley the occupation of ancient sites seems to have been linked to the continuing Byzantine presence until the early decades of the seventh century, during which period considerable agricultural restructuring took place in order to supply the neighbouring Byzantine coastal towns, such as *Castrum Truentinum*, *Castrum Novum*, *Ostia*, *Aterni*, *Hortona*, and *Histonium*. Although

[9] T. W. Potter, 'Population hiatus and continuity: the case of the south Etruria survey', in H. McK. Blake, T. W. Potter, and D. B. Whitehouse (eds.), *Papers in Italian Archaeology* (Cambridge, 1978), pp. 99–116; T. W. Potter, *Storia del paesaggio dell'Etruria meridionale. Archeologia e trasformazione del territorio* (Rome, 1985).

[10] V. Fiocchi Nicolai, 'Discussione', in Francovich and Noyé, *La storia dell'alto medioevo italiano*, pp. 403–6.

[11] G. Gazzetti, 'La villa romana in località Selvicciola (Ischia di Castro—VT)', in N. Christie (ed.), *Settlement and Economy in Italy 1500 BC to AD 1500: Papers of the 5th Conference of Italian Archaeology* (Oxford, 1995), pp. 297–302.

declining, the port structures allowed this supply system to function until a later period. Three different zones coexisted, therefore, each with a different economic organization: an inland area with simple forms of settlement by *vici* where subsistence farming was carried out; a second inland area where settlement was linked to production for the centres under imperial authority; and a third area on the coast and immediate hinterland where a number of large complexes still survived.[12]

In Apulia, the Gothic War and the later Lombard invasion also brought discontinuity as a consequence both of the conquest and of the conflict itself.[13] The mid-sixth century was a period of severe crisis in the countryside: in the Salento area and the Oria district desertion of settlements was widespread; in the Gargano area numerous settlements were reoccupied by small, often poor communities, as can be seen in the cemeteries and remains of buildings in recycled wood or stone. In some cases (Avicenna, Melfi-Leonessa, Campi Salentina-Santa Maria dell'Alto, S. Miserino, and Rutigliano-Purgatorio), during the sixth and seventh centuries, villages developed around small religious buildings constructed on or near older villas.

The beginning of the Middle Ages: the formation of villages and hilltop architecture

Archaeology now provides us with a clear picture of a process of change whose different elements were in fact closely interconnected. By about the mid-seventh century the production of pottery that had formerly been connected in its forms, techniques, and distribution networks to the ancient world finally ceased. The new wares that developed in the eighth and ninth centuries were completely different from the previous ones. For that reason the new ceramics are, however, difficult to classify and date, because they were products

---

[12] A. Staffa, 'Alcune considerazioni sulla presenza longobarda nell'Italia centrale adriatica (secc. VI–VII)', in Brogiolo, *II congresso nazionale di archeologia medievale*, pp. 117–26.

[13] J. M. Martin and G. Noyé, *La Capitanata nella storia del Mezzogiorno medievale* (Bari, 1991).

of new systems of production even in the regions still under Byzantine dominion, such as the Salento area in Apulia and Sicily. It is in precisely these regions that scholars have greatest trouble in dating the changes in the seventh and eighth centuries because of a scarcity of fossil guides, other than those provided by imported pottery and Byzantine coins. The situation is the same for Tuscany, Liguria, and the entire Po area. Undoubtedly more evidence has become available in the last twenty years, but the fact remains that African and Oriental sigillata pottery, amphorae, and red-slip wares were not replaced with similar products; different materials (wood, glass, and recycled metal) were used instead.

In the Lombard regions, tomb ornaments were no longer used, and the Christianization of the funerary rituals led to the construction of private churches; in many regions there was a shift away from settlements on the plains to a new pattern in which, after many centuries, mountain and hilltops once again played an important role, and not only for reasons of defence. The settlement pattern of both housing and artisan structures that had survived the fifth-century crisis dissolved between the sixth century and the first half of the seventh century. All this points to the conclusion that the second half of the seventh century was a turning point. Although this general picture is convincing, it must nonetheless be noted that this period has not yet been investigated in many regions. The scarcity of the archaeological evidence leads us to suppose that the landscape contained several different regional variants in a generalized picture of decisive change in habitat structures. The outcome was the emergence of a new network of settlement that followed strongly centralized forms.

Tuscany has the most obvious traces of hilltop villages inhabited continuously for long periods of time. These represent successful forms of settlement, in which clear social distinctions that evolved during the ninth and tenth centuries were a prelude to their later transformation into castles. Similar developments were occurring elsewhere. In Piedmont, recent findings have revealed that the castles were built on early medieval nucleated villages. In Sabina, at Casale San Donato, the *incastellamento* developed on early medieval settlements involving the fortification of pre-existing wooden villages.[14]

---

[14] J. Moreland et al., 'Excavations at Casale San Donato, Castelnuovo di Farfa (RI), Lazio, 1992', *Archeologia medievale*, 20 (1993), pp. 185–228.

Nor does this seem to be a totally new phenomenon.[15] In Abruzzo and Molise (S. Maria in Civita) there are also widespread similar cases of *incastellamento* involving the direct participation of the lay and ecclesiastical landowners.[16]

Archaeological evidence suggests that the appearance of a hierarchy within the hilltop villages between the ninth and tenth centuries and the rise of strong lordships in the formation and development of the *curtense* or manorial system were closely linked. First mentioned in documents of the eighth century, the *curtis* has been interpreted by historians as the first step in a process of reorganization of landed lordship that was represented archaeologically by the castle. But the *curtis* was essentially a system of relationships between private individuals, based on a strict social hierarchy. It is thus difficult to believe that the *dominicum*, the area retained for the lord's personal use, could have been made up of only one or a few isolated houses. It is more likely that the demesnes were located in centralized hilltop sites, of which material traces have survived. In these centres, a substantially egalitarian initial phase gave way to a period of distinct social division that followed the same chronology evident in written sources, and provides proof that the aristocratic groups of the late eighth and ninth centuries had already started a process of reorganizing landed property and power relations. The final stage in the process of landscape formation was the castle, which was superimposed on a variety of earlier types of settlement, both consolidating existing forms and, as in the case of Rocca San Silvestro, constructed in previously uninhabited areas.

The formation of hilltop villages took place in parallel with the foundation of royal and aristocratic monasteries. During the seventh and eighth centuries, a network of ecclesiastical settlements (churches and monasteries) had developed throughout the countryside to ensure closer control of the population. These two aspects coexisted throughout the entire late Lombard and Carolingian eras, which was also precisely the 'golden age' of the large monasteries such as S. Vincenzo al Volturno. Founded between the end of the seventh and beginning of the eighth century on the remains of a late Roman

---

[15] *Contra* P. Toubert, *Les structures du Latium médiéval. Le Latium méridional et la Sabine du XIe siècle à la fin du XIIe siècle* (Rome, 1973).

[16] Barker, *A Mediterranean Valley*, pp. 258–70.

village on the land of the duke of Benevento, the monastery flour-
ished at the time of Charlemagne, when it found itself at the centre of
bitter dispute since it was located on the border between Frankish
territory and the duchy of Benevento. Abandoned after a Saracen raid
in 881, it was rebuilt during the eleventh century, but survived only
for a brief period and never regained its previous splendour. The
complex structures of the abbey and the presence of frescoes, stained-
glass windows, and workshops make S. Vincenzo al Volturno not
unlike a city (it is estimated that about 500 monks may have lived
there in the ninth century). The church founded by Abbot Joshua at
the end of the eighth century was an imposing building, one of the
largest in Italy, and demonstrates the particularly privileged condition of the community, as well as the direct interest of Charlemagne
in an important border garrison.[17]

In Tuscany, too, the abbey of S. Salvatore al Monte Amiata,
founded by royal decree in the eighth century, had by the ninth
century expanded its influence as far as the Tyrrhenian coast through
the foundation of *cellae*, small dependent monasteries that functioned on the model of the *curtis*.[18]

Between the seventh and ninth centuries, resettlement of the population and the redefinition of the settlement networks deeply affected
the Italian countryside. The relations between the system of churches
and monasteries on the one hand and the world of the hilltop villages
on the other were dialectic in form. In the former, an ancient model
prevailed: around the religious centre a small scattered settlement
grew up that was destined to grow; in the latter, social relations
within the village communities were redefined. For some centuries
these two models confronted each other, but the fact that as early as
the tenth century many of the large monasteries were already starting
to decline and the parish churches had been brought within the
castles, and not vice versa, indicates how profitable the investment
of the landed lordship in the hilltop sites had been.

It is by no means easy to trace the events linked to the formation of
early medieval nucleated settlements in northern Italy since this has

---

[17] R. Hodges (ed.), *San Vincenzo al Volturno*, i: *The 1980–86 excavations* (London,
1993); R. Hodges (ed.), *San Vincenzo al Volturno*, ii: *The 1986–90 excavations* (London,
Rome, 1995).
[18] M. Ascheri and W. Kurze (eds.), *L'Amiata nel medioevo* (Rome, 1989).

not yet been sufficiently studied. In the Trentino region, for example, the analysis of the transformation of the rural landscape stops at the seventh century. The situation for Lombardy and Veneto is similar, with the exception of a few fortified centres such as Castelseprio and Monselice, for which continuing habitation has been ascertained. Piadena[19] is a splendid example of a new and short-lived early medieval village; the church of S. Tomè di Carvico, the only case of a religious building constructed in wood that has already been discovered in Italy,[20] was abandoned during the seventh century, and is evidence of the decline of the small settlement network that had arisen nearby. Similar cases in Tuscany indicate the spread of short-lived settlement sites for a somewhat later date (ninth–tenth centuries), which usually lasted only a few decades and were even built in wooded areas on land that was ill-suited to agriculture.

In Emilia-Romagna, too, investigations have not proceeded much beyond questions related to the villas of late antiquity, and therefore only general observations can be made. It does not seem possible to interpret the rapid shrinkage of settlement (about three-quarters of the sites of late antiquity) as evidence of a total collapse of the countryside: indeed, in the same period new nucleated settlements were being founded in parallel to the network of Byzantine and Lombard *castra*. The case of Modena provides perhaps the clearest example of the final decline of a system. The existence of well storage suggests the habitat was deserted because of war, after which a new settlement network was formed based on strategically positioned, protected inhabited areas. This factor, highlighted by the location of the Lombard cemeteries, appears linked to the role of the Modenese territory in the middle of the seventh century as a border area.[21]

There are still unanswered questions about the formation of early medieval villages. Some areas, however, are beginning to provide important new findings. In the Garda area near Verona, surface evidence shows that the villages grew up in connection with areas already inhabited in late antiquity, and continued to be engaged in

[19] A. Breda and G. P. Brogiolo, 'Piadena, loc. Castello 1984. Lotti 2 e 3', *Archeologia medievale*, 12 (1985), pp. 181–8.

[20] G. P. Brogiolo, 'Edilizia residenziale in Lombardia (V–VIII secolo)', in G. P. Brogiolo (ed.), *Edilizia residenziale tra V e VIII secolo* (Mantua, 1994), pp. 103–14.

[21] G. P. Brogiolo and S. Gelichi, *Nuove ricerche sui castelli altomedievali in Italia settentrionale* (Florence, 1997), pp. 101–17.

agricultural activities. The presence of Lombard cemeteries suggests that the origins of some villages can be dated to the seventh century.[22] In Piedmont, too, archaeological research has begun to uncover some initial material. A unique example is the building with a front portico, perhaps defended by a wall, which has been uncovered at Trino Vercellese and which dates from between the fifth and sixth centuries. Built on a previous Roman site, it is at the moment the only example in the region of a settlement occupied continuously since Roman times,[23] while in other cases the fortifications of late antiquity were reoccupied during the seventh century, with the addition of walls and towers in the tenth and eleventh centuries. There are also the two *curtes* of Benevagienna and Orba, which were fortified in the tenth century, where excavations have uncovered the boundary wall that surrounded a small, perhaps densely populated space. Nevertheless, it must be specified that the appearance of nucleated and protected habitats did not completely absorb the pre-existing population, which was divided up into villages and isolated houses.[24]

The picture for southern-central Italy is instead much more clearly defined. The existence of early medieval villages in Lazio has been known for some time, and it has been suggested that the foundation of the papal *domuscultae* may be interpreted as an attempt to revitalise depressed areas rather than a sign of rural repopulation. The excavation work at Mola di Monte Gelato, perhaps part of the *domusculta* of *Capracorum*, and at S. Cornelia has provided important evidence.[25] The excavations in upper Sabina seem to confirm the presence of villages: at Casale San Donato the site excavated was an active one, with considerable circulation of goods and at least fourteen types of pottery produced locally and elsewhere.[26] In the Viterbo district[27] and at the border with Abruzzo,[28] survey work on some

[22] Mancassola and Saggioro, 'Ricerche sul territorio tra tardoantico e altomedioevo', pp. 127–31.

[23] M. M. Negroponzi Mancini (ed.), *San Michele di Trino (VC). Dal villaggio romano al castello medievale* (Florence, 1999).

[24] Cantino Wataghin, 'Il territorio', pp. 142–50.

[25] *Capracorum*: Potter, King, *Excavations at Mola di Monte Gelato*; S. Cornelia: N. Christie (ed.), *Three South Etrurian Churches* (London, 1991).

[26] Moreland et al., 'Excavations at Casale San Donato'.

[27] T. W. Potter, 'Recenti ricerche in Etruria Meridionale. Problemi della transizione dal tardoantico all'altomedioevo', *Archeologia medievale*, 2 (1975), pp. 215–36.

[28] E. Hubert (ed.), *Une région frontalière au Moyen Âge. Les vallées du Turano et du Salto entre Sabine et Abruzzes* (Rome, 1995).

fortified sites seems to reveal the existence of a complex settlement network based entirely on villages. In Abruzzo it has been shown that continuing and discontinuing settlement coexisted, with an early shift to hilltop sites. In the Lombard era this transfer was largely due to unstable conditions in an area in a continual state of war. Some of these villages managed to take root and survive; others were destined to disappear.[29]

In Apulia, the situation in the countryside seems different. The hinterland was generally abandoned between the seventh and tenth centuries in favour of the large port towns, especially on the central Adriatic coast (Barletta, Trani, Bari), which gradually grew into cities. The widespread reoccupation and vast repopulation of the country-side took place only from the eleventh century as a result of Byzantine initiative.[30] In Sicily, systematic and accurate archaeological survey at Monreale, around Entella, and at Eraclea Minoa show an increase in the desertion of settlements around the fifth century, with a survival of the larger settlements, where sixth- to seventh-century African red-slip pottery and tenth- to eleventh-century polychrome glazed earthenware have come to light. Populations were grouped in villages based on the late antiquity settlement network, with no direct relations with the pre-existing structures. Recent studies in the Segesta district seem to confirm the absence of abrupt interruptions follow-ing the Islamic conquest in the ninth century, and settlement made up of nucleated but unprotected villages, many of which were already declining between the end of the tenth and the beginning of the eleventh century, following the foundation of Calathamet.[31]

Tuscany is the region in which the formation of medieval land-scapes has been most systematically studied. During the seventh cen-tury, all the poorer forms of settlement were deserted, including those that had grown up around the churches. The population shifted to the hilltop villages that were inhabited continuously until the thirteenth century. Amongst the sites excavated, the most legible

[29] A. R. Staffa, 'Alcune considerazioni sulla presenza longobarda nella media Italia adriatica (secc. VI–VII)', in Brogiolo, *II congresso nazionale di archeologia medievale*, pp. 117–26.
[30] C. D'Angela and G. Volpe, 'Aspetti storici e archeologici dell'alto medioevo in Puglia', in Francovich and Noyé, *La storia dell'altomedioevo italiano*, pp. 361–78.
[31] A. Molinari, 'Il popolamento rurale in Sicilia tra V e XIII secolo: alcuni spunti di riflessione', in Francovich and Noyé *La storia dell'altomedioevo italiano*, pp. 299–332.

are Scarlino (Grosseto), Montarrenti, and Poggibonsi (Siena).[32] While at Poggibonsi the village arose from a previous late antique rural complex, in the other two cases settlement took place spontaneously. The absence of tangible signs of an internal social hierarchy points to the limited power of the aristocracy in the Lombard age. On the Maremma coast, at Scarlino, beneath the Romanesque structures of the castle of the Alberti family, a group of huts inhabited for a long period between the middle of the sixth to the seventh century has been discovered, to which a stone church was added in the Carolingian age. The huts show signs of several reconstructions and previous levels eroded or cancelled over three centuries. At the beginning of the tenth century, there were two kinds of such dwelling of different sizes: the basic structures were wooden poles, the upper parts were made of branches cemented with clay, with roofing in straw and vegetal binding, dirt flooring, and fireplaces surrounded by stones and located near the entrance as they had no draught system. The chronology of the hut village (seventh–tenth centuries) shows a rural nucleus that in its latest documented evidence (973) is called *curtis*. In the late Carolingian period, the topmost area contained a large hut, smaller buildings, and the church: these elements make it an important structure, a status which is reinforced later by the location of the eleventh-century lordly building. This may have been the centre of the *curtis*, perhaps the demesne house; the other buildings, peasant huts, are instead set on the western and south-eastern slopes.

Located between the diocese of Volterra and Siena, Montarrenti evolved as a village of huts between the mid-seventh and the mid-eighth centuries, and became a centre for collecting agricultural products in the Carolingian age. The first phases of occupation of the site show the presence of oval wooden huts covering the whole hillside surface. Already in this phase the village was surrounded by two wooden palisades defending the upper and lower slopes. Pottery demonstrates that there were local production centres and varied demand. Between the mid-eighth and the ninth centuries, the

---

[32] R. Francovich (ed.), *Scarlino, i: Storia e territorio* (Florence, 1985); R. Francovich and R. Hodges, 'Archeologia e storia del villaggio fortificato di Montarrenti (Si). Un caso o un modello?', in R. Francovich and M. Milanese (eds.), 'Lo scavo archeologico di Montarrenti e i problemi dell'incastellamento medievale. Esperienze a confronto', *Archeologia medievale*, 16 (1989), pp. 15–38; M. Valenti, *Poggio Imperiale a Poggibonsi (Siena). Dal villaggio di capanne al castello di pietra* (Florence, 1996).

function of the topmost area changed: a stone and mortar wall replaced the wooden palisade, and the huts were replaced by a rectangular wooden storehouse. The topmost area was used for the storage of agricultural provisions and their manufacture, as shown by the discovery of a mill and a small oven used to dry grain. The presence of an area with structures for the storage of surplus products and for artisan activity at a higher location with respect to the dwellings suggests that the complex was a nucleus of landowners able to exercise prerogatives of territorial lordship. A new economic structure evolved in the village with the concentration of agricultural produce and service structures (the granary and the oven) on the higher part of the hill, surrounded by stone walls. It would be plausible to identify the elements of the centre of a *curtis cum clausura* in these eighth–ninth-century structures. Perhaps after a fire in the storehouse (second half of the ninth century), the topmost area continued to be inhabited, with the construction of new wooden buildings.

Poggibonsi is a village of two hectares that was inhabited for almost three centuries. It was composed of huts made of wood, clay, and straw defended naturally by a steep cliff almost 100 metres high and set between two burial grounds, one to the south-east and the other to the north-west. The sequence of the buildings shows that the dwellings were built over one or two generations. Those constructed in the Lombard era indicate a village without hierarchical differences, whose inhabitants were engaged in agricultural and animal husbandry. A decisive change is visible from the middle of the ninth century: a large central building appears, similar to the longhouse, with an interior storehouse for agricultural produce, a slaughterhouse surrounded by smaller huts, a farmyard, an area for artisan activities and the storage of surplus production. Finally, the amounts of meat consumed in the different parts of the site point to the fact that this was becoming an important status symbol. The centre of the settlement may have been used as the landowner's residence, suggesting this might be the centre of a *curtis*.

Around the mid-seventh century the processes of transformation that brought about both the definitive dissolution of the ancient landscapes and the emergence of new nucleated hilltop settlements came to maturity. The new settlement networks spread rapidly throughout many regions in the peninsula thanks largely to the peasant population and without any real obstacles, thus forming the first phase of the medieval landscapes. It was on this network that the new elite of the eighth and ninth centuries settled, determined to impress their presence on the landscape and to promote new forms of agricultural management. It is important to point out that the signs of recovery were felt in the hilltop villages and not in the more dispersed settlements. It was, in other words, in the village community that unmistakable signs of hierarchy in material structures mirrored the rise of a new social structure. The process continued through subsequent phases alongside the transformation of landed lordship into territorial lordship. The decline of the Italic kingdom in the tenth century permitted the rise of local aristocracies in different territorial contexts, and led to the formation of castles—a tangible sign of the new social hierarchies.

8

The cities

Sauro Gelichi

The cities of the Italian peninsula from the fourth to the tenth centuries: current research

The 1980s marked a turning point in research into the Italian cities of the early Middle Ages, providing us with new information on the building materials used and extending our knowledge of the layout and organization of public and private spaces. This turning point coincided with a renewed interest in urban archaeology, and hence with the initiation of a series of excavations on the sites of the ancient cities of the peninsula—both those which had been subsequently abandoned (for example, Luni near La Spezia) and those which continued to develop as urban settlements (Rome, Naples, Brescia, Pavia, and Verona).

The extended time-period which interested archaeologists led to the production of a body of significant information, the quality and quantity of which would have important consequences for the ways in which the cities of the early Middle Ages have been studied. In effect, up to only twenty years ago such cities were essentially seen as entities whose survival or disappearance depended almost always on their continuing performance of the economic or juridical functions that were considered their very *raison d'être*. There were very few specific studies of actual material structures or the urban organization of space, and interest tended to be focused on more general topographical concerns—such as the identification and location of important public structures and infrastructures (city walls, streets, palaces). The roots of such an approach were to be found, in part, in a historical topography that drew mainly on the analysis of written sources and, in part, on models that archaeologists and scholars had gradually developed through their study of the cities of classical antiquity. Thus the picture of the early medieval city was so ill-defined that, at the sixth *Settimana di Studi sull'Alto Medievo* (held at Spoleto in 1959), two historians—Dupré Theseider and Bognetti—could give totally conflicting accounts of it, without the incongruencies appearing strange.[1]

The mass of new data that has since emerged has enabled scholars to propose new models for interpreting the development of early medieval cities which are less conflicting than they might at first appear. In fact, a recent article on the subject has argued that despite the slight differences of nuance or emphasis, the various accounts now given agree as to the essential characteristics and features of the city of the early Middle Ages.[2] Naturally, however, the use of such terms as 'decline', 'rebirth' or 'reconstruction'[3] in describing the developments concerned means that the theoretical categories being applied are a long way from those of the modern anthropological doctrine that holds all cultures to be equal and thus denies the application of 'decline' or 'progress' to describe what is simply 'change'. Such contemporary anthropological notions are particularly clear in the work of English-speaking archaeologists and historians, as one can see from a recent collection of studies on European cities[4] which opts for the more neutral term 'transition'. Whichever term is to be preferred, there is no denying that the debate between those who focus on the continuing inheritance of classical antiquity (the 'continuists') and those who choose to emphasize features indicating rupture and change ('rupturists' or 'catastrophists') has been useful

[1] E. Dupré Theseider, 'Problemi della città nell'alto medioevo', and G. P. Bognetti, 'Problemi di metodo e oggetti di studio nella storia delle città italiane dell'alto medioevo', in *Sett. CISAM* 6 (Spoleto, 1959), pp. 15–46, 59–97.

[2] B. Ward Perkins, 'Continuists, catastrophists and the towns of post-roman Northern Italy', *Papers of the British School at Rome* 45 (1997), pp. 156–76.

[3] The title of a collection of essays edited by R. Hodges and B. Hobley is *The Rebirth of Towns in the West: AD 700–1050* (London, 1988). This includes the essay by B. Ward Perkins, 'The towns of Northern Italy: rebirth or renewal?', pp. 6–27, which considers the former term suitable for the many European cities that had effectively disappeared during the early Middle Ages, but adopts the less emphatic term of 'renewal' for the urban centres of northern Italy.

[4] N. Christie and S. J. Loseby (eds.), *Towns in Transition: Urban Evolution in Late Antiquity and the Early Middle Ages* (Aldershot, 1996).

in that it has brought the essential characteristics and features of the shift towards the Middle Ages into sharper focus.

However, in our own specific field it should be pointed out that whilst there has been quite extensive and intensive archaeological research in the urban centres of northern Italy, the same cannot be said of the centres of central and southern Italy (with the one exception of Rome). This fact has had a far from marginal effect on attempts to summarize results, which have necessarily tended to focus on the situations and behaviour patterns that obtained in the urban centres of the North.[5] Nevertheless, in general terms it is true to say that, whatever unexpected new information may be provided by future research, the revolution in urban archaeology that took place in the 1970s–80s laid the basis for a more reliable understanding and reconstruction of the architecture and layout of the early medieval city. What is more, archaeologists have become increasingly aware that the dualism continuity/discontinuity is not only a rather limiting instrument of research but is also based on a misleading comparison between two stereotypes. Just as the 'city of classical antiquity' cannot be identified exclusively with the urban model that became established during the first imperial age, so the 'city of the early Middle Ages' cannot be reduced to a single model: it clearly evolved over the period that ran from the seventh to the tenth centuries.

Territorial divisions and the number of cities

Many of the cities of classical antiquity survived into the early Middle Ages, a time which also saw the foundation of other settlements that aspired to the title of city (and sometimes are referred to as such in written documents). Those cities that still existed had sizeable populations and were the seat of public and ecclesiastical (episcopal) authority; they also continued to be the chosen place of residence of the aristocratic elite and—with certain variations—key centres of trade. During the Carolingian period Italy was still dotted

[5] G. P. Brogiolo and S. Gelichi, *La città nell'alto medioevo italiano. Archeologia e storia* (Rome, 1998).

with cities; indeed, the density of surviving or new cities was probably much higher than that one would find in most of the Islamic or Byzantine territories that gave onto the Mediterranean. Hence, one of the undoubted features of the evolution that took place in the peninsula during the early Middle Ages was that the urban model continued to play a central role in the economic and institutional organization of territory.

More detailed analysis reveals that this continuing importance was subject to regional variations. For example, in northern Italy it has been shown that most of the inhabited centres of classical antiquity survived into the early Middle Ages—and, indeed, in some areas (particularly the north-eastern region) they were joined by newly founded urban centres. In regions such as Lombardy and Emilia-Romagna, almost all the present-day cities which are centres of administrative districts were first established as Roman colonies or *municipia*. However, the situation was not the same everywhere: for example, in lower Piedmont numerous cities were (often quite early on) abandoned, never to be resettled—probably because, from their very foundation, a number of the Roman settlements seem to have been superfluous to the actual needs of the population and thus ceased to exist once they no longer fulfilled institutional roles as expressions of Roman government. The same situation can be seen in the central–Apennines area, where a number of the Roman *municipia* did not survive beyond the fifth century (one might cite *Trebula Mutuesca* and *Amiternum*, the decline in the latter apparently reflecting a concomitant decline in rural settlement[6]).

In its turn, the ancient *Regio VII* (later named *Tuscia*) reveals variations that are a good illustration of this 'disjointed' process of development, with cities responding in different ways to the process of Romanization (which in the south tended to be radical and violent, in the north more gradual, drawing on the collaboration of the local elites). The refoundation of certain centres of southern *Tuscia* during the first imperial age was in effect only a temporary

[6] S. Gelichi, 'La città in Emilia Romagna', in R. Francovich and G. Noyè (eds.), *La storia dell'alto medioevo italiano alla luce dell'archeologia* (Florence, 1994), pp. 567–600; C. La Rocca, '*Fuit civitas prisco in tempore*. Trasformazioni dei *municipia* abbandonati nell'Italia occidentale nell'XI secolo', in *La contessa Adelaide e l'XI secolo in Italia settentrionale* (Susa, 1993), pp. 238–78; E. Migliario, *Uomini, terre e strade. Aspetti dell'Italia centroappenninica tra antichità e alto medioevo* (Bari, 1995).

phenomenon: many of these cities were again in crisis during the end of the second and beginning of the third century, due to the demise of their political-military role and the fact that industry and trade in the surrounding territory had broken free of their hegemony (such was the case, for example, with *Cosa*). It would only be much later on (during the Byzantine period) that these centres would regain their original function (if at all), and even then it is doubtful whether one could still define them as cities. The recovery in the urban centres of the northern coast (Luni, Lucca, and Pisa) and inland areas (Florence, Arezzo, and Chiusi) was very different; for a variety of reasons, these enjoyed renewed vitality from the late classical period onwards and would subsequently become key political and economic centres during the Lombard and Carolingian ages.

All in all, however, it is clear that the waning of the Roman system and its structure of *municipia* had undoubted repercussions on urban settlement at the time. There were profound changes in the structure and layout of cities, which were particularly evident in the level of urban adornment and in the quality of urban life. Indeed, in many cases the very site of the classical city was abandoned, to become an empty space that would gradually be resettled by less substantial institutional entities (walled and unwalled villages, *curtes*). What emerges, therefore, is clearly a fragmented picture: the survival of an urban settlement seems to have depended increasingly on local factors, and thus cities became an expression of a particular regional situation. It is also interesting to note that, in many cases, the reason for the problems faced by the urban system can, in part, be traced to factors that pre-date the collapse of the Roman empire. The system of *municipia* throughout Italy was promoted by Rome essentially for political and administrative reasons; and many of these cities continued to perform these functions and enjoy a certain standard of urban life only as long as the patronage of imperial Rome and the local aristocracy made it possible.[7] In other words, this means that many of these cities did not become autonomous catalysts of settlement—for example, in the central-Apennines area, most spontaneous settlement continued to be centred in pre-Roman villages. In such circumstances, it is obvious that cities of this kind could not

[7] E. Gabba, 'La città italica', in P. Rossi (ed.), *Modelli di città. Strutture e funzioni politiche* (Turin, 1987), pp. 109–26.

survive the process of 'natural selection' triggered by the collapse of Roman rule; one might say that their ultimate demise was already inscribed in their original DNA. Naturally, this explanation cannot be extended automatically to cover the whole of Italy. It is, for example, clear that the new economic functions being taken on by settlements in surrounding territory also played a fundamental role in the process. In the Po valley the increasing importance of river trade not only helped to maintain such ancient settlements as Cremona and Mantua, but also led to the foundation of new cities and even stimulated the development of areas that had been of only marginal importance in the Roman network of urban settlements (for example the Ferrara area, which during the early Middle Ages saw the foundation of such cities as Comacchio and Ferrara itself). The situation in the Veneto region is here particularly significant— and not only because this was the period of those settlements that would ultimately give rise to the birth of Venice. In this region the Lombard occupation did lead to the abandonment of centres (in border zones above all, the occupation led to a clear breakdown in urban settlement); however, that process was counterbalanced by the fact that in both Lombard and Byzantine-controlled areas there were measures to stimulate the growth of existing centres and to create new settlements.[8]

Archaeological research has yet to produce as clear a picture of what was happening in the south of Italy; however, certain regional and local characteristics are coming into sharper focus. A first general analysis would seem to suggest that the network of ancient cities here held up much less well than in the north of Italy. By the sixth century some 50 per cent of ancient urban settlements had been abandoned. Taking Calabria alone, one can observe that in the fourth century almost a third of cities had disappeared, lost their urban functions to other centres, or been transformed into agglomerations that were

[8] P. Delogu, 'Longobardi e romani: altre congetture', in S. Gasparri and P. Cammarosano (eds.), *Langobardia* (Udine, 1990), pp. 111–67; G. P. Brogiolo, 'Towns, forts and the countryside: archaeological models for Northern Italy in the early Lombard period (AD 568–650)', in G. P. Brogiolo, N. Gauthier and N. Christie (eds.), *Towns and their Territories between Late Antiquity and the Early Middle Ages* (Leiden, 2000), pp. 299–323; C. La Rocca, '*Castrum vel potius civitas.* Modelli di declino urbano in Italia settentrionale durante l'alto medioevo', in Francovich and Noyé *La storia dell'alto medioevo italiano*, pp. 545–54.

very different to the cities of classical antiquity. The continuing health of certain urban settlements or specific territorial areas (for example, central Campania or central-northern Apulia) was substantially due to the level of interest and investment forthcoming from central government (which would continue to invest resources into those cities that played an important economic role, controlled important natural resources, or occupied strategic positions).[9] One compensation for this widespread early decline in urban development is that—from the late classical period onwards—rural settlements (*vici* or *villae*) recovered a number of their former functions.

As regards other specific centres, there is still no clear explanation for the fortune they enjoyed during the early Middle Ages. Cities such as Salerno and Benevento obviously benefited from the presence of the court of a Lombard duke and its concern to give fitting material expression to its prestige (the various building projects undertaken included such public structures as the city walls). However, there is no sign of particular vitality in early medieval Naples, even if there is an indirect suggestion of that vitality in the archaeological evidence which shows the structural layout of the city to have been very similar to that of cities in the north of the peninsula.[10] On the contrary, both written sources and a long-standing tradition of scholarly research have underscored the role and importance of contemporary Amalfi; however, whilst we can understand the function and characteristics of this almost legendary commercial centre, we have a much vaguer idea of the place's material layout and structure.

---

[9] G. Noyé, 'Les villes des provinces d'Apulie-Calabre et de Bruttium-Lucanie du IVe au VIe siècle', in G. P. Brogiolo (ed.), *Early Medieval Towns in the Western Mediterranean* (Mantua, 1996), pp. 97–120; P. Arthur, 'La città in Italia meridionale in età tardoantica. Riflessioni intorno alle evidenze materiali', in *L'Italia meridionale in età tardo antica. Atti del trentottesimo convegno di Studi sulla Magna Grecia* (Naples, 1998), pp. 167–200 (esp. pp. 173, 185–6).

[10] P. Arthur, 'Naples: a case of urban survival in the early Middle Ages?', *Melanges de l'École Française de Rome* 103(2) (1996), pp. 759–84.

Old and new public spaces

As the Romans conquered the Italian peninsula, they founded or refounded urban centres that were to serve as pivotal components in the organization of the Roman state. This process involved the application of fairly standardized schemata and models to the layout and structure of urban settlements. There is no change in the characteristic features of the Roman city from the age of the republic to that of the empire, and perhaps it is this essential homogeneity that helps us to identify the first early signs of disruption that appeared towards the end of the second century and beginning of the third.

The Roman city had a structured layout that was more or less regular: it was built around a number of straight roads that intersected at right angles, forming a series of spaces (*insulae*) that were destined to serve different functions and purposes. This road grid would house private residences and the public buildings of civil government and religious worship (paid for by public—and imperial—funds, as well as by private donations, these public buildings were often particularly prestigious structures). Street paving and a good water supply (guaranteed by aqueducts and a system of waste pipes, together with an efficient drainage system) meant that living standards in the city were fairly high, whilst the location of cemeteries outside the city maintained a clear distinction between the space of the living and that of the dead. It is obvious that such massive investment in public building works, which also had an effect on the building of private residences, left its mark on the urban fabric for centuries to come (only in the era of the communes in the thirteenth century would there be comparable commitment to urban building). Indeed, the scale of such work was so vast that the changes made in the years to come appear all the more macroscopic and evident.

There can be no doubt that the appearance of Italian cities changed over the period that runs from the late imperial age to the early Middle Ages. Let us now look at the forms that change took.

Around twenty years ago, Bryan Ward Perkins published his

excellent summary of the way public buildings in northern and central Italy changed from the late classical period to the tenth century[11]—a process which is documented not only by written sources but also by the evidence unearthed by archaeologists. What is clear is the fact that during the early Middle Ages not all public buildings and public spaces were either destroyed or reconverted to serve other functions. For example, city walls would remain a constant feature of the urban landscape throughout the early Middle Ages. The restoration of these walls occurred during the late classical age, when tensions caused by internal conflict and the growing number of barbarian incursions were on the increase; however, whilst essentially defensive in purpose, this restoration could also embody a statement of ideology. The refortified walls were often the ancient structures (sometimes, indeed, pre-Augustan); but if these were either absent or totally unserviceable, new walls might be built from scratch. Sometimes, the city walls would enclose an area that was smaller than that of the original urban settlement, leaving entire districts of the city as extra-mural; however, this phenomenon was nowhere near as widespread in Italy as it was in Gallia. Indeed, there are—admittedly exceptional—cases (such as Milan and Ravenna) where the building of the walls actually marked an extension of the city's perimeter. The walls in Milan—built in the fourth century, during the period of Maximian's rule—enclosed the area of the circus, which had served as the venue for the celebrations of imperial power; whilst in Ravenna, the extension of (the still well-preserved) city walls seems mainly to have been intended to provide the city with the space necessary for certain important functional structures (a *palatium*, a circus, a mint, and various places of worship).[12]

However, though city walls were an important part of the urban landscape in the early Middle Ages, there are only very few cases of entire circuits of walls being built. Perhaps the restructuring work on

[11] B. Ward Perkins, *From Classical Antiquity to the Middle Ages: Urban Public Building in Northern and Central Italy, AD 300–850* (Oxford, 1984).

[12] S. Gelichi, 'Ravenna, ascesa e declino di una capitale', in G. Ripoll and J. M. Gurt (eds.), *Sedes regiae (ann. 400–800)* (Barcelona, 2000), pp. 109–34.

the walls of Benevento dates from the Lombard period, whilst the extension of the walls of Salerno is attributed to Arechis II, and the renewal of the urban defences of Oderzo dates from the period of Byzantine rule (however, the structures discovered in a recent dig are part of a defensive structure placed within the city, not part of a project to refortify the city walls themselves). The early Middle Ages also saw the construction of the first walls around the Rivoalto nucleus that would subsequently become the city of Venice, fortifications which John the Deacon dates around the time of Duke Peter the Tribune (for the moment, they are only known to us through archaeological finds of dubious attribution). However, the most significant project of new city walls undertaken in Italy during this period was the work of a pope, Leo IV, who commissioned the Leonine walls that were to protect the Vatican from the growing number of incursions by Saracen raiders.[13]

Although city walls were considered an indispensable instrument in the protection of built-up urban areas, the early Middle Ages also saw the construction of fortifications within the urban area. These were veritable castles, some of them built for private individuals (for example, the *castrum aureum* built near the ancient Balbo crypt in Rome) or for bishops (for example, the fortified episcopal palaces at Reggio Emilia and Modena).

Numerous imperial and royal palaces survived into the early Middle Ages and were restored or rebuilt. Written sources suggest that the palace in Pavia was still standing in the eleventh century. The *palatium* in Ravenna—initially the seat of imperial power, then of the Ostrogothic kings—would become the residence of the

---

[13] Benevento: M. Rotili, *Benevento romana e longobarda. L'immagine urbana* (Benevento, 1986); Salerno: P. Delogu, *Mito di una città meridionale (Salerno, secoli VIII–XI)* (Naples, 1977); Oderzo: D. Castagna and M. Tirelli, 'Evidenze archeologiche di Oderzo tardoantica ed altomedievale: i risultati preliminari di recenti indagini', in G. P. Brogiolo (ed.), *Città, castelli, campagne nei territori di frontiera (secoli VI–VII)*, (Mantua, 1996), pp. 121–34. On the building of the Venice walls and their historical context, see S. Gasparri, 'Venezia tra l'Italia bizantina e il regno italico. La *civitas* e l'assemblea', in S. Gasparri, G. Levi and P. Moro (eds.), *Venezia. Itinerari per la storia della città* (Bologna, 1997), pp. 61–82. On the Leonine walls, see S. Gibson and B. Ward Perkins, 'The surviving remains of the Leonine wall', *Papers of the British School at Rome* 42 (1979), pp. 30–57.

exarch of Italy during the period of Byzantine rule, and only began to be dismantled in the Carolingian period (we know that Charlemagne took some of the building's decorative fixtures for his own palace at Aachen). New palaces were also built, inspired by openly classical models: for example, Arechis II's *palatium* at Salerno, in which the chapel was decorated with *opus sectile* and with a squared-script inscription in bronze letters of a text written by Paolo Diacono.

Some of the other infrastructures of the Roman city were less fortunate, though there is some evidence that the aqueducts were still in operation in the early Middle Ages (for example, we know that in the eighth century work was carried out on the aqueduct of Brescia, to carry water to a *balneum* in the monastery of San Salvatore). Place names that refer to water channels can still be found as late as the year 1000, and sometimes even later; overall, however, the last sizeable maintenance work on these infrastructures dates from the period of Byzantine rule. The same is also true of sewers and drainage systems, many of which were not repaired when they became blocked.

The question is much more ambiguous when one comes to consider roads. There is no doubt that the use of paving stones or other hard-wearing materials (*opus signinum*, rubble, etc.) came to a halt (they would only make their reappearance at the time of the communes in the thirteenth century); however, especially in urban areas, roads as such must have survived and—together with property boundaries—served to maintain that regular layout that can still be seen in many Italian cities (particularly in the north).

What did disappear for good were those public spaces that had played such an important role in the civic life of a Roman city: forum, baths, circus, theatres, amphitheatres, and, above all, places of pagan cult. The written sources of the early Middle Ages give no indication of the location of public baths, except for a reference to those built for Vittore (bishop of Ravenna from 537 to 544/6) in his palace—hence even these really date from the late classical period—and a vaguer mention of the closure of 'the baths' at the time Damianus was bishop of Ravenna towards the beginning of the eighth century. However, this does not mean that private baths disappeared altogether—as we can see from both written documents and archaeological evidence. For example, both the baths discovered within the monastic complex of S. Salvatore in Brescia (perhaps connected with San Salvatore in Pensilis) uneart ruins of the Balbo crypt date from the Middle Ages.[14]

Written sources may confirm that Roman circuses continued to be used for the ritual celebration of power during the Lombard period—for example, the ceremony in which Agiluf took his son as 'co-ruler' was held in the circus of Milan; however, most of the great buildings associated with Roman games or other expressions of power were soon dismantled and 'requarried'. Given their location—outside the centre of the city, on the very edge of the built-up urban area—these buildings were often included within the circuit of the city walls and became a key point in the new system of defences. This would seem to be the case with the amphitheatre in Verona, which is still clearly visible in the famous *Icnografia Ratheriana* of the city and shown incorporated within the extension of the urban area that is attributed to Theoderic.

Along with many other administrative buildings, these complexes might also be used as burial areas, or else were divided up and became private property; this is clearly the case with the theatres of Verona and Lucca (the latter still clearly identifiable from the urban layout of the city, even if its original fabric almost totally disappeared over the centuries). A similar fate befell the famous theatre of Marcellus in Rome, before restoration work resulted in a (partial) return to its original form. There is scant information on the other monuments of this kind: sometimes the only remaining trace is in a place name (as is the case with Altopascio, near Pisa), whilst excavations have also brought further information to light (for example, the recent work at Bologna, where again the theatre was incorporated within the fifth-century system of urban defences).[15]

Obviously, as these places of entertainment, political celebration, and public life began to lose their original function, they were reconverted to serve other purposes, subjected to the same dismantling

[14] G. P. Brogiolo, *Brescia altomedievale. Urbanistica ed edilizia dal IV al IX secolo* (Mantua, 1993); L. Saguì, '*Balnea* medievali. Trasformazione e continuità della tradizione classica', in L. Saguì (ed.), *Archeologia urbana a Roma. Il progetto della 'Crypta Balbi'. 5. L'esedra della 'Crypta Balbi' nel medioevo (XI–XV secolo)* (Florence, 1990), pp. 98–116.

[15] J. Ortalli, *Il teatro romano di Bologna* (Bologna, 1986).

and recycling that one can also see at the sites of pagan cult. It has traditionally been argued that, after the Edict of Constantine in 314, there was a concerted programme to reconsecrate pagan temples as Christian churches. However, not only was there opposition to the new religion itself (particularly amongst the aristocracy), it is also clear that the progress of this conversion of pagan temples was far from straightforward and uniform. As has been recognized recently, the establishment of Christian spaces within a city might well have very diverse explanations—not least amongst which were purely utilitarian considerations or simple changes in ownership. Nevertheless, it is clear that—thanks to both the church hierarchy and converted aristocrats—from the fourth century onwards the new religion began to leave its mark in urban and suburban areas alike. Basilicas for cults and religious gatherings, baptisteries for the performance of the rites of baptism and residences for the new priesthood and clergy were sited in the former;[16] the recognized burial places of saints and martyrs, funeral basilicas, and new Christian cemeteries in the latter. In their turn, these new places of cult would become key points in the topography of cities in the early Middle Ages, determining both patterns of settlement and road layout.

The replacement of the public and religious buildings of classical antiquity by buildings that served for the celebration of Christian rituals is also reflected in changes in public commissions and patronage. It is clear that the new aristocrats of the late classical period and the early Middle Ages invested resources in the construction of the great monuments of Christianity—building projects whose chief support came from bishops and (after Constantine) from kings and emperors themselves.

[16] P. Testini, G. Cantino Wataghin and L. Pani Ermini, 'La cattedrale in Italia', in Actes du XI Congrés International d'Archéologie Chrétienne (Rome, 1989), pp. 5–229.

Open spaces and the problem of the ruralization of cities

One of the main features that distinguishes the structure of the classical city is the very density of the urban fabric (even if this does not necessarily imply greater population density, given that buildings might be used for something other than housing). This density of urban fabric was clearly documented by past archaelogical studies—though one has to admit that such studies tended to focus on the outline and description of prestigious buildings and complexes rather than recording, where present, those non-built-up areas that were not intended for residential or monumental use. A comparison of the data we have regarding the cities of classical antiquity with what archaeology has revealed about the cities of the early Middle Ages indicates a sharp reversal in trend: not only were the later cities built of materials which were more perishable (and thus less likely to survive for identification by archaeologists), they were also less dense in built-up areas. Confirmation of this also comes from written sources, which speak of open areas used as gardens, fields, or pasture land for flocks and herds—a development that has already been conjectured upon by Gian Piero Bognetti in a discussion that has led to talk of the 'ruralization' of cities (not only in the north of Italy, but also in some centres of the south—for example, Naples; indeed, it has even been argued that the increasing consumption of goats and sheep that can be documented in fifth- and sixth-century Naples is proof of the increasingly rural nature of the city centre).

So the countryside—complete with wild, uncultivated areas—makes its appearance within the city, and according to some scholars this makes it difficult to draw a sharp distinction between the urban and the rural. However, ultimately this overemphatic reading seems unjustified, even when one tries to draw a distinction between the political-cultural developments in the cities of the Byzantine regions and those under Lombard rule (since all seem to evolve following roughly the same pattern).[17] Nevertheless, there is no doubt that there

---

[17] V. Fumagalli, 'Langobardia e Romania. L'occupazione del suolo nella Pentapoli altomedievale', in Ricerche e studi sul 'Breviarium Ecclesiae Ravennatis' (Codice Bavaro) (Rome, 1985), pp. 95–107; S. Gelichi, 'Note sulle città bizantine dell'Esarcato e della Pentapoli tra IV e IX secolo', in Brogiolo, Early Medieval Towns, pp. 67–76.

was an increase in the area of open spaces within the early medieval city, and that therefore there is some justification for the application of the adjective 'rural'. But in what sense is one to understand this 'ruralization' of the city? It is clear, for example, that during the early Middle Ages cities may have been 'rural' but remained very different from either walled or unwalled villages—in size, in population density, and in function. Many cities were the heirs of classical foundations and thus, compared to the newly created areas (be they rural or urban), maintained features that revealed their origins. It is not uncommon to find written records mentioning how the still-visible remains of classical antiquity served as a clear (if not always well-interpreted) reminder of the ancient status and origin of the settlement.

In effect, ruralization should be seen as a phenomenon that affected only some areas within the urban fabric, radically changing the function and structure they had had during the classical period. It was not only that areas for purely rural use were now present within the city (there is documentary evidence of gardens existing within Roman cities), but that the urban fabric became organized around certain settled areas (be they public or private); and it was this which led to the fragmentation or polarization that was to be one of the key features of the early medieval city. Thus one can accept the term 'ruralization' insofar as it registers the objective reduction in the qualitative differences between rural and urban life; indeed, if we are to look at the cities of northern Italy alone, evidence regarding housing would seem to suggest that those differences had almost entirely disappeared by the tenth century.

Residential buildings and housing

Undoubtedly, residential building and housing is one of those areas in which one can note a clear change in technology, materials, and design from the period of classical antiquity to that of the early Middle Ages. In spite of the ambiguity in the terminology used by some of the extant written sources, housing in the early Middle Ages seems to have been very different from that which existed before. Unfortunately, archaeological studies of this area have only recently achieved a level of detail and sophistication which makes it possible to outline and compare different models of housing. However, whilst our knowledge of the whole range of housing is not yet complete, the general outlines seem sufficiently clear for us to identify the main differences in building types and when they occurred.

One certain area of difference is that of building materials. In the periods of the Roman republic and empire, all housing both within and without cities was constructed in non-perishable materials (be it brick or stone, according to area resources); and even if recent arch-aeological research has shown that wood and clay were being more frequently used sooner than had previously been thought, they were still being employed in structures with plaster-faced walls, roof tiles, clay moulded anchor decoration, mosaics, and, in the most refined cases, *opus sectile* flooring. Such materials were used in single-family housing of medium-high quality, which extended to cover quite a large ground area with a series of porticoed courtyards (each building might often occupy the area of an *insula* created by a city's roads). This model was derived from the *domus* of Greek and Roman trad-ition, and was accompanied by more modest structures which tended to imitate its layout and functional characteristics.[18] In the larger cities (above all Rome and Ostia) there were also examples of more plebeian housing, generally small in size and located on the first floor of the large residences that occupied entire city blocks. The single-family unit of housing—which was also to be found in rural areas—went into decline around the third century, when a number of such complexes were destroyed and/or abandoned, never to be rebuilt. And though this model of housing did not disappear altogether, it was now accompanied more and more frequently by other types of structure built using less durable materials.

The passage towards the building types that would become typical of the early medieval city is rather complex and occurs over various stages. The first step was fragmentation in the use of what, in classical antiquity, had been single housing units, with the (often partial) readaptation of spaces using recycled building materials and rela-tively low-quality building technology. Following extant written

[18] F. Guidobaldi, 'L'edilizia abitativa unifamiliare nella Roma tardoantica', in A. Giardina (ed.), *Società romana e impero tardoantico*, ii: *Roma. Politica, economia, paesaggio urbano* (Rome, 1996), pp. 165–237.

sources, this process has been seen in relation to the quartering of troops that occurred during the war between the Byzantines and the Goths, or simply as the result of occupation by squatters. Although there must have been many individual causes for this development, the basic framework within which they became operative was that of a general weakening of the urban middle classes (who were less and less able to afford the maintenance of such large buildings). This weakening of the middle classes must have led to the sale, confiscation or donation or buildings; and when—as was most often the case—the new owners were bishops or ecclesiastical foundations, the structures were split up so that they could be exploited more profitably (slightly later written sources, of the ninth and tenth centuries, make this abundantly clear).

Within this process of change, reasonable-quality private homes to a smaller scale continued to be built; indeed, in the Ostrogothic period one sees the emergence of new building types, with the construction of two-floor houses complete with pilasters and porticoes, often set within open spaces and looking out onto a public road. So far this type of housing has only been discovered in the north of Italy, and it probably developed in rural areas or *castra*. The most significant examples excavated so far are those at the *castrum* of Monte Barro and the complexes of buildings in Via Alberto Mario (Brescia), Via Dante (Verona), palazzo Tabanelli (Trento), and—perhaps—the structures excavated in Parma, Santa Brigida.

Another aspect of the change in building types is that, right up to at least the middle of the sixth century, the ancient standards of housing were maintained in the residences built for an aristocratic elite of state functionaries and the rich *possessores* who lived in urban areas. Their homes are a clear example of continuing imitation of the lifestyle of the aristocracy of classical antiquity, and comprise amply laid-out structures that are opulently decorated with paintings, mosaics, and *opus sectile* work that is often of very high quality. As has so rightly been pointed out, it is very difficult to distinguish between these residential buildings and those that are a direct expression of royal or imperial power; numerous examples are to be found in those areas around what were centres of power in the late classical period: fourth-century Milan and fifth/sixth-century Ravenna.[19]

[19] N. Duval, 'Comment reconnaître un palais impérial ou royal? Ravenne et Piazza Armerina', *Felix Ravenna* 115 (1996), pp. 29–62.

Little is yet known about the housing of later periods. Written sources—above all, those relating to the pentapolitan area and the exarchate (that is, the coastal region under Byzantine rule)—suggest the continuing existence of fairly good-quality housing, given that they use a technical terminology drawn from the domestic architecture of classical antiquity. However, more than once one gets the impression that such terminology does not actually reflect reality, and continues to be applied simply because it has become part of the fossilized language used in the chancelleries of episcopal courts.[20]

Recent excavations in Rome have unearthed two-storey brick buildings with a ground-floor portico that can be dated from the Carolingian period;[21] and it is likely that in the north of the country too, the local aristocracy aspired to types of housing that were rather more 'upmarket' than those which archaeologists have so far discovered. Some indication of this comes from the extant written sources referring to both the Byzantine and Lombard areas (above all, the documents relating to the city of Lucca).

However, a general downturn in building standards is undeniable. Houses such as the recently discovered structures in Via D'Azeglio in Ravenna (which were still being restored at the beginning of the sixth century) would soon be impossible. What is more, in the north of Italy the dominant models of housing would rapidly become purely wooden structures (perhaps with clay and thatch) comprising a single multi-purpose room and formed using a framework of horizontal beams and vertical posts. Examples of such buildings have been found in newly founded cities (for example, Ferrara) and in such ancient cities as Fidenza and Parma (some of them even date from later than the tenth century). In those cases where the wooden components have happened to survive, one can see that the structures required fairly skilled joinery work, which leads one to suspect there may well have been a market for already-finished pieces. One should, however, point out that we have very little information on the elevation of these buildings, nor is there even substantial agreement on when structures of this type first made their appearance. It is

[20] M. Cagiano de Azevedo, 'Le case descritte nel *Codex Traditionum Ecclesiae Ravennatis*', *Rendiconti dell'Accademia dei Lincei* 27 (1972), pp. 159–81.

[21] R. Santangeli Valenzani, 'Edilizia residenziale e aristocratica urbana a Roma nell'altomedioevo', in S. Gelichi (ed.), *Atti del I Congresso nazionale di Archeologia Medievale* (Florence, 1997), pp. 64–70.

interesting to note that such buildings are also to be found in the rural settlements of the day (walled and unwalled villages); this underlines the increasing similarity between the rural and urban which has already been referred to—a similarity that, at both a cultural and material level, would only be substantially reversed with emergence of the communes in the eleventh century.

The early medieval perception of cities

As we have already seen, where cities did survive there was a notable change in their appearance. The inhabited centres of the Roman republic and early empire were something different to the urban entities that formed over the period of late antiquity and the early Middle Ages. Now one must look at the way the people of the time saw their cities, and their level of awareness of the changes that I have illustrated.

This question has been the subject of a recent collection of essays, one of which uses written and archaeological sources to give a more precise account of the changes in this awareness over time.[22] A first phase is to be identified with the period of late antiquity, between the fourth and fifth centuries. This, it is argued, is when the first symptoms of urban transformation were taken by contemporaries to be striking evidence of overall decay—something which finds expression in the famous metaphors in which cities are compared to living beings in decline (*semirutarum urbium cadavera*, says Ambrose of some of the cities of the old *Regio VIII*,[23] whilst Rutilius Namatianus describes some of the cities of the Tyrrhenian coast as dying like *mortalia corpora*[24]); archaeological sources too provide pertinent, though less emphatic, expressions of the same point of view. It is interesting to note how all of this reveals a deeply felt malaise and,

[22] G. P. Brogiolo and B. Ward Perkins (eds.), *The Idea and the Ideal of the Town between Late Antiquity and the Early Middle Ages* (Leiden, 1999), esp. G. P. Brogiolo, 'Ideas of the town in Italy during the transition from antiquity to the Middle Ages' (pp. 99–126).

[23] Ambrosii, *Epistolae*, XXXIX, 3, in O. Faller (ed.), *Ambrosii Opera, Pars X* (Vienna, 1968).

[24] Rutilii Namantiani, *De reditu suo*, i. 413–14, in A. M. Duff and J. W. Duff (eds.), *Minor Latin Poets* (London, 1934).

most particularly, an awareness amongst the aristocratic classes that their cities were undergoing social and structural changes.

The following period—that of the Ostrogothic kings, and of Theoderic in particular—is almost unanimously viewed in contemporary sources as a time of peace and stability, of great urban renewal and a return to the restoration of public buildings and infrastructures. However, recent study has shown that, when looked at more closely, the building programme undertaken by the Gothic king turns out to be rather modest in scale.[25] Hence, a large part of the stress sources put on his role must be attributed to intelligently concerted propaganda, even if there is no denying that the special and favourable conditions during his reign must have had beneficial effects on many aspects of private building work and on the development of the urban fabric as a whole (as we have seen, there were certain improvements in building techniques and in the types of housing being constructed). However, it is clear that this favourable situation was soon to end. The long and extenuating war between the Goths and the Byzantines, which involved most of the regions of the peninsula in a conflict lasting more than twenty years, plus the subsequent invasion by the Lombards (and the years that followed immediately afterwards), were almost always viewed by contemporaries as a time of unrelieved woe. The violence of long and bloody sieges, and the subsequent sacking of cities, is often compared to the devastating fury of the forces of nature. The general picture that appears is one of Italian cities that only just survive the savagery of the period.

Then, after 680—a crucial period in the history of Italy—a different idea of cities begins to make its appearance in written documents. The Lombard kings attempted to establish a certain continuity with the past by the restoration or creation of places that could serve to legitimize their authority; and in contemporary writers we see not only a celebration of kings such as Cunipert and Liutprand as the restorers of cities, but also a return to a totally idealized image of the city. Liutprand is also striking for his role as a founder of cities such as Cittanova, a few kilometres to the north-west of Modena (a celebratory inscription credits the Lombard king with the foundation of

[25] C. La Rocca, 'Una prudente maschera *antiqua*. La politica edilizia di Teodorico', in *Teodorico il grande e i Goti d'Italia. Atti del XIII Congresso internazionale di studi sull'alto medioevo* (Spoleto, 1994), pp. 451–515.

this settlement, which in ninth-century charters will appear under the name *Civitas Geminiana*). However, even though this site had a certain institutional importance—first as the seat of a royal court and then as the temporary residence of a Carolingian count—this status has, so far, not been borne out by archaeological evidence (all that excavations of the 1980s revealed were the remains of a *castrum* built near the site by Gotefredus, bishop of Modena, in 904).[26]

So, as we have seen, the attitude of contemporaries—known to us only through the ideas expressing the ideology of certain aristocratic groups—would seem really to be an expression of trends and aspirations. And this would appear to be true both when the opinions voiced are a criticism of the profound material and functional transformations that are taking place in cities and when they emphasize urban decline and decay in general. However realistic a picture they may give of the actual state of settlements at this time, such opinions also express the way contemporaries experienced and perceived the long transitional period that would end in the Middle Ages—and naturally they do so in a way that is not always totally unbiased and objective.

[26] S. Gelichi et al., 'Studi e ricerche archeologiche sul sito altomedievale di Cittanova', in *Modena dalle origini all'anno mille. Studi di archeologia e storia*, i (Modena, 1989), pp. 577–60.

Lay and ecclesiastical culture

Claudia Villa

The Lombard domination: a past to legalize the present

The cultural history of the two centuries from the arrival of the Lombards in Italy to the collapse of their kingdom in 774 has long posed problems of evaluation. As early as the eighteenth century the Italian antiquary Gerolamo Tiraboschi (1731–94) noted the very limited quantity and quality of literary productions surviving from this era, which led him to question the judgement of Ludovico Muratori (1672–1750). Muratori had been more attentive to juridical aspects and so readier to think well of the two centuries of Lombard domination, and saw in the long period of peace evidence that the groups indentified as Lombards and Romans had been able to live and work together. Even a cursory glance at the period suggests that Muratori was hardly wrong to draw attention to the great legislative initiatives of the age and also to the educational leadership that was provided from the beginning of the eighth century within the Lombard kingdom given by the group of 'Italians', such as Peter of Pisa, Paul the Deacon, Paulinus Patriarch of Aquileia and, likely enough, Desiderius' courtier Fardulfus, who had a radical impact on Frankish culture while they worked under Charlemagne. But Tiraboschi and others who have studied the Lombard period have also pointed out that what was produced in the way of literature amounted to little more than a few occasional poems.

For a more informed assessment of Italian culture in the early Middle Ages we can now turn instead to the results of 'excavations' among the collections of ancient Latin codices in the libraries of the period. Because these manuscripts were solid objects skilfully made from sturdy parchment, they were able to survive many complex and now unkown adventures unharmed. These highly resistant materials made the manuscripts highly durable, and they passed through the hands of generations of mostly unknown readers. They were also brought together in collections where they were protected from the harm wrought by time and, most probably, preserved in good order with the aim of reproducing culture. In short, they were preserved because they were considered to be essential features of the educational process, and served for the teaching of grammar or history in a culture that relied heavily on tradition.

The codices that have come down to us from the period between the fifth and the seventh centuries have now become 'homeless': they are books that were produced and stored in places of which we still know too little. But as we shall see, these places were not only monastic centres. Indeed, among their users we find all those with literary training, such as judges, notaries, and others involved in the law and public functions, all of whom were professionally engaged in passing on tradition and written culture.

We should start by asking, however, how the authors of this period themselves understood the transmission of culture since this will enable us to establish the cultural canons and principal points of reference of Lombard culture. Dating from the late eighth century, Paul the Deacon's reflections on the arrival of the Lombards in Italy offers an initial overview. He narrated the events that took place in the sixth century when the Lombards had replaced the Goths, and he listed the men most worthy of being remembered, thereby implicitly establishing the canon of late antiquity which still today constitutes a starting point for our understanding of the early Middle Ages. After recounting an episode that demonstrated the qualities of King Alboin,[1] Paul immediately listed other great men of the period, naming the Emperor Justinian, the statesman Cassiodorus, the grammarian Priscian, the chronologist Dionysius Exiguus, and the poet Arator. Since every social group produces its own models,

[1] Pauli, *Historia Langobardorum*, i. 24.

alongside Alboin Paul constructed a gallery of ancestors, and he chose among his predecessors outstanding examples of a legislating sovereign and great masters of the disciplines of rhetoric, grammar, mathematics, and prosody that were indispensable for the cultural development of the prince's counsellors and, at a lower level, of the functionaries of civil administration. Revealing very clear criteria of selection, this ideal gallery displays the values of a juridical and civil culture grounded in the study of grammar and rhetoric that was the foundation of Lombard civilization. And when his narrative reached the seventh century, Paul recalled the new masters of grammar, naming in particular Felix, who was honoured by King Cunipert, and his nephew Flavian, who was Paul's own master.

The panorama set out by Paul offers a useful starting point for reconstructing cultural developments in Italy from the middle of the sixth century to the end of the eighth. It is particularly important for an understanding of which places were equipped to ensure cultural continuity and the material preservation of books into the eighth century.

If we date the beginning of the early Middle Ages from the entry of the Lombards into Italy in 568, we would probably fix on the capture of Pavia. But if we had to choose a date that would serve to help us understand how books came to be preserved and the origins of the institutions that preserved them, then we should start not from the founding of the monastery at Bobbio in 612 but from the earlier and quite miraculous decision not to raze Pavia that was taken around 570. This was the moment when under Alboin's leadership the new conquerors decided to settle in the ancient Gothic capital, with the result that both the king's court and the administration of the realm ceased to be itinerant. Consequently, in trying to locate the origins of the sense of tradition that was shared by the Lombards we should recall that the people who now inhabited what had been Theoderic's palace were 'now confident of a better future'.[2] The mosaic representing the Gothic king that still presided over the royal tribunal in the tenth century was a symbol of this hope: in the application of the law and civil administration, justice represents a future founded on tradition.

King Agilulf initiated a programme of public building, including

[2] Ibid. ii. 27.

the royal palace at Monza, in which he was buried, and it was with his permission that St Columban founded the monastery at Bobbio. Nothing is known about the cultural activities at Bobbio in the first centuries of its existence, but it certainly included the recovery and accumulation of manuscripts which were brought here from many different places and which by the time of the Ottonian emperors, four centuries later, constituted one of the great libraries of the tenth century, whose catalogue still survives.

Thirty years after the foundation of Bobbio and seventy after the capture of Pavia, from the palace of that city Rothari published the famous edict of 643. This document bears witness to the legislative projects and juridical learning of the team of experts from whom originated the allusions to the Justinian Code that make the prologue to Rothari's edict one of the most important written documents of the seventh century. Rothari and his judges used juridical formulas and terminology that demonstrate their acquaintance with the parallel texts of Justinian and of Theodosius (*renovare, emendare*) as well as technical terms attested by Cassiodorus and Festus. One of the central themes was the idea of a renovation (*renovatio*), a concept deeply rooted in many spheres of medieval culture (*renovatio imperii, renovatio studii, renovatio librorum*) that expressed the desire to innovate without breaking with tradition, since the idea of *renovatio* is inseparable from the need for historical memory.

The legislative activity of the Lombard kings did not end with Rothari's edict but was carried forward by subsequent rulers down to the great juridical revival of the eleventh century. Grimoald and Liutprand, and especially Ratchis and Aistulf, explicitly drew attention to the presence of the judges (*iudices*) who aided them.[3] This is also connected with the important place held by the grammatical tradition which as a result of the influence of the monks of Bobbio, became a central feature in north Italian culture. Since legislation called for reflection on tradition and demanded discussion of custom and practice, a training in grammar was indispensable for producing a class of specialists capable of interpreting the ruler's will and the intent of the legislation translating them in proper form. This same class was also called on to organize various forms of consensus, and

---

[3] Ratchis, *Prologue*: 'Here begin the laws established by King and Lord Ratchis of one mind with our judges'; 'in our council with all the judges'.

especially to produce laudatory verses, metrical epitaphs, and celebrations of civic life to accompany festivals and other public events. A good example of this is the *Carmen de Synodo Ticinesi*, a celebration of King Cunipert, who acted as moderator at the synod held in Pavia in about 698 that brought to an end of the 'Schism the Three Chapters'.

What emerges is a picture of a culture that relied on the grammatical, rhetorical, and prosodic tools that can be found in surviving early medieval miscellanies. These were collections of classical materials that were brought together and rewritten for specific educational purposes. They enable us to understand why particular attention was given to spelling and the use of texts like the *Appendix Probi*, transferred into a codex in the seventh century, which was of importance for those who needed to distinguish the proper forms of late Latin which was already being severely undermined by Romance influences.

The sequence of legislating Lombard kings is particularly significant, and this also revealed the existence of civic centres or family traditions in which the officials who compiled and then enacted the written laws were educated. The oldest copies of the edict are from the seventh century, at St Gall (Stiftsbibl. 730) and from the eighth century, at Vercelli (Biblioteca Capitolare, 188). These are written in uncial, a fine ornamental hand, whose survival is an indicator of the tenacious hold of tradition, because this was the script used in the ancient manuscripts of the Digest of Justinian. The same style was also adopted in the oldest codex of Paul the Deacon's *Historia Langobardorum*, which was executed in the author's lifetime and is now at Perugia. Even centuries later, the codices of the *Leges Langobardorum* carried effigies of the rulers, as can be seen in the important examples conserved at Modena (Biblioteca Capitolare, tenth century, O.I.2) and, for Benevento, in the early eleventh-century Cava manuscript (Archivio della Badia, 4).

It has to be remembered, too, that the transcription of juridical codices raised the possibilities of copying errors and of arbitrary changes. These were especially serious in the case of legal texts; the authors of Lombard laws were perfectly aware of this, and made it a requirement that copies of texts be reproduced only with the authorization of a royal notary. These concerns help explain why Carolingian philologists engaged so heavily in labours of extensive textual revisions and the collation of the texts of classical authors. It is also important to stress the degree to which the interest in history was connected to jurisprudence, since the codices containing the Lombard laws also conserved the *Origo gentis Langobardorum*. In other words, historical memory was put to work so that the past might legitimize present undertakings.

The Latinization of Lombard culture fixed once and for all the linguistic model and the stylistic discipline of Latin based on the relatively 'modern' texts produced by the grammarians, rhetoricians, and prosodists of late antique Rome and of the recent past under Theoderic, from which also came the manuals prepared for the education of court officials. The most important example was Cassiodorus. His *Institutiones* were copied in the eighth century in the area around Benevento and later at Nonantola, and set out a programme based on the seven liberal arts accompanied by a bibliographical listing of authors on the basis of a scheme that follows exactly the readings laid down by Paul the Deacon. Within this schema, attention was focused on the ancient customs and habits that Paul himself drew attention to in his well-known and widely distributed epitome of Festus Pompeius, dedicated to Charlemagne with the declared intent of making the usages and practices of the pagans better known.

The South of Italy provided even clearer examples of the ways in which the creation of an administrative capital preceded the cultural impetus that derived from the founding of an important monastic centre. Towards the end of the sixth century the Lombards had reached the southern part of the peninsula. Around 592–3, King Arechis I laid waste to Velia Busento and Blandia in Lucania which would form the basis of his own principality, and in 596–7 he conquered Crotone. In the following centuries southern Italy played a key role in the conservation of traditions derived from the classical texts that finally found their way to Montecassino. But even in this case, the monastery's library was never simply a lifeboat for saving books and traditions. Even though it later became the most famous monastic foundation in southern Italy, Montecassino was silent throughout much of the Lombard period. After being destroyed between 577 and 589, it was refounded by a nobleman named Petronace in 720, with the support of many other Lombard lords as part of the intensive activity of renewal during the reign of Liutprand. Paul claimed that the books of the Holy Scripture and St Benedict's own manuscript copy of the Rule were brought there from Rome,[4] but that should be qualified because the attraction exercised by the capital was what determined the early influence of the liturgy of Benevento at Montecassino.

This is also borne out by the fate of such a great institution as the Vivarium. Founded by Cassiodorus, who died while the Lombards were besieging Naples (c.585), the Vivarium had ceased to be active in the first decades of the seventh century. That was the moment when the dukes had became firmly ensconced at Benevento, which makes it necessary to reconsider Benevento's role in the diaspora of the Vivarium's library. In the late eighth century the codex of Cassiodorus that is now at Bamberg (State Library Pat.61) was taken from the archetype—that is, the oldest manuscript—of the *Institutiones*, while in the fifteenth century the Capitoline Library of Benevento still possessed the text, which certainly came from the Vivarium, that is now in the Vatican (Lat. 5704).

Soon after the death of Cassiodorus the Lombards reached Calabria, getting as far as Reggio, if Paul the Deacon is to be believed. A letter from Gregory the Great to John of Squillace in 591 states that they continued to move through the region between Crotone and Reggio until the frontier with the eastern empire became fixed at Cosenza. From the beginning of the seventh century, Gregory the Great's letters to the Lombard dukes show that they had chancelleries capable of maintaining correspondence with the pope; and Paul the Deacon himself reproduces the letter, which may have been conserved in a Benevento archive, in which Gregory calls on Duke Arechis I to help with the transport of timber from *Bruttii* to Rome. A general transfer of books and of the men needed to maintain and interpret them, from the Vivarium to Benevento, cannot therefore be ruled out at a time when Montecassino could not have played any part in the conservation of the texts and translations that had re-emerged in this area. The abbey became important for only a brief period between 750 and 756, when it was the refuge of King Ratchis and his entourage. It was at that time that Paul the Deacon, who was probably Ratchis' adviser (*consiliarius*) on affairs of state (*omnia arcana imperii*), also withdrew permanently to the monastery. But Paul had also been in the

---

[4] Pauli, *Historia Langobardorum*, vi. 40.

service of the duke of Benevento, for whom he composed epigrams, dedicatory verses, and a *Historia Romana* for his pupil Adelperga, wife of Arechis and daughter of the Lombard king Desiderius.

If Benevento had a greater role than has hitherto been recognized in the transmission of classical culture, the royal seat of Pavia was soon to become another important point of reference. The close similarities between Lombard laws and those of the Anglo-Saxons have suggested that the latter imitated the former; and archaeological finds show that these exchanges would include books as well. The most important confirmation of the involvement of royal officials in the commerce in books comes from the Mozarabic prayer book which is now at Verona but around 730 was in the possession of a certain Maurezo Canaparius, an administrator of King Liutprand. From a little later, but still at Verona, the 'Veronese Riddle' appears to have been composed as a calligraphic exercise, in which the questioner describes the act of writing by way of a metaphor using linguistic forms that are recognizably Romance and adopting images that are part of the poetic repertory that we find also in Paul the Deacon's writings.

There is thus much still to be learnt about the role of the Lombard ruling class in the conservation of collections of books from late antiquity. All efforts to connect the Master Flavian with specific interventions in the grammar manuals and collections have proved in vain, but Paul the Deacon's testimony is in any case sufficient to establish the importance that the court gave to the grammarians who produced instructive texts which were perfectly in keeping with current needs and models of teaching and which finished up in the library of Bobbio. The metrical and rhythmic experiments in some of their epigraphic writings indicate that these canny intellectuals were endowed with a practical culture that contained some elements of eclecticism.

Two late eighth-century miscellanies reveal what was required in the education of a good official. One is in the Bibliothèque Nationale at Paris (Lat. 7530): it comes from the Benevento area and has traditionally been connected with the teaching of Paul the Deacon. The other is in the State Library at Berlin (Diez B 66), and is a collection of texts that are almost exclusively from the North of Italy. These include Peter of Pisa's grammar, a small set of poems addressed to him, songs by Angilbert, a celebration, from between 792 and 796, of the victory of King Pippin of Italy over the Avars, and also a brief passage with a classification of the writings in use among the Romans or the Anglo-Saxons. These materials suggest that the manual was in use at the court of Italy. This makes the astonishing list of classical authors it contains of special importance, since this corresponds closely with the much later collection in the Capitolare Library at Verona, which was the site of one of Theoderic's palaces that was later inhabited by the Lombard kings and by King Pippin himself. The two codices have a number of authors in common and are basically chancellery manuals, and it is not surprising, in a society that produced two important hymns dedicated respectively to Milan and to Verona, to find in them instructions for writing the praises of cities. They also contain models for versification in the form of a sailor's song that seems to have been the model for the later 'Song of the Modena Watchmen'.

A society that employed the didactic instruments of late antiquity also took pleasure in quotation, and in re-creating grand styles for religious buildings and those associated with civil power. The decoration of the Tempietto at Cividale, the remarkable classicism of the temple of Clitumno or S. Salvatore at Spoleto, and the surviving fragments of court art at Arechis' Benevento show that the arts and architecture that the ruling class in Italy in the seventh and eighth centuries chose to patronize provide further evidence of the desire to conserve. They demonstrate deep familiarity with the ancient world, and make it reasonable to suppose that the conservation of classical writings had a similar function.

The Frankish court

In the second half of the eighth century Italian-trained intellectuals were an important presence at the court of Charlemagne. Indeed, even before the fall of Pavia in 774, relations between the ministers of Austrasia and the Lombard court were so close, according to Paul the Deacon, that the young Pippin of Heristal was sent there as the pupil of Liutprand.[5] The prestige of the Lombard Italian cities in the eighth century was evident from the later connection

[5] Pauli, *Historia Langobardorum*, vi. 53.

between Charlemagne and Peter of Pisa, who was certainly retained by the court at Pavia, which also hosted the young Alcuin, who himself later met Charlemagne at Parma. The forced exile to one of the royal abbeys (Corbie or St Denis) of the last Lombard king, Desiderius, along with his followers—among whom we may very plausibly include Fardulfus, later the very learned abbot of St Denis—was also part of this process of reciprocal cultural exchange. So too were the diplomatic missions and broader cultural projects that after 774 involved continuous and lengthy journeying on the part of high Frankish dignitaries such as Adalard and Wala, both cousins of the emperor and abbots of Corbie, not to mention Angilbert, later lay abbot of St Riquier, who was the first minister (*primicerius palacii*) to the very young Pippin, King of Italy, and, according to Alcuin, the pupil of Peter of Pisa. Angilbert's songs form part of the complex miscellany of the Berlin codex Diez B 66, along with other poems taken from a lost manuscript of the *Anthologia Latina*. For this reason, it is in the circle of these royal officials who were deeply interested in cultural issues, and hence constantly in contact with the books that have been preserved in Italy to the present, that we should look for the ownership of the main source for the *Anthologia*, the large and complex eighth-century uncial manuscript now held in Paris (Lat. 10318).

An education similar to that of the Lombard officials would have been appropriate for Carolingian officers. The first were the *scabini*, officials with specific juridical competence, the second were the *iudices*, responsible for reproducing and emending juridical texts, and finally the custodians of the lay archives. It has long been acknowledged that the Carolingian renaissance was nourished by books that had been conserved, and even studied and corrected, in Italy. Thus during what was described as the 'book revival' (*renovatio librorum*) in the ninth century, much of the cultural inheritance from the classical world that had survived up to that time was transferred into neat and clear Carolingian script. Seneca's *De Beneficiis* and *De Clementia*, in the exempla of the important manuscript that is now in the Vatican Library (Palat. Lat. 1547), illustrates this process. The codex was the work of a group of copyists who were active at the beginning of the ninth century in northern Italy, perhaps in the area in which St Ambrose's liturgy was in use. Recent studies have shown that the manuscript underwent careful revision before being copied into what

is now the Vatican Reg. Lat. 1529, which was soon in use in the school
of Heiric at Auxerre. The subject matter of Seneca's texts must have
reflected very closely the concerns and interests of civil adminis-
trators, and the attention paid to Seneca in the second half of the
ninth century in northern Italy is also demonstrated by another
manuscript that is now in the Querini Library at Brescia (B II 6).
This was the result of a philological operation designed to re-
establish the pristine state of the text, by putting back together two
sections of the *Letters to Lucilius* that had hitherto survived in parallel
traditions. It is interesting to note that the first section of letters in the
Querini text is closely related to the codex produced in the first third
of the ninth century that is now in the Laurentian Library in Florence
(76. 40) and has recently been linked with the court of Charlemagne's
son, Louis the Pious.

The most wide-ranging testimony we have of the strong commitment to the creation of a network of centres of learning comes from
Lothar's capitulary of Olona, issued in 825, which lists the cities that
had teaching centres in which students could enrol. This document
also gave recognition to Pavia, which had invited the Irish master
Dungal as a teacher: he subsequently bequeathed his books to Bobbio
and was probably the author of the corrections in the important
'oblungus' text of Lucretius that is now at Leiden (Voss Lat. F. 30).

A culture at the service of power also emerges from the very
important miscellany of classical poetical texts, among others poems
by Horace, that is now in the City Library at Berne (n 363). In the
marginal notes there is a mass of references to contemporary figures
such as Aganon, bishop of Bergamo, and Angilberga, wife of the
Emperor Louis II. The traces in the margin of Servius' scholium on
Virgil seem to have been left by a reader who had the task of gathering information on Roman marriage customs at a moment at which
Lothair II's concubinage and his repudiation of Theutberga meant
that matrimonial issues were of immediate concern to members of
the royal family including Angilberga herself. The presence in the
codex of a song in praise of the Milanese bishop Tado also links the
scribe of the Bernese manuscript with the monastery of St Ambrose
in Milan where the Carolingian kings of Italy were buried.

The mid ninth-century cultural initiatives associated with Louis II
and Angilberga have not yet been fully studied. In this period
important foundations like the monastery of S. Salvatore at Brescia,

where the emperor's daughters were educated, were still maintained by the sovereign or else were the private concerns of aristocratic families. This overlapping of court and church influences may explain the presence of collections of lay texts. Likewise, the court promoted the circulation of books dedicated to the spiritual life; Angilberga, for example, passed on her name in a psalter donated to S. Sisto at Piacenza, a monastery that she had founded, and another important psalter was donated to her by Bishop Notting. It is now the catalogue of the library of the monastery of St Gall (n 267), and was also used by a certain Magister Rihbertus. Even these liturgical texts were subject to the practice of textual emendation repeating the formula: 'corrected and emended by the mostly saintly Priest Jerome with verses and sentences divided by obelisks and asterisks'. Finally, the empress's name also appeared in the seventh-century Juvencus in the Parker Library at Corpus Christi College, Cambridge (304, fo. 75^v), and is further evidence that books were studied in the royal palace.

'Like the Emperor, though in a different way', as the scurrilous author of the *Epitome Chronicorum Casinensium* adds,[6] Angilberga loved the palatine count Hucpaldus from whom Boniface of Tuscany was directly descended. In the eleventh century this marquis, who was a member of the Canossa family, made gifts to the abbey of Pomposa, a foundation that was famous for its library rich in lay codices. Finally, mention should be made of the library of Duke Eberhard of Friuli, which was exclusively constructed for the needs of his chancellery and contained the books of the *Leges*, a copy of the *Liber Pontificalis*, the encyclopedic *Liber Glossarum*, and Orosius' *Historiae*.

Among the classical authors who were studied in Italy in the ninth century were many of those listed in the later eighth-century Berlin manual Diez B 66. In the closing decades of the ninth century a precious example of a codex library was prepared in or around Milan, now preserved at Paris (Lat. 7900A), that brings together texts of Terence, Horace, Lucan, and Juvenal (accompanied by Martianus Capella) in a teaching version, with comments to assist the reading of these difficult works. The similarity between this list and those of a century earlier demonstrates the persistence of a canon of reading. In these texts, the commentary is primarily concerned to draw attention

---

[6] *Epitome Chronicorum Casinensium*, ed. L. Muratori, (Milan, 1750), p. 370.

to grammatical and stylistic matters but also seeks to enrich the knowledge of antiquity with mythological and historical information.

It is also important to bear in mind the significance of the need for an education in juridical culture, which was probably transmitted within the families of individuals associated with law and civil administration. The episcopal courts as a result probably also played a part in the transmission of the classics. This would help explain, for example, the presence of secretaries' notes in the codices, indicating forms of shared knowledge passed down through a notarial tradition. In the ninth and tenth centuries, the manuscripts of classical authors were often very similar, in terms of format and presentation, to the juridical manuscripts of the same period. Occasionally we find collections of texts of minor or even very minor authors that were designed for apprentices and were exclusively lay in character. These might be brief glossaries, grammatical or rhetorical definitions, astronomical diagrams, tables of kindred and affinity, accounts, or tests of penmanship by the apprentice. These remind us too that monks were not the only readers.

To complete this overview of Italian culture, we should also briefly indicate how the tradition of Benevento continued to focus attention on the memory of that city's notable concentration of grammarians. In the important grammatical miscellany now in the Casanatense Library at Rome (n. 1086), which in many sections is close to the Paris manuscript Lat. 7530, we find the work of a certain Master Orso, who may later have become bishop of Benevento. Likewise, Master Ildericus, who may have been a pupil of Paul the Deacon and for a short time the abbot of Montecassino, wrote a grammar that has come down to us. But the loss of the archives rules out further enquiries, and makes it impossible to estimate how representable was the high level of literacy shown by the laymen who subscribed the private charters in Salerno.

Culture and power in the tenth century

In the tenth century, Italian writing took an unexpected turn towards a self-conscious style, adopting tropes from hermetic writings, at times employing extremely recherché vocabulary, syntactic convolutions that verge on the incoherent, and the indiscriminate use of languages other than Latin. These were the products of intellectuals, bishops, and churchmen who were nevertheless still connected with the diocesan and imperial courts, in some cases as chancellors. The common feature of these writings is a stylistic ambition and a parading of rhetorical tropes that resulted in a pompous and highly artificial mode of expression, reflecting a taste and a preciosity in keeping with the solemnities of an ecclesiastical court.

Two bishops who were at the forefront of this movement were constantly involved in political affairs. One was Ratherius, who was active at Verona where the chapter library had significant holdings that were dispersed in the fourteenth century. The other was Liutprand, bishop of Cremona, who was connected to the court of Pavia. Liutprand dedicated himself to chronicling his times to satisfy both his taste for narration and his personal animosity towards King Berengar II and his wife, Willa. Liutprand was a great writer, whose ability to spin and to twist a tale with rhetorical skills indicates a very high level of familiarity with classical culture. His favoured trope was the *antapodosis* or *redditio contraria* that had been theorized by, among others, Quintilian, whom he may have read in the ninth-century codex produced with secretarial notes in northern Italy that is now in the Ambrosian Library in Milan (E 153 sup.). Liutprand's ability to parody the lofty theme of the birth of the *puer* and the coming of the Golden Age in Virgil's Fourth Eclogue can be appreciated when he recounts the bawdy episode in which Willa 'gives birth' through the discovery of a precious golden belt that she had hidden from the king and that comes to light through the offices of a servant who pretends to be a gynaecologist. Likewise, we learn a good deal about relations in aristocratic families from the lewd tale of the deformed priest: here what is important is not so much that he was Willa's favourite on account of the exceptional size of his male member, as that the priest, who was subsequently castrated, was the tutor to Berengar's daughters. This provides evidence of a tradition of domestic teaching following the same model adopted within the royal family. In the same century, the anonymous 'Panegyric to Berengar' has been attributed to Bishop John, Berengar's arch-chancellor. The poem was probably composed at Verona and was glossed by the author himself, perhaps for use in teaching. It exhibits close knowledge of epic texts, and is clearly intended as a model for similar compositions in praise of kings.

It is worth recalling the persistence in northern Italy of the First Decad of Livy, which comprises books dealing with imperial history and Roman tradition. At Piacenza, the site of the imperial monastery of S. Sisto, the bishop, John Filagatus, managed to assemble on behalf of Otto III a small collection that, along with Livy, also included Orosius and two glossaries. Together with other important holdings that were later taken from southern Italy by the emperor Henry II, these books crossed the Alps and went to enrich the library at Bamberg. Another important figure was Duke John of Naples, whose cultural interests were described by the priest Leo in his translation from the Greek of the *Romance of Alexander*. The duke created a rich library which also contained copies of Livy, and it may be that he also owned the copy of Servius' scholium on Virgil, now in the Vatican (Lat. 3317), transcribed as continuous text in Beneventan script with notes in Carolingian. A page of Livy from the First Decad, which is now in the State Library at Prague (CSR, VII.A.16 (1224)-IX), is also traditionally ascribed to this collection.

In the tenth century, the tradition of Italian masters who were active north of the Alps continued. They included Gunzo of Novara, who complained in his woebegone *Epistola ad fratres Augienses* of the pride of the monks of St Gall and of the derision heaped on him for his improper use of Latin. The grammarian Stephen of Novara, whom the emperor called to teach at Würzburg, by contrast modelled his epitaph on those of Terence, and tells us proudly that he was educated at Pavia, which is a clear sign that the prestige of the school of the old Lombard capitae continued. The city's archives also continued to receive important documents, such as when Elbuncus, bishop of Parma, had four copies of his will produced, one each for the bishoprics of Piacenza, Reggio, and Modena and one 'to bear witness in the royal court of Pavia'.

Many very ancient codices were also being used, read, and

annotated in the tenth century. Two short fragments of Livy were
inserted into blank spaces in the famous copy of Orosius produced at
Ravenna in the fifth century (now in the Laurentian Library in Florence). A note giving the Latin equivalent of a Greek term was made
by the 'Master of the Pickle', who annotated in a Benevento hand
the famous Justinian codex in the Pisan-Florentine manuscript also
now in the Laurentian Library. The continuing use from the time
of Theoderic onwards of these ancient books indicates the need to
create an uninterrupted sense of tradition in a society in which
these codices were not forgotten and continued to be used.

From the books that have survived and from the traces that their
readers left in the margins of the codices, it is evident that from the
sixth to the tenth century Italian culture focused particularly on
grammar and rhetoric. This anticipates what would come to full
flower in the eleventh century, when the revival of civil law stimulated
a renewal of the scholastic system. The juridical culture at the service
of the civil authorities had played its part in conserving the classical
inheritance, and the books owned by both aristocratic families and
ecclesiastical bodies provided the cultural base of well-defined social
groupings.

10

Private charters

Attilio Bartoli Langeli

Quantity and quality of Italian documents in the early Middle Ages

The written documents that we shall be concerned with in this chapter include all the forms of written texts that have survived from this period, particularly those whose function was to establish and provide evidence in forms acknowledged and recognizable as legal by all, whether compiled by public corporations or by private individuals. There were two fundamental types of documents depending on who produced them: one group comprised diplomas, liens, permits, and orders issued by a public, secular, or ecclesiastic authority, the other agreements, contracts, and other legal instruments drawn up on behalf of private individuals. 'Public deeds' included those documents that were issued by the authorities, who participated directly in their compilation and made their authorization evident through such devices as the affixing of a seal, the use of a particular style of handwriting, or the adopting of certain marks. Since, in the case of 'private charters', the persons involved were private figures, legal validation was conferred by the observance of certain formalities by their professional compilers, i.e. public notaries. Private charters were for the same reason also 'public' documents, because they compelled society as a whole to recognize the rights that they established or enforced.

As historical sources, private charters can provide a huge amount of information. They deal with the actual relationships between individuals (contracts and obligations) and between persons and things (property rights); they demonstrate how the legal systems of historical societies functioned, illustrating how the actions of members of those societies were represented in formalized terms. The amount of information they can give us depends on how much written documentation has survived, which is clearly only a fraction of what was originally produced. Michael T. Clanchy has suggested that the number of documents and writings surviving from the Middle Ages in England, including both originals and copies, represents 1 per cent of the total production. For Italy, that estimate is perhaps a little exaggerated, but nonetheless the loss of archives and documents leaves us with only a fragmented glimpse of how documents were really used in the early Middle Ages. Form, material, and the means of transmission are all integral features of the study of written documents, but we will start by trying to evaluate the size and quality of the legacy of documentation for the early Middle Ages in Italy.

The documents of the early medieval period in Italy take the following shape: no more than about fifty documents survive from the sixth and seventh centuries, nearly all on papyrus, and nearly all from Ravenna. There is almost complete silence from the rest of Italy until about 710, when Lombard written documents began to appear. From then on the number of documents available increased progressively, thanks especially to the rich collection of Lucca: two-thirds of all Italian documents from the eighth century have been conserved here in the archives of the bishopric and the cathedral. The remaining documents are distributed unevenly in different centres of the *Regnum*, the most important of which are in the city churches of Pisa, Milan, Piacenza, and the Tuscan monastery of S. Salvatore al Monte Amiata. Later collections survived in other centres (for example, Verona, Bergamo, Pavia, Asti, Pistoia, and again Ravenna), while the production of written documents also expanded in the great abbeys of central–southern Italy: Farfa, Casauria, Montecassino, and Cava dei Tirreni. The geography of production in a number of widely scattered sites lasted for a couple of centuries, and it was only around the year 1000 that archives began to be created in ways culminating in a quantitative and typological explosion of written documentation between the twelfth and thirteenth centuries, which radically changed the profile of the Italian sources.

Starting from about 500 in the eighth century, the total number of documents that have survived rose to about 9,000 in the eleventh century, with roughly the same number for the next century, following a geometric progression that continues in subsequent centuries. In terms of geographical distribution some 35 per cent of the total came from northern Italy (including the region of Emilia), 50 per cent from central Italy (the Tuscan towns, Farfa, and Casauria), and 15 per cent from southern Italy (Montecassino, Cava dei Tirreni). About three-quarters consist of originals on single sheets of parchment, the remainder being copies, most of which came from monastic archives.

By way of comparison, for the same three centuries France has a total of 800 documents, half of which are imperial and royal deeds (a much higher percentage than in Italy). Thus the Italian documentary legacy is quite substantial, albeit fragmentary. It comes exclusively from ecclesiastical and religious institutions, although from only very few of the many which not only existed at that time but were also thriving. There are a number of reasons for this. In this era, secular society and religious society were very closely integrated in both individual and institutional terms. This is clearly demonstrated by the so-called *pro anima* donations. These could be drawn up either *inter vivos* or *post obitum*, and were used to found religious sites. Lay noblemen gave their property to churches (or, in some cases, even went so far as to become members of a religious community themselves) in order to establish a stable and long-lasting relationship between themselves and their families and these religious institutions. This brought about a major expansion in the size and importance of ecclesiastical property, and since most of the early medieval legal documentation relates to estate and property matters, the bishoprics, churches, and monasteries became the principal centres for commissioning, producing, and receiving written documents.

Another factor was the archival tradition, which was totally ecclesiastical in origin. While many documents originated from kings or other secular authorities, only those that were addressed to and preserved by churches or monasteries have survived. The political capitals and seats of local government have left no documentary traces. This was often because of fires, raids, or other forms of destruction, as happened when the royal palace at Pavia was burnt down in 1024. Public archives were also easily dispersed through the actions of the personal wielding of power. But other, more structural factors were decisive. For a start, political rulers in the early Middle Ages did not possess an 'archival consciousness', an understanding of the relationship between archival records and the functioning of the institution. But both the urban cathedrals and the major non-urban religious centres did possess this awareness. This represents only one of the aspects of the ecclesiastical monopoly over written culture and Latin, the only language that could be used for writing. For a very long time ecclesiastics were the only keepers and users of documents and books, and for these precious materials they created special although rudimentary structures: the library, the archive, the scriptorium. The greater part of this tradition of ecclesiastical documentation has been broken up and dispersed, so that what has survived is greatly inferior to its original scale, but it is still sufficient to demonstrate the organic ties that linked religious structures and documents. The Church was not a separate entity, but one that gave legal form and substance to the society of the time. The business of preserving of documents, however uneven a path it followed, was inherent in that relationship and function.

Language, handwriting, and culture of the notaries

The main body of Italian documents is composed of 'private charters' or notarial documents, although to speak of 'notaries' and 'notarial documents' is somewhat inexact. Many of those who drafted documents for private individuals did not call themselves *notarius*: it could be done, for example, by a *presbiter*, or priest, or by a relative or friend of the person commissioning the deed. In other words, Italian 'notaries' did not constitute a distinct social body, at least not until the ninth century, and then only in some cities like Ravenna, Rome, and Naples where there was a strong Byzantine tradition. In the rest of Italy, both clerics and laymen drafted documents, without any precise distinction of function or activity. Both were educated at the cathedral schools in the different towns which trained literate laymen and specialists in law as well as the clergy. It was not until the end of the ninth century that the *domni imperatoris* or *sacri palacii* notaries, who were employed above all to write *placita*, began to appear throughout the kingdom; the title *notarius* (and/or *iudex*) *sacri palacii* was then long used in Italian towns to describe royal judges and notaries well after the time of the destruction of the palace of Pavia in 1024.

Since what is known about the notaries comes from their documents, the study of these documents enables us to understand the characteristics of the culture that provided for basic legal needs of Italian society for four centuries. What first strikes anyone who reads an Italian early medieval document are the handwriting and the language. Let us begin with the handwriting.

The handwriting used in Italian documents from the eighth to the tenth centuries, and in some cases persisting beyond the eleventh century, belongs to the style palaeographers describe as 'new cursive'. This style of writing has a very linear history. New cursive is the form that Roman minuscule assumed in about the fourth–fifth century in the documentary, administrative, and common writings of the empire, and it became the most widespread and free style of late ancient Latin writing. This style was distinctive by virtue of the speed of execution that enabled writing to be *currenti calamo* (with a flowing hand instead of with single strokes), and in its precise structural characteristics: the line without contrast that develops vertically, the specific design of some letters (e.g. the open *a* and the tall *c* and *e*) and, above all, the ligatures that altered the form of the joined letters which were nearly added to the alphabet as separate letters. This style of writing paid little attention to legibility especially when writing documents, since they were texts for keeping, not for reading.

As a consequence, more often than not the handwriting used by notaries appears as a disorderly mass of marks that are very difficult to read. It might instinctively be thought that these writers were semiliterate, low-grade scribes barely capable of holding a pen. But that was not the case, as is evident from the fact that they remained faithful to 'their' handwriting for a long time, even after European culture came under the influence of the Carolingian writing centres and converted to a new style, the Caroline minuscule. This was an ancient-style minuscule, which seems to have been devised as an exact opposite to cursive: it was based on the perfect design and separation of the letters (*litterae absolutae*), and was devised primarily as an instrument of orthographic reform to reinforce the principles of legibility and textual accuracy that formed part of the attempts of the Carolingian cultured elite to bring about the restoration of written Latin. The new style had a powerful hegemonic and unifying capacity, and conquered many areas that had formerly been linked to the cursive tradition: especially centres of book production, but also many of those producing documentation north of the Alps and, from the second half of the ninth century, the major chancelleries.

The Caroline minuscule, however, had a relatively weak impact on the writing habits of Italian notaries, who remained faithful to the cursive style. Variations in individual uses and styles did nothing to soften the extremely obstinate conservatism with regard to handwriting on the part of the Italian notaries. This is even more evident if we bear in mind that the first evidence in Italy of the Caroline minuscule began to appear at the bottom of the documents in the signatures of the witnesses, which is indicative of a changing situation and one that was open to a variety of cultural and handwriting influences.

Now we come to language, to the notaries' Latin. This is best explained by comparing the text from two different documents chosen at random: one drawn up in the Como area by *Austrolf notarius* in April of the year 748 and, at the other extreme (both chronologically and geographically), another document written in Foligno in December 1085 by *Sere notarius*[1]. The first charter begins: 'Constat se Alexandro de Sporticiana accepisse et accepi ad te Arighis de Canpilioni auri solido uno', whereas someone with a good knowledge of Latin would have written: 'Constat me Alexandrum de Sporticiana accepisse et accepi a te Arigho de Canpilione auri solidum unum.' The same can be said about the second one: 'Constat me Benedicto filio quoddam Anso odierna die propria expontanea mea bona voluntate dedimus atque tradedimus [. . .] a tibi Mainardos abas et a tui sucesoribus', where one would expect: 'Constat me Benedictum filium quondam Ansi hodierna die propria et spontanea mea bona voluntate dedimus atque tradidimus a te Mainardo abate et a tuis successoribus.' As we can see, the Latin cases and objects are optional: sometimes the so-called tricasual declension is applied (nominative, ablative-accusative, genitive-dative), and often objects with prepositions, i.e. the 'single case', are preferred. The verb endings are best not mentioned. As far as phonetics is concerned, in

---

[1] Respectively: R. Marichal, J. O. Tjäder, G. Cavallo and F. Magistrale (eds.), *Chartae Latinae Antiquiores*, xxviii *(Italy IX)* (Zurich 1988), no. 848; G. Cencetti (ed.), *Le carte dell'abbazia di S. Croce di Sassovivo*, i (1023–1115) (Florence 1973), no. 46.

Austrolf there is a marked tendency toward the softening of dentals (*udilitatibus* in place of *utilitatibus*, *prado* instead of *prato*), as well as toward metaphony, or the exchanging of vowels (*pigneri* instead of *pignori*, *cridituri* instead of *creditori*). In Sere these phenomena are attenuated, as his language is more disciplined from a phonetic and lexical viewpoint, making the purposeful distortion of the syntax even more significant.

The language of these texts, like many others, is quite poor. There are very few words or constructions that are free of grammatical, syntactical, or phonetic faults. We should not compare this Latin with classical Latin. It is another Latin, which owes little to classical models, and coexists and contrasts with literary language. It is a language based on tradition and not on a school; it is not governed by rules but has its own system, which gives it an unmistakable tone. Its foundation and starting point dates from Rothari's Edict. This codification of 643 was the result of a triple translation: from oral to written, from Germanic to Latin, and from memory to document. The consuetudinary law and traditional memory of the Lombards, which had been preserved for centuries through the means typical of oral cultures, needed a new and stronger foundation: they became texts written in Latin. But written in *that* Latin: a very 'poor' Latin, teeming with phonetic, grammatical, and syntactical irregularities. These irregularities are made even more evident by the fact that the genealogical and narrative insertions in the laws, and lengthier historical works and epics, are written in a Latin that is correct, and at times of the highest literary quality, such as the *Historia Langobardorum* by Paul the Deacon (contrary to what took place in Gaul, for example, where 'Merovingian Latin' invaded literary territory as well). Furthermore, there was an undeniable revival of the Latin cultural tradition in Lombard Italy between the seventh and eighth centuries, but even kings such as Liutprand and Ratchis had their laws written in a language even less literary then that of Rothari.

Lombard law imposed this Latin as the language of the institutions, of the kingdom, and of law. And it was preserved in the documents, and especially in the *chartae*, as the legacy of many generations of notaries, without being touched by any form of political or cultural change. There is no doubt that it was a deliberately archaic language, consciously adopted in keeping with a tradition: the choice of this Latin was a matter of culture, not of a lack of culture. The fact that for more than four centuries the notaries unfailingly continued to use this juridical Latin—as well as their attachment to cursive handwriting—indicates an identity of culture and class, a declaration of faithfulness to a tradition. The imprinting of the Lombard experience on Italian history was indeed formidable: notwithstanding changes in culture, in systems of power, and in ideological structures, for nearly half a millennium legal style in Italian society was expressed in documents written in the 'Lombard style'.

'Chartae' and 'brevia'

But what did the Italian notaries write? This is the central concern of those who study the types and forms of document. We shall leave out the documents that the notaries 'of the king' or 'of the sacred palace' drafted for public persons—sovereign deeds, drawn up and 'issued' directly by the authorities—and the *placita*, the documents of the royal judicial courts, to focus instead on *chartae* and *brevia*: the two types of document used by notaries for private individuals and ecclesiastical institutions.

Strictly speaking, the term *cartula* or *charta* means nothing more than a sheet of parchment; but between the eighth and twelfth centuries it indicated a precise type of document. The *charta* was the principal documentary instrument available to Italian society from the Lombards onwards, and served mainly for property transfers in the form of sales, donations, last wishes and exchanges.

The use of the *charta*, which became widespread in the era of Liutprand, gained additional strength in terms of legality, procedure, and notarial organization from the contribution of the Franks. The Lombard-Frankish model of the *charta* lasted through the entire eleventh century and beyond in Italy, although outside Italy it never became firmly established and fell into disuse in the time of Otto I, when notarial writings were rejected in favour of sealed documents. In the Italian peninsula, however, this practice of documentation survived and was widespread for over four centuries; in southern Italy, where the *charta* took on particular significance, it continued to be dominant for even longer.

What did the *charta* consist of? We can only attempt a simplified answer. The protocol consisted of an invocation, which was both symbolic (the *signum crucis*) and verbal (*In nomine domini Dei*), and was chronologically dated: the year (at first the year of the reign), the month and the day, and the indiction. The text is based on the subjective construction, although it can be introduced by a declarative formula such as *Constat me* (but *manifestus sum ego, presens presentibus dixi*, are also frequent). The *tenor* follows a basic formula, which over time became increasingly precise. This sets out the factual elements of the deed: names and relations of the parties taking action, description of the property, and its price. There is always a guarantee regarding the observance of the contract. The eschatocol consists of the formula of the *rogatio*, by means of which the request made by one of the parties to the notary to draft the document is declared; the topological dating, regarding place, expressed with the formula of the *actum*, closed by the *apprecatio* 'feliciter'; the corroborations, i.e. the signatures of those taking part in the deed.

More details should be given regarding these signatures. The salient fact of the original *charta* is the number of persons taking part, each of whom personally declares himself and 'writes' in the first person. In the *tenor*, the *ego* of the person selling, donating, etc. dominates. In the eschatocol things get crowded: there is the *ego* of the actor (and, where applicable, of the transferee or the consenting party), the *ego* of the witnesses, and in closing the *ego* of the notary. All of these persons participate, with different roles and in regulated forms, both in the carrying out of the deed (the sale, the donation) and in its written realization, both in the action and in the documentation. When speaking of the 'dispositive' character of the Lombard-Frankish *charta*, an allusion is made to this permeation between action and documentation; and if one speaks of 'formalism' it is because the *charta* presents the documented deed as a performance or representation. There is the main character, who recites the words and does the deeds required by the circumstances (the *actor*, a very apt term); there is the chorus (the witnesses); and there is the person in charge, the director who signs the work (the notary).

Let us begin with the signature of the notary. The most frequent among the formulas used by the notary are the following: *post traditam complevi et dedi* (*cartulam* is implied), where the expression *post traditam* is often contorted, for example, into *postradita*. The procedures followed by the notary to complete the documentary process are declared: the *traditio*, the *completio*, the delivery to the transferee. In essence, these procedures were as follows: after writing the text, the notary would read it to the contracting parties, to receive their approval; and the *charta* would be delivered to the person commissioning the document. Now let us go back to the problem of language. The *completio* was the formal moment of an oral character in the documentary procedure. If the Latin of the *chartae* leaned toward the vernacular, it was because the notary had to render an account of what he had written to the contracting parties. They understood little of this Latin, but they knew it was the language of documents, which gave validity to their will; and they at least heard their own names, the key words of the deed, and the description of the land being pronounced in the way that they themselves would pronounce those words.

In this ceremonial act, which we can imagine to have been standardized, the only part that was really slow came from the need to have several persons sign it: in fact, the notary's signature is preceded in the *charta* by the signatures of the witnesses (*Ego . . . testis subscripsi* and such), or by their *signa crucis* ('†') followed by the notary's statement (*Signum manus . . .*).

The written participation of the witnesses is also decisive for understanding the *charta* system and the changes it underwent over time. At the beginning they were necessary. A law of Ratchis (744–9) set out the requirements for a document to be valid in these words: 'if someone made for someone else a *cartula* of sale for any kind of thing, and it was written by a public scribe, it is to be validated by qualified witnesses and both the seller and the witnesses have signed it or set their hand to the same *cartula*.' The intervention *propria manu* of the witnesses was the major source of authenticity available to Italic society; in the language of the notaries of the time, signatures gave the document *monimem, cautela, stabilitas, perennis securitas, firmitas, confirmatio, vigor, robur*. For this reason the charter was *roborata, corroborata, firmata, manufirmata*, meaning that it was signed at the bottom by the witnesses as well as by the notary. Both the witnesses and the notary gave this 'private' deed a de facto 'public' character. This could be seen even more in southern Lombard Italy, where from the eleventh century onwards the signature of a judge became a constant feature of the *chartulae*, taking on the function of privileged *roboratio*, while for a long time the signature of the notary who drafted the deed was not required. Even when there were only two or three witnesses, they nonetheless represented the entire community in the document. Their *manufirmatio* effectively stood for the presence, participation, and recognition of the community in the deed of the individual, and thus made it strong, valid, and authentic.

This is the significance of the Lombard-Frankish custom regarding signatures. All the same, there is considerable variety in the documents from the period: thus there are documents with autograph signatures and signatures by *signum manus* (where the witness was illiterate) but also documents with *signa manus* only, on which the 'X' is often drawn not by the witnesses but by the notary himself. These different ways of proceeding depended on the lengthy process required for the compiling the document: the witness stage was separated from the drawing up of the document by the notary, who could, according to the circumstances, surrogate it either entirely or partially. This means that the hand of the notary alone was sufficient to impart full value to the document, so that the balance between the two factors of the *roboratio*, the notary and the witnesses, began to swing slowly in the direction of the strength and autonomy of the notary (although only in central and northern Italy). In other words, increasing importance was given to the role of the notary, who gained a new status, so that in its final form the witness no longer signed the *charta* and everything was done by the notary.

Many of the typical features of the *charta* remained the same: the language and the writing; the legal statement of the authors; the formula *signum manus*, evoking the signature of the witnesses; the presence of the acting *ego* and the writing *ego*, the one confined to the *tenor*, the other the master of the eschatocol—the sign of a new distinction between action and documentation. The final step came when the witnesses were shifted to the sphere of action, within the *actum*, and the *tenor* was converted from the subjective to the narrative form in the third person and in the past tense: only one *ego* thus remained, that of the notary, who also became formally the absolute protagonist of the process of documentation. In the meantime, traditional Latin and the severe cursive style was also abandoned in favour of a grammatically correct text and standard handwriting. All of these elements contributed to the emergence of a new system of documents, the *instrumentum publicum* that placed greater importance on textual form.

This was not the outcome of the internal evolution of the *charta*, but was a response to other notarial forms of drafting documents, which were independent and therefore dynamic compared to the static traditional model. In essence, these became the *brevia*.

The term *brevia* covered a variety of different forms. It often referred to lists, continuing the ancient tradition of writings in the form of a list for use in public administration (such as military and tax rolls, lists of *dignitates*, and registers for public accounting). For example, the inventories of assets (lands, incomes, tenant farmers, servants) produced by numerous abbeys and bishoprics were called *brevia*. But in the eighth and ninth centuries the term *brevia* was also applied to documents or writings testifying to a legal action carried out on a certain day by certain persons. These deeds normally did not relate to property transfers, however, but generally to 'minor' or temporary contracts: wedding donations, obligations, *mundia*, i.e. emancipations, the division of assets, investitures, limited-term licences and refutations.

In these cases the title of *breve* might be accompanied or replaced by that of *notitia*, or *memoratorium*, *notitia brevis commemoracionis*, and the like. The way in which they were drawn up and their structure also varied, some being similar to the *charta* (with the signature of witnesses) while others were completely free in form. Some *brevia* were not even signed by the notary. In this way solutions emerged that were quite different from the dominant type of document: these included the objective form and the use of the past tense and also the reference to witnesses with the formula *in presentia*, while the text was written in standard, grammatical Latin indicating that outside the *charta* it was possible not to use legal Latin.

Outside the *charta*: there is no other way of considering these writings for which there was no common model. What actually happened was that there was a need to document a deed that, by its nature, did not permit or necessitate the formality of the *charta*. As a result, the drafter could proceed freely and empirically to make a written statement that nonetheless achieved its purpose of certifying, proving, 'making known'.

The disparate forms of the *brevia* between the eighth and ninth centuries confirm the primary role of the *charta*, the only notarial text worthy of being called a document, the guarantor of the legal and patrimonial construction of society, which was fully valid because it was the result of a regulated procedure and text.

The *brevia, notitiae,* and *memoratoria* had no claim to substitute or supplant it, but they filled a role that was not and could not be filled by the *charta.* In case of legal dispute, they did not constitute legal proof, but were used as mere reminders of a specific event. The same can be said about other written documents used by ecclesiastical institutions, such as *cartulari* and polyptics: the former were books containing transcriptions of documents, often placed in a chronachistic frame (in Italy there are very few of these *cartulari* in comparison with France and England). The polyptics were lists and inventories of lands, men, and rents belonging to an institution.

On the other hand, the *charta,* subscribed by witnesses, could guarantee the legal validity of its contents and its probatory value. Because of its procedural and formal rigidity, the *charta* left an open area in which specific needs for documentation could be met in a flexible form. From these unstructured and varied beginnings, the *breve* established itself as a documentary model in the towns of central–northern Italy from the ninth century down to the twelfth century. It became a parallel, so to speak, to the *charta,* and historians have referred to the '*charta–notitia* dualism' that was first introduced and christened by Heinrich Brunner more than a century ago and later defined in more precise terms by Oswald Redlich.

The eleventh-century *breve* had characteristics that made it a true alternative to the *charta,* and it is natural to define each by comparison with the other. The *charta* was directly and immediately valid because its *traditio* and *completio* coincided with the completion of the negotiation; the *breve* was a document whose function was exclusively probatory, attesting a deed that was already complete in itself. One emphasized the connection, and the other the separation between action and documentation. One referred to the 'actors' who express their will in the first person, the other simply to clients. This was reflected in the texts: a subjective form in the *charta,* a narrative form in the *breve;* different forms of statement by the witnesses, since their roles differed—in one they were guarantors before the act–document assembly (*signum manus*), in the other as persons present at the deed (*in presentia* or *interfuerunt testes*); a different signature for the drafter because his role was different, in one case the 'director' of the entire operation (*post traditam complevi et dedi*), in the other a privileged witness and 'narrating voice' (*interfui et scripsi*). The necessary compactness of form and substance of the *charta* contrasted with the flexibility of the *breve*, the narrative form of which allowed all kinds of variation and enabled it to record the deed and its precedents unconditionally. In short: formalism with the *charta*, realism with the *breve*.

The *breve* imposed a new way of documenting that was both practical and flexible and hence gradually came to erode the longstanding primacy of the *charta*. The values of the *memoria* and of the *veritas* substituted constitutive effectiveness as the purpose of the documentary deed. The considerable broadening of the sphere of documentation and of documentable deeds (with narration 'everything' could be documented) resulted in the multiplication of types of negotiation and their corresponding documentary forms in response to changing social, civic, and institutional needs. The full responsibility assumed by the notaries defined their own cultural and technical profile, and at the same time consecrated their authority before the community, constituting what later will be called *publica fides*. Added to this came the great developments in jurisprudence and the renaissance of classical Roman law which both justified and rationalized the procedural innovations. The different factors of change were all to be found in the diffusion of free forms of documentation *ad memoriam retinendam*.

Italian early medieval society was characterized by a more intense use of written documents than in any other society of the period. Even if the relative wealth of written sources was simply a consequence of their conservation rather than production, this would still provide firm evidence of the significant extent to which they were used. Obviously, consuetude and orality still retained their primary role: a huge number of institutional, personal, and juridical relationships were never sanctioned in written form. The latter was applied mainly to transactions deviating from the established path of property transmission, especially when ecclesiastical institutions were involved.

The Lombard kingdom played a fundamental role in generalizing the practice of writing documents, starting from the moment in which it accepted, through a political decision, the traits transmitted by the local culture. The Edict of Rothari of 643 marks the passage of the Lombard kingdom from memory to written documents. Between the seventh and the eighth centuries the relation between law and *charta* was established, following an original documentary model that owed its shape to Justinian law. The strength of these foundations conferred on the *charta* a resistance that would make its effects felt up to the twelfth century. As a consequence, it gave the notaries (heirs to the *scrivae* of Lombard custom, responsible of the juridical truth of documents) an increasingly important role.

The development of the role of notaries in Italian society is thus characterized by two tendencies: on one hand, the stubborn fidelity to its origins, shown by its use of 'juridical Latin'; on the other hand, the dynamic and flexible capability to adapt to the needs of a changing society, an aspect in which the *charta* was proving itself inadequate. This lead to the adoption of new types of document, to an increased responsibility of the composer of the documents, and, finally, towards the twelfth century in northern Italy, to the end of the *charta* and of Lombard legal experience, while in the South, the early medieval documentary models persisted much longer, as shown by the lasting use of the subscriptions of witnesses.

11

Epigraphs

Flavia De Rubeis

The evolution of aristocratic epigraphy

The principal feature of the written culture of the Roman world was its uniform character, but it left a complex and sometimes fragmented cultural heritage for Italy of the fifth and sixth centuries. Areas of continuity alternated with others in which the tradition of epigraphic writing became deeply differentiated in both form and content. This process of fragmentation would not be reversed until the eleventh century, implying that the Lombard period was the fundamental moment in the transition from the old to the new epigraphic tradition in Italy.

In 568/9 the Lombards made their way into Italy and rapidly settled in its northern regions, penetrating as far as central and southern Italy. During their conquest they underwent many cultural changes, and in particular acquired the use of the written word with all its functions. In the course of little over a century, writing became a distinctive feature of the Lombard kingdom.

The development of epigraphy in Lombard Italy can best be understood from two different perspectives. The first focuses on the correlation between social structure and epigraphy, while the second is concerned with the relationship between epigraphic and book scripts, and in particular between distinctive scripts (that is to say, writings that differentiated separate texts in a codex) and display scripts.

In ancient Rome, display scripts were commonly employed by every level of society, each of which adopted its own style of writing and used it for different purposes. Monumental inscriptions, for instance, were used for purposes of commemoration, for the celebration of special events, or for honouring people. Such inscriptions were therefore put on display in large open areas where they would be visible to as many people as possible. Funerary inscriptions which listed the deeds and honours of the deceased were of equal importance in terms of the volume and quality of writing. Everything on these lists appeared according to a strict schema. This had been established during the republican period and brought to perfection in the imperial era, setting out a formal balance between text, content, and layout. These official inscriptions were produced in substantial quantities, in contrast to the small number of inscriptions produced by more humble social groups. Graffiti on walls, plaster, public columns or on tablets, tiles, and bricks were addressed to a much wider audience, however, and were often carved without following any precise criteria of script or layout.

An important early transformation in this apparently uniform written culture came with the use of palaeo-Christian epigraphy in funerary inscriptions. Both the content and the formal layout of the inscriptions changed. Production became less formal, and the requirements of the new Christian cult led to a simplification of the texts, to the point that only the name of the deceased and the day of death were recorded. The layout ignored all the formal rules for the use of the capital script that had been followed in previous centuries. After the introduction of new forms of funerary epigraphy, major changes in the style of writing took place in fourth-century Rome as a result of reforms introduced by Pope Damasus and his calligrapher, Furius Dionysius Filocalus. These changes were closely linked to the recovery of the relics of the martyrs and their celebration through epigrams composed by the pope himself. In compiling these texts, Filocalus developed a new calligraphic script. Starting from the epigraphic capital, decorations were now added to cross-strokes and feet, diacritics took on a curved shape, and in general the letter-form narrowed downwards. This script, known as 'Damasan' after the Pope, or 'Filocalian' after the scribe who designed it, rapidly gained popularity for texts other than Pope Damasan's festive poetry. It was soon adopted for funerary inscriptions for the Roman clergy, which were written in metrical form. In this way, the premise was laid for the development of a new elite script that could easily be distinguished from that used for other scripts. This distinction was symbolically set in stone by Pope Gregory the Great's funerary inscription (604), which is remarkable precisely for its use of a pure epigraphic capital.

In Rome in the period from the sixth to the eighth centuries the reduction in the use of written inscriptions led to a qualititative and quantitative decline of epigraphy. This was mainly due to the crisis of public administration which deprived the written word of its public function. But the economic crisis that accompanied the political and administrative upheavals inevitably made itself felt on the stone-workers' trade, since fewer customers could now afford to commission works of high quality, while the political circumstances also caused illiteracy to increase rapidly.

Although on a modest scale, the production of inscriptions with public functions nevertheless continued. The official epigraphy of these centuries presents a rather different image from that of the preceding period, however. The output of inscriptions created for public purposes dropped dramatically from the Roman palaeo-Christian era, when as many as 45,000 inscriptions were produced in Rome alone, to quite insignificant numbers. However, numerous dedicatory, didascalic, or celebratory inscriptions in Rome show that, in response to the elite, and especially ecclesiastical demand, use was made of a capital that tended to become rectangular in shape. As the capital became taller the curves were shifted towards the extreme ends of the letters, while eyes were reduced in size and cross-strokes moved upwards. While inscriptions of this type reflected predominantly elite demand, scripts adopting uncial letter-forms (the roundly shaped book-script which was used from the fourth to the ninth centuries) began to be employed in commissions originating from a variety of different social groups. This meant that the capital schema was broken in ways that allowed for the diversification of graphic forms. This process of differentiation would continue: in the eighth and ninth centuries it led, on one hand, to a production of inscriptions commissioned by the popes, whose writing continued to be based on the use of the capital, and, on the other, to a medium- or low-level range of inscriptions, in which the writing was disorganized, forms were rather loose, and layout careless. But these scripts should not be considered as 'minor', or of inferior quality. It was more a matter of the development of a more mature pattern that was no longer a capital script but one that consisted of hybrid majuscules organized as a graphic system. Only in the ninth and tenth centuries would the capital letter-forms (which in preceding centuries had been used exclusively for papal business) be used by a wider range of social classes. At the same time, the papal capital tended to reflect changes that were occurring in medium or lower level inscriptions. In the funerary inscriptions of Pope Hadrian II and of Leo Cubicularius, for instance, which date from the beginning of the ninth century, the distinctive writing style that had characterized papal output in the seventh and eighth centuries had vanished.

Parallel to what had happened in Rome, Ravenna also developed an 'elite script' at the turn of the seventh and eighth centuries. To a large extent this was based on the capital, even though the formal rigour typical of the preceding centuries began to relax. The vertical extension of the script seems to have played an important part in this development, and the script maintained a capital of subtle design, which nevertheless tended to concentrate the text and compress it into ever tighter spaces. A good example of this is the inscription of Archbishop John V (726–44) conserved at S. Apollinare in Classe in Ravenna.

The relative continuity of traditions evident in the development of script production in Rome and Ravenna has to be contrasted, however, with the situation in northern Lombard Italy, and the differences between these regions became greater over time. In their use of writing to commemorate the dead, the Lombards set in motion an extraordinary process of transformation which drew on all scriptorial traditions of the Italian territories. During the sixth and seventh centuries, Lombard funerary practices (which were always inseparable from the transmission of social status) focused on the deposition of grave-goods in burial tombs: the memory of the dead was therefore linked to the funeral and its audience. In the same period, long after the classical scriptorial procedures had attained their fullest development and at a time when the traditional Roman stone-carvers' workshops had largely disappeared (and with them their techniques), a form of funerary epigraphy developed that was quite new in both content and graphic expression. This marked the beginning of a long-term process, but within a century the practice of depositing grave-goods inside the tomb was being supplanted by a written epitaph that set out the memory and the status of the deceased on the outside of the grave in a form that was directed to a wider audience and also designed to last over time.

Two different pre-existing cultural traditions merged to create the basis for the great Lombard funerary epigraphy: on one hand, early Christian customs and on the other, traditions drawn from Roman models. As in Rome and in Ravenna, where an elitist model of writing had developed—closely associated respectively with the output of the popes and high-ranking clerics—Lombard society quickly acquired and elaborated various modes of writing that were used for remembering the dead of different social ranks. The initial model, made up of a concise biography of the deceased, became an authentically aristocratic epigraphy, distinguished both by its content (a fixed narrative structure, listing the place of birth, social status, physical appearance, and the main *gesta* of the dead) and by its graphic form. The text was framed by a large cornice that was sometimes enhanced by a great central cross, the hands of which were used as partitions of the text. The script, a remote derivation of the epigraphic capital, was soon canonized: in the inscription for King Cunipert (from the early eighth century) it already appears as well structured, vertical in shape, with narrow strokes embellished with many ornamental cross-feet. As a counterpart to this elaboration, inscriptions were also produced that employed a script that degraded towards forms increasingly contaminated by minuscules or uncials. As in Rome, this development ended with graffiti that used script in an unstructured and disorganized way, in which 'aristocratic' scripts stood side by side with uncials or minuscules of various derivations. An example of these writings can be seen in the inscriptions on the columns in the basilica of SS. Felice and Fortunato in Vicenza, which consisting solely of the names of the dead and the date of their burial.

By the end of the eighth century the situation in central and northern Italy was fairly clear-cut: despite some changes, the Rome–Ravenna axis continued to provide the model for the epigraphic capital used in elite inscriptions, while for medium- or low-level inscriptions a variety of different graphic systems was being used which, although derived from the majuscule, were often contaminated by book-hands. In the territories of the Lombard kingdom this process quickly led to a conscious use of the written word as a means of social identification and not simply as an instrument for the graphic transmission of a text.

In southern Italy, elite funerary practices developed with particular vigour in the duchy of Benevento. The scripts typical of northern

Italian elite production adorned the tombstones made for the dukes of Benevento. Letter-forms were compressed in width, resulting in curves and cross-strokes being moved towards the extremities of the letters. The great cornices found in northern Italy are rare in the South, and are frequently reduced to simple listels. They were used, on the other hand, in the Byzantine territory: for example, in the epitaph for the Neapolitan duke Bono, dated to 834, in which the presence of a cornice is reminiscent of Lombard models and the script betrays the influence of Lombard traditions. This is even more evident when comparing the script of Bono's epitaph with the completely different funerary epigraph of the Neapolitan archdeacon Theofilactus (d. in 671), where shapes that have already started to develop vertically are flanked by traditional epigraphic capitals. Furthermore, if we compare Bono's inscription with contemporary inscriptions for the princes of Benevento the similarity of the scripts is striking, as is the intrusion of elements derived from book-hands.

Therefore, while in northern Italy the aristocratic script derived exclusively from epigraphic customs, although based on the same model, the southern scripts register a significant influence of book-hands. This important difference forces us to reconsider the distinctions that have traditionally been drawn between the output of lay stone-carving workshops and ecclesiastical *scriptoria*.

Scriptoria and epigraphy

The second set of perspectives concerns the relationship between book-hands and epigraphic script, which enable us to understand better the changes in graphic style that occurred in southern Italy as a whole. In these territories graphic production before the ninth century was characterized by a form of script that seemed to be a generic continuation of the Roman epigraphic capital (for instance in Benevento in the fifth, seventh and eighth centuries, where the funerary poem for Bishop David, dated 726, was written in pure capitals). The change took place when, between the eighth and ninth centuries, book-scripts entered into the epigraphic systems using a capital that was associated with the Beneventan and Neapolitan elites. It seems that *ordinatores* (the specialists in composing the layout of an epigraphic text) with a book culture participated in the elaboration of these texts. The same can be said about content, and it is important here to emphasize the links with the funerary poetry that Paul the Deacon wrote at the Beneventan court. There clearly must have been contacts between the workshops of the (presumably lay) stone-carvers and the (probably ecclesiastical) *scriptoria*. But this seems to have been true more generally for lay and ecclesiastical literary culture in this part of Italy, a good example of which is again provided by Paul the Deacon and his connections with the Lombard ruling classes at Benevento.

In southern Italy the development of elite scripts was closely associated with that of distinctive book-scripts. This contrasts with the impact that Carolingian graphic culture would have in northern Italy. Here the Lombard canon was abandoned and a re-elaborated Carolingian epigraphic capital, possibly transmitted by book-hands, was introduced. It seems clear that in northern Italy the models developed during the Lombard period were developed within the context of elite workshops, operating within a single graphic culture that had come down from the epigraphic heritage. By contrast, epigraphic production in southern Italy had found alternative ways for defining its own style, inspired by book-hands that in turn were giving rise to what became known as the 'Beneventan' script. In this context, the evolution of the epigraphic capital at the monastery of San Vincenzo al Volturno is telling. Between the late eighth and early ninth centuries its first production of epigraphs seems to have been modelled by book-hands; later, a peculiar capital was selected from which developed an authentic 'Volturno style'. This suggests that the monastery had a *scriptorium* which initially provided epigraphic scripts with models derived from their bookhands; later, this epigraphy began to influence in some degree the monastery's distinctive scripts. A similar process may also have occurred in Benevento, where other ecclesiastical *scriptoria* were certainly active in the ninth century.

In the ninth century, cultural life at Benevento was dominated by Bishop Orso, to whom many sylloges of texts have been ascribed. The codices produced in this period bear display scripts in capitals and uncials executed in double tracing, and are also remarkable for the narrowing of certain letter-forms like for instance the 'O'. A capital script with many uncial inclusions was used for the elite funerary inscriptions of Chisa, Sicone, Radelchis, and Radelgarius (all members of the Beneventan ruling elite), which suggests the possibility of a conscious use of this style and close links with ecclesiastical culture. This hypothesis is reinforced by the scarcity of examples of mixed epigraphic/book systems in manufactures commissioned by those of lower status, which by contrast tended to use unofficial majuscule derived from the capital.

Between the end of the ninth century and the beginning of the tenth a new graphic tradition had been established in Italy which defined the canon that would remain in use down to the late eleventh century. In northern Italy, the epigraphic capital, which Carolingian culture brought back into use, wholly replaced the Lombard capital (as can be seen in the case of the late ninth-century funerary inscription of the priest Tafo of Brescia). In southern Italy the epigraphic script, a capital based on Lombard style, continued to have a significant book-hand component. In Rome, on the other hand, the epigraphic capital was restored to use at every level of society.

This phenomenon finds perfect correspondence in the manuscript book-hands: the Caroline minuscule used in northern Italy reflected the political homogeneity of the Carolingian period, but was counterbalanced in southern Italy by the 'Beneventan' script used in all levels of written production and hence in charters, codices and inscriptions.

Glossary

Annona: Elaborate system of food supply organized by Byzantine central authorities in the sixth and the seventh centuries, to provision the numerous military posts along the coasts of the Mediterranean.

Book-hands: Manuscript books: originally a roll of papyrus or parchment which between the second and the fifth centuries changed into a codex manuscript, made of sheets of papyrus or parchment, and later parchment only, prepared for writing, folded in numbered fascicles, and bound together.

Book-scripts: Librarian script: the different kinds of writing script used in the course of centuries for manuscripts text rolls or codices. These include bilinear scripts (majuscule), with letters compressed in two lines, or four-linear (minuscule), with vertical ascending and descending elements coming out of the margins of writing. They may show different degrees of poise (*ductus*), readability and accuracy depending on the use for which the manuscripts were intended and on the geographical and cultural characteristics of the place of composition.

Castrum: Fortified military sites built by or with the aid of the public authorities between the end of the fourth and the end of the eighth centuries. They differed from later medieval castles (tenth to thirteenth centuries), since the latter were built by individual lords to control their own subjects and territories.

Curtis: Within the Lombard territories this was an enclosure which from the seventh and the eighth centuries was often described by the adjectives *regia* or *ducalis* to indicate a complex of royal, or ducal, estates. After the eighth century, and especially during the Carolingian age, the term was increasingly used for either an administrative centre (or the building in which it was situated) or a landed estate. The latter were usually divided into two sections: one run directly by the owner (the *dominicum*) and one administered by families of farmers/tenants (*massaricium*) in exchange for money, products, or services, and illustrated the highly fragmented character of the *mansus* or farm estates. It was generally the case that while the *dominicum* was normally tilled by servile labour the *curtis* was also farmed by the tenants of the *massaricium* through obligatory and unpaid labour services (*corvées*) that were part of the the relationship of coercion that bound the serfs to the landlord (*dominus*).

Display scripts: All scripts used as texts for collective reading, or for distance reading in outdoor or indoor places, that were designed to last over time.

The graphic systems used were generally easy to read and the format of letters was usually large .

Distinctive scripts: Scripts used within a manuscript for purposes of identification, the introduction or conclusion of a text, and to enable inner partitions to be found easily. They varied in terms of the written graphic typology of the text, geographical or cultural period and area, by the use of different inks, the amplified format of single letter, the use of different graphic systems, and initial decorated letters and/or enlarged formats.

Domusculta: Type of agrarian/rural estate peculiar to Lazio, organized and promoted by the early medieval papacy in order to solve the crisis of provisioning the city of Rome after the seizure of papal estates in Sicily and southern Italy by the Byzantine emperors. The *domuscultae* were established in close proximity to the city, and in their original form were short-lived.

Epigraphic capital: Roman epigraphic script was canonized between the second and first centuries BC. In its canonized form it is characterized by a square letter module, by the presence of geometric forms such as right angles, section of circles and *chiaroscuro* effects traced with a triangular section. It is also used in book-scripts as distinctive scripts, frequently associated with the script model derived from uncial script.

Glazed pottery: Well known and widely diffused in late antiquity, especially in northern Italy, glazed pottery remained in use within the Byzantine empire, from where it was probably reintroduced to Italy during the eighth century. The multi-coloured samples found in Sicily, dated between the end of the tenth and the twelfth centuries, belong to an Islamic cultural mould and typically have a thin glazing on both sides, made from a white mixture with decorations painted in green, brown, and yellow. The great variety of shapes and decorations found seems to point to many different centres of production.

Incastellamento: The long process that shaped the typical medieval landscape, characterized by the clustered and fortified hill-top villages. Using evidence from written records the French historian Pierre Toubert argued in the 1970s that castles were built from the beginning of the tenth century onwards on uninhabited hill-tops on the initiative of local lords, thereby marking a break with the pattern of rural settlement that had survived from the Roman period to the early Middle Ages. He claimed that the processes of 'climbing' and 'clustering' around a centre were contemporaneous. Archaeological evidence now suggests that the process of 'climbing' occurred earlier and in different places from 'clustering', although the building of castles still constituted the final act in the hierarchical stratification of the village community and coincided with the formation of a landed ruling class.

Placita: Public court proceedings for the settlement of legal disputes. *Placitum* was also the name of the public charter drawn up when the dispute had been settled.

Red-slip pottery: Also called 'early medieval red-painted' to distinguish it from similar products of the imperial age. This pottery is a reliable indicator of changing economic conditions in the sixth and the first half of the seventh century. Its very wide diffusion was a response to the decline in Mediterranean trade and consequently of imports of *sigillata* pottery. Manufactured using technologies similar to those employed for making the *sigillata*, this pottery indicates the reactivation of centres of production and distribution networks at a regional and sub-regional level. In southern Italy, pottery decorated with red *ingobbio* bands was found throughout the Middle Ages.

Sigillata **pottery**: The term *sigillata* was never used in antiquity and refers to a wide range of pottery products produced between the second and the seventh centuries that shared some common features. In the late antique period, the most common *sigillata* pottery in Italy came from northern Africa (and is generally known as 'African red-slip').

South Etruria survey: The first major landscape archaeology project in Italy that was organized by the British School at Rome after the Second World War. Directed by John Ward-Perkins, a large group of researchers for the first time searched for traces of human settlement in rural areas. From the early 1950s to the late 1970s the entire rural area around Rome was thoroughly inspected, and every subsequent project has been deeply indebted to this first serious effort to understand the ways in which the rural landscape was being changed in this period.

Villae: Archaeologists use the term 'villa' to describe a variety of settlement types that range from luxury residential building to the site around which a medium-sized farm was organized, inhabited by the owner, who would consume *in loco* what was produced on the land. The different components of the villa system (the 'rural' one (the farm), the 'urban' one (the residential complex) and the 'productive' one (the *fructuaria*)) were found in many different combinations. This has caused considerable confusion, and means that many sites described by the same name were not in fact comparable. In some areas the *villa* operated on the base of slave labor, and from the first half of the first century BC to the first century AD constituted the driving force of economic development, while in others it was only a status symbol in tightly knit settlement networks where small and medium landownership prevailed.

Well-depots: Wells, pits, or hidden stores where pottery and other objects were deposited wrapped in cloth to hide them during the early Middle

Ages. They are completely different from the waste pits where garbage was thrown. Those who hid their wealth in well-depots believed they would recover it in the future, so they provide archaeologists with information about which objects were considered worth hiding and hence of high value.

Further reading

General

The principal English-language bibliographies for each chapter are listed below. Recent general studies of the period include: C. J. Wickham, *Early Medieval Italy* (London, 1981), which is by far the best comprehensive overview; C. Azzara, *Le invasioni barbariche* (Bologna, 1999) is a very useful introduction. An archaeological approach to Lombard Italy is N. Christie, *The Lombards* (Oxford, 1995). Classical works are E. Gibbon, *The Decline and Fall of the Roman Empire*, abridged version (Harmondsworth, 1981) and L. M. Hartmann, *Geschichte Italiens im Mittelalter* (4 vols., Gotha, 1900–15), a detailed narrative still valid in many respects. On the late Roman empire, the standard handbook for events and structures is A. H. M. Jones, *The Later Roman Empire, 284–602: A Social, Economic and Administrative Survey* (3 vols., Oxford, 1964); E. Stein, *Histoire du Bas-Empire*, i (Paris, 1959), ii (Paris, 1949), is most reliable for the history of events to 565. On public building policy, see B. Ward-Perkins, *From Classical Antiquity to the Middle Ages: Urban Public Building in Northern and Central Italy, AD 300–850* (Oxford, 1984). A classic in social and structural history is G. Tabacco, *The Struggle for Power in Medieval Italy: Structures of Political Rule*, (Cambridge 1989). Recent overviews are P. Cammarosano, *Nobili e re. L'Italia politica dell'alto medioevo* (Rome, 1998), and P. Cammarosano, *Storia dell'Italia medievale. Dal VI all'XI secolo* (Rome, 2001). For Byzantine and Lombard Italy, see T. S. Brown, 'Byzantine Italy, c. 680–c. 876', in R. McKitterick (ed.), *The New Cambridge Medieval History, ii: c. 700–c. 900* (Cambridge, 1995), pp. 320–48, and, in the same volume, P. Delogu, 'Lombard and Carolingian Italy', pp. 290–319. On Carolingian Italy, see also G. Tabacco, *Sperimentazioni del potere nell'alto medioevo* (Turin, 1993).

Chapter 1

S. Gasparri, *Prima delle nazioni. Popoli, etnie e regni fra antichità e medioevo* (Rome, 1997) is a good overview with an eye to recent debates about early medieval ethnicity. Detailed but often outdated is T. Hodgkin, *Italy and her Invaders* (8 vols., Oxford, 1880–99). Discussion of the significance of ethnic distinctions in the period is found in W. Pohl, 'Telling the difference: signs of ethnic identity', in W. Pohl and H. Reimitz (eds.), *Strategies of Distinction: The Construction of Ethnic Communities, 300–800* (Leiden, 1998), pp. 17–70. W. Pohl, *Le origini etniche dell'Europa* (Rome, 2000) is an essay collection, focusing on Huns, Goths, and Lombards. On Rome and the barbarians, see:

P. S. Barnwell, *Emperor, Prefects and Kings: The Roman West, 395–565* (London, 1992), underlining the Roman character of the post-Roman kingdoms; J. R. Martindale (ed.), *Prosopography of the Later Roman Empire*, ii (AD 395–527), (Cambridge, 1980); iiiA and iiiB: (AD 527–641) (Cambridge, 1992) is a valuable work of reference; see also J. Matthews, *Western Aristocracies and Imperial Court A.D. 364–425* (Oxford, 1975).

On the barbarian settlement, see W. Goffart, *Barbarians and Romans, A.D. 418–584: The Techniques of Accommodation* (Princeton, NJ, 1980), arguing that barbarians received tax shares instead of land, while W. Goffart, *Rome's Fall and After* (London, 1989) is an essay collection with original insights. On the Huns, the standard work, with some lacunae, is O. Maenchen-Helfen, *The World of the Huns* (Berkeley, Calif., 1973); E. A. Thompson, *The Huns* (2nd edn., Oxford, 1999) is still a very readable classic. On the Goths, the fundamental study and still a standard work is H. Wolfram, *History of the Goths* (Berkeley, Calif., 1988). See also P. Amory, *People and Identity in Ostrogothic Italy, 489–554* (Cambridge 1997), arguing that Gothic identity was only ethnographic ideology; while P. J. Heather, *The Goths* (Oxford, 1996) is a valuable introduction. *Teoderico il Grande e i Goti d'Italia. Atti del XIII Congresso internazionale di studi sull'Alto Medioevo* (Spoleto, 1993) collects conference proceedings including some good English papers. On Byzantines and Lombards the standard work is T. S. Brown, *Gentlemen and Officers: Imperial Administration and Aristocratic Power in Byzantine Italy A.D. 554–800* (Rome, 1984), an excellent survey, especially of socio-economic developments. Lombard history is summarized by J. Jarnut, *Geschichte der Langobarden* (Stuttgart, 1982), while T. F. X. Noble, *The Republic of St. Peter: The Birth of the Papal State 680–825* (Philadelphia, 1984) is a very readable introduction, especially on the relationship between the Roman Church and the Lombard kings. W. Pohl, 'The empire and the Lombards: treaties and negotiations in the sixth century', in W. Pohl (ed.), *Kingdoms of the Empire: The Integration of Barbarians in Late Antiquity* (Leiden, 1997), pp. 75–134; and W. Pohl, 'Memory, identity and power in Lombard Italy', in Y. Hen and M. Innes (eds.), *The Uses of the Past in the Early Middle Ages* (Cambridge, 2000), pp. 9–28, discuss specific topics.

The ninth and tenth centuries received much less attention on the perspective of ethnicity. General introductions are: P. Delogu, 'Lombard and Carolingian Italy', in R. McKitterick (ed.), *The New Cambridge Medieval History*, ii (Cambridge, 1995), pp. 290–319, and G. Fasoli, *Le incursioni ungare in Europa nel secolo X* (Florence, 1945). *Il secolo di ferro: Mito e realtà del secolo X (Sett. CISAM 38*, Spoleto, 1991) is a collection of papers, some in English. For ethnic identity in northern Italy, see A. Castagnetti, *Teotisci nella 'Langobardia' carolingia* (Verona, 1995). A good introduction on southern Italy in the ninth and tenth centuries is B. Kreutz, *Before the Normans: Southern Italy in the Ninth* and Tenth Centuries (Philadelphia, 1991). See also R. McKitterick, 'Paul the Deacon and the Franks', Early Medieval Europe, 8 (1999), pp. 319–39, arguing that Paul may have written his Lombard history for a Frankish audience; and C. Wickham, 'Lawyer's time: history and memory in tenth- and eleventh-century Italy', in C. Wickham, Land and Power: Studies in Italian and European Social History, 400–1200 (London, 1994), pp. 275–94, with inspiring discussion on the role of memory in social relations. Two recent textual analyses, including tenth-century perception of ethnicity are G. Gandino, Il vocabolario politico e sociale di Liutprando di Cremona (Rome, 1995) and A. Berto, Il vocabolario politico e sociale della 'Istoria Veneticorum' di Giovanni Diacono (Verona, 2001).

Chapter 2

On transmission of royalty, see M. McCormick, Eternal Victory: Triumphal Rulership in Late Antiquity, Byzantium, and the Early Medieval West (Cambridge, 1986); M. Humphries, 'Italy, A.D. 425–605', in A. Cameron, B. Ward-Perkins, and M. Whitby (eds.), The Cambridge Ancient History, xiv: Late Antiquity: Empire and Successors, A.D. 425–600 (Cambridge, 2000), pp. 525–51; P. Delogu, 'Il regno longobardo', in P. Delogu, A. Guillou, and G. Ortalli, Longobardi e Bizantini (Turin, 1980); S. Gasparri, 'Kingship rituals and ideology in Lombard Italy', in F. Theuws, and J. L. Nelson (eds.), Rituals of Power from Late Antiquity to the Early Middle Ages (Leiden, 2000), pp. 95–114. For Lombard public administration, see S. Gasparri, 'Il regno longobardo in Italia. Struttura e funzionamento di uno stato altomedievale', in S. Gasparri and P. Cammarosano (eds.), Langobardia (Udine, 1990), pp. 237–305. A general overview is D. Harrison, The Early State and the Towns: Forms of Integration in Lombard Italy, A.D. 568–774 (Lund, 1993).

On the changing role of the queen: P. Stafford, Queens, Concubines and Dowagers: The King's Wife in the Early Middle Ages (London, 1983; 2nd edn. 1998); A. Foessel, Die Königin im mittelalterlichen Reich. Herrschaftsausübung, Herrschaftsrechte, Handlungsspielräume (Sigmaringen, 2000); C. La Rocca, 'La reine et ses liens avec les monastères dans le royaume d'Italie', in R. Le Jan (ed.), La royauté et les élites dans l'Europe carolingienne (du début du IXe siècle aux environs de 920) (Lille 1998), pp. 269–84; F. R. Erkens, 'Die Frau als Herrscherin in ottonisch-frühsalischer Zeit', in A. von Euw and P. Schreiner (eds.), Kaiserin Theophanu. Begegnung des Ostens und Westens um die Wende des ersten Jahrtausends (Cologne, 1991) ii, pp. 245–59. On the female royal monastery of S. Salvatore in Brescia see S. Fonay Wemple, 'S. Salvatore/ S. Giulia: a case study in the endowment and patronage of a major female monastery in northern Italy', in J. Kirschner and S. Fonay Wemple (eds.), Women of the Medieval World (Oxford, 1985), pp. 85–102.

On Pavia and the public palaces: C. Brühl, Fodrum, Gistum, Servitium *regis. Studien zu den wirtschaftlichen Grundlagen des Königtums im Frankreich und in den Fränkischen Nachfolgestaaten Deutschland, Frankreich und Italien vom 6. bis zur Mitte des 14. Jahrhunderts* (Cologne, 1968); D. A. Bullough, 'Urban change in early medieval Italy: the example of Pavia', *Papers of the British School at Rome*, 34 (1966), pp. 82–130; S. Gasparri, 'Pavia longobarda', in *Storia di Pavia, ii: L'alto medioevo* (Pavia, 1987), pp. 19–65; A. A. Settia, 'Pavia carolingia e post-carolingia', in *Storia di Pavia ii: L'alto medioevo* (Pavia, 1987), pp. 69–158; A. A. Settia, 'Pavia nell'età precomunale', in *Storia di Pavia, iii Dal libero comune alla fine del principato indipendente (1024–1535)* (Pavia, 1992), pp. 9–25; F. Bougard, 'Les palais royaux et impériaux de l'Italie carolingienne et ottonienne', in A. Renoux (ed.), *Palais royaux et princiers au Moyen Âge* (Le Mans, 1996), pp. 181–96.

On Carolingian Italy, public authority, and justice: C. Wickham, 'Land disputes and their social framework in Lombard-Carolingian Italy, 700–900', in W. Davies and P. Fouracre (eds.), *The Settlement of Disputes in Early Medieval Europe* (Cambridge, 1986), pp. 105–24 (repr. in C. Wickham, *Land and Power: Studies in Italian and European Social History, 400–1200* (London, 1994) pp. 229–56); F. Bougard, *La justice dans le royaume d'Italie de la fin du VIIIe siècle au début du XIe siècle* (Rome, 1995); F. Bougard, 'La cour et le gouvernement de Louis II, 840–875', in Le Jan, *La royauté et les élites*, pp. 249–67.

On royal gifts: D. Harrison, 'Political rhetoric and political ideology in Lombard Italy', in W. Pohl, H. Reimitz (eds.), *Strategies of Distinction: The Construction of Ethnic Comunities 300–800* (Leiden, 1998), pp. 241–54.

General overviews can be found in: G. Tabacco, 'L'avvento dei Carolingi nel regno dei Longobardi', in Gasparri and Cammarosano (eds.), *Langobardia*, pp. 375–403 and G. Sergi, 'The kingdom of Italy', in T. Reuter (ed.), *The New Cambridge Medieval History, iii: c. 900–c. 1024* (Cambridge, 1999), pp. 346–71. On Berengar's gifts, see B. H. Rosenwein, 'The family politics of Berengar I, king of Italy (888–924)', *Speculum*, 71 (1996), pp. 247–89; B. H. Rosenwein, 'Friends and family, politics and privileges in the kingship of Berengar I', in S. K. Cohn Jr. and S. A. Epstein (eds.), *Portraits of Medieval and Renaissance Living: Essays in Memory of David Herlihy* (Ann Arbor, Mich., 1996), pp. 91–106 (these two contributions are reprinted in abbreviated form in Rosenwein, *Negotiating Space: Power, Restraint and Privileges of Immunity in Early Medieval Europe* (Ithaca, NY, 1999), ch. 7). See also A. A. Settia, 'Economia e società nella Pavia ottoniana', *Archivio storico lombardo*, 121 (1995), pp. 11–28.

Chapter 3

For the Gothic period: P. Amory, *People and Identity in Ostrogothic Italy, 489–554* (Cambridge, 1997); for Byzantine Italy and Rome the fundamental works are T. S. Brown, *Byzantine Italy, c. 680–876*, in R. McKitterick (ed.), *The New Cambridge Medieval History, ii: c. 700–c. 900* (Cambridge, 1995), pp. 320–48, and T. S. Brown, *Gentlemen and Officers: Imperial Administration and Aristocratic Power in Byzantine Italy, A.D. 554–800* (Rome, 1984); also very important are: T. F. X. Noble, *The Republic of St. Peter: The Birth of the Papal State 680–825* (Philadelphia, 1984); G. Arnaldi, 'Le origini del patrimonio di S. Pietro', in C. Vivanti (ed.), *Storia d'Italia*, vii/2 (Turin, 1987), pp. 3–151; and R. Markus, *Gregory the Great and his World* (Cambridge, 1997). Still useful is P. Llewellyn, *Rome in the Dark Ages* (London, 1971).

General overviews of the Lombard and Carolingian period in Italy are: P. Delogu, 'Lombard and Carolingian Italy', in *The New Cambridge Medieval History, ii*, pp. 290–319, and D. Harrison, *The Early State and the Towns: Forms of Integration in Lombard Italy A.D. 568–774* (Lund, 1993); to evaluate the first period of the Lombard settlement in Italy, it is important to consult W. Pohl, 'The empire and the Lombards: treaties and negotiations in the sixth century', in Pohl (ed.), *Kingdoms of the Empire: The Integration of Barbarians in Late Antiquity* (Leiden, 1997), pp. 75–133. For a methodologically interesting use of archaeological sources, see A. A. Settia, 'Longobardi in Italia: necropoli altomedievali e ricerca storica', in R. Francovich and G. Noyé (eds.), *La storia dell'alto medio evo italiano alla luce dell'archeologia* (Florence, 1994), pp. 57–70, and C. La Rocca, *Segni di distinzione. Dai corredi funerari alle donazioni 'post obitum' nel regno longobardo*, in L. Paroli (ed.), *L'Italia centrosettentrionale in età longobarda* (Florence, 1997), pp. 31–54. On aristocratic power in Lombard-Carolingian Italy, see C. Wickham, 'Aristocratic power in Eighth-century Lombard Italy', in A. Callander Murray (ed.), *After Rome's Fall: Narrators and Sources of Early Medieval History* (Toronto, 1998), pp. 153–70, and S. Gasparri, 'Istituzioni e poteri nel territorio friulano in età longobarda e carolingia', in P. Chiesa (ed.), *Paolo Diacono e il Friuli altomedievale (secc. VI–X)* (Spoleto, 2001), pp. 105–28.

On *Longobardia Minor*, see G. A. Loud, *Southern Italy in the Tenth Century*, in T. Reuter (ed.), *New Cambridge Medieval History, iii: c. 900–c. 1024* (Cambridge, 1999), pp. 624–45; P. Delogu, *Mito di una città meridionale* (Naples, 1977); J.-M. Martin, 'Éléments préféodaux dans les principautés de Bénévent et de Capoue (fin du VIIIᵉ–début du XIᵉ siècle): modalités du privatisation du pouvoir', in *Structures féodales et féodalisme dans l'Occident méditerranéen (Xᵉ–XIIIᵉ siècle). Bilan et perspectives de recherche* (Rome, 1978); H. Taviani, *La principauté lombarde de Salerne (IXᵉ–XIᵉ siécle). Pouvoir et société en Italie lombarde méridionale* (Rome, 1991).

On Carolingian and post-Carolingian Italy, see especially V. Fumagalli, *Le origini di una grande dinastia feudale. Adalberto-Atto di Canossa* (Tübingen, 1971) and V. Fumagalli, *Terra e società nell'Italia padana. I secoli IX e X* (Turin, 1976). A quantitative and prosopographic analysis of immigrant and institutions from the Frankish kingdom is E. Hlawitschka, *Franken, Aleman-nen, Bayern und Burgunder in Oberitalien (774–962)* (Freiburg im Breisgau, 1960). Analyses of regional contexts are G. Sergi, 'I rapporti vassallatico-beneficiari', in *Atti del X Congresso internazionale di studi sull'alto medioevo* (Spoleto, 1986), pp. 137–63; J. Jarnut, 'Ludwig der Fromme, Lothar I. und das Regnum Italiae', in P. Godman and R. Collins (eds.), *Charlemagne's Heir: New Perspectives on the Reign of Louis the Pious (814–840)* (Cambridge, 1990), pp. 349–62; A. Castagnetti, 'Immigrati nordici, potere politico e rapporti con la società longobarda', in S. De Rachewiltz and J. Riedmann (eds.), *Kommunication und Mobilität im Mittelalter. Begegnungen zwischen dem Süden und der Mitte Europas (11.–14. Jahrhundert)* (Sigmaringen, 1995), pp. 27–60; S. Gasparri, 'Les relations de fidélité dans le royaume d'Italie au IXe siècle', in R. Le Jan (ed.), *La royauté et les élites dans l'Europe carolingienne (du début du IXe aux environs de 920)* (Lille, 1998), pp. 145–57. For an overview of Caroling-ian aristocracy, excluding Italy, see S. Airlie, 'The Aristocracy', in McKitterick, *The New Cambrige Medieval History, ii*, pp. 431–50; on the Unruochings: C. La Rocca and L. Provero, 'The dead and their gifts: the will of Eberhard, count of Friuli, and his wife Gisela, daughter of Louis the Pious (863–864)', in F. Theuws and J. L. Nelson (eds.), *Rituals of Power: From Late Antiquity to the Early Middle Ages* (Leiden, 2000), pp. 225–80. For the concept of *militia*, see M. De Jong, 'Power and humility in Carolingian society: the public penance of Louis the Pious', *Early Medieval Europe*, 1 (1992), pp. 29–52, and H. Keller, 'Militia. Vassalität und frühes Rittertum im Spiegel oberitalienischer miles-Belege der 10. und 11. Jaherhunderts', *Quellen und Forschungen aus italienischen Archiven und Bibliotheken*, 62 (1982), pp. 59–118.

G. Sergi, 'The kingdom of Italy', in T. Reuter (ed.), *The New Cambridge Medieval History, iii*, pp. 346–71, is an outline of the kingdom of Italy during the tenth and eleventh centuries; see also *Formazione e strutture dei ceti dominanti nel medioevo: marchesi conti e visconti nel regno italico (secc. IX–XII)*, (2 vols.,) (Rome, 1988–1996), and, for an institutional approach, R. Pauler, *Das Regnum Italiae in ottonischen Zeit. Markgrafe, Grafen und Bischöfe als politische Kräfte* (Tübingen, 1982) and G. Sergi, *I confini del potere. Marche e signorie fra due regni medievali* (Turin, 1995). A classic for the *incastel-lamento* is A. A. Settia, *Castelli e villaggi nell'Italia padana. Popolamento, potere e sicurezza fra IX e XIII secolo* (Naples, 1984). Studies for regional areas are A. Castagnetti, *Il Veneto nell'alto medioevo* (Verona, 1990), H. Keller, *Adelsherrschaft und städtische Gesellschaft in Oberitalien (9. bis 12. Jahrhun-dert)* (Tübingen, 1979) and F. Menant, *Lombardia feudale. Studi sull'aris-tocrazia padana nei secoli X–XIII* (Milan, 1992). Studies on individual kin groups: M. Nobili, 'Le famiglie marchionali nella Tuscia', in *I ceti dirigenti in Italia in età precomunale* (Pisa, 1981), pp. 79–105; F. Bougard, 'Entre Gandolf-ingi et Obertenghi: les comtes de Plaisance aux Xe et XIe siècles', *Mélanges de l'École Française de Rome*, 101/1 (1989), pp. 1–66; R. Merlone, *Gli Aleramici. Una dinastia dalle strutture pubbliche ai nuovi orientamenti territoriali (secoli IX–XI)* (Turin, 1995) and S. M. Collavini, *'Honorabilis domus et spetiosissimus comitatus'. Gli Aldobrandeschi da conti a 'principi territoriali' (secoli IX–XIII)* (Pisa, 1998).

Chapter 4

Many of the most important regional rural studies are referred to in the footnotes to the text. Useful integrations are: B. Andreolli et al., *Le campagne italiane prima e dopo il Mille* (Bologna, 1985); M. Montanari, *L'alimentazione contadina nell'alto medioevo* (Naples, 1979); L. Provero, *L'Italia dei poteri locali, secoli X–XII*, (Rome, 1998); P. Squatriti, *Water and society in early medieval Italy* (Cambridge, 1998); G. Tabacco, *I liberi del re nell'Italia carolingia e post-carolingia* (Spoleto, 1966); P. Toubert, *Dalla terra ai castelli* (Turin, 1995); C. Wickham, *Land and Power* (London, 1994).

Chapter 5

For the history of the church in late antiquity and early medieval Italy, fundamental works can be found in the series entitled *Storia della chiesa*, such as that edited by A. Fliche and V. Martin (Turin, 1976–9), or the one edited by H. Jedin (Milan, 1975–80). English readers can also consult the *Oxford Dictionary of the Christian Church*, (Oxford, 1974). See also the entry 'Italie', in *Dictionnaire de spiritualité*, vii, (Paris, 1971), coll. 2142–2311, and the incisive, problematic essay by G. Miccoli, 'La storia religiosa', in *Storia d'Italia*, ii: *Dalla caduta dell'impero Romano al secolo XVIII*, i (Turin, 1974). Some recent essays are C. La Rocca, 'Cristianesimi', in *Storia medievale* (Rome, 1998) and A. Rigon, 'Le istituzioni ecclesiastiche della cristianità', in S. Collodo and G. Pinto (eds.), *La società medievale* (Bologna, 1999). Useful recent collections are: G. De Rosa, T. Gregory and A. Vauchez (eds.), *Storia dell'Italia religiosa*, i: *L'antichità e il medioevo* (Rome, 1993); G. Filoramo and D. Menozzi (eds.), *Storia del cristianesimo*, ii: *Il medioevo* (Rome, 1997) and G. M. Cantarella, V. Polonio and R. Rusconi, *Chiesa, chiese, movimenti religiosi* (Rome, 2001).

On the concept of 'popular religion', see R. Manselli, *Il soprannaturale e la religione popolare nel medioevo* (Rome, 1985). For an introduction to the various expressions of religiosity in the early medieval west, see S. Boesch Gajano, 'Pratiche e culture religiose', in G. Ortalli (ed.) *Storia d'Europa, iii: Il medioevo. Secoli V–XV* (Turin, 1994). On hagiographic research for the early middle ages, see S. Boesch Gajano (ed.), *Agiografia altomedievale* (Bologna, 1976); the classic general study is P. Brown, *The Cult of the Saints* (Chicago, 1981). On the formation of ecclesiastical territories (dioceses and provinces), see C. Violante, *Ricerche sulle istituzioni ecclesiastiche dell'Italia centro-settentrionale nel medioevo* (Palermo, 1986); a recent overview of the situation in southern Italy can be found in G. Vitolo, 'L'organizzazione della cura d'anime nell'Italia meridionale longobarda', in G. Andenna and G. Picasso (eds.), *Longobardia e longobardi nell'Italia meridionale. Le istituzioni ecclesiastiche* (Milan, 1996).

The impact of the Lombard invasion on the network of episcopal sees in Italy can be reconstructed from G. P. Bognetti, 'La continuità delle sedi episcopali e l'azione di Roma nel regno longobardo', in *L'età longobarda*, iv (Milan, 1968); on the preceding situation, see the classic work by F. Lanzoni, *Le diocesi d'Italia dalle origini al principio del secolo VII* (Faenza, 1927). The *episcopalis audientia* is studied by G. Vismara, *Episcopalis audientia* (Milan, 1937); by the same author, 'La giurisdizione civile dei vescovi nel mondo antico', in *La giustizia nell'alto medioevo (secoli V–VIII), Sett. CISAM*, 41 (Spoleto, 1995). On the sanctification of the bishops and their role in city worship, see A. Orselli, *L'immaginario religioso della città medievale* (Ravenna, 1985) and P. Golinelli, *Città e culto dei santi nel medioevo italiano* (Bologna, 1991); on the 'Germanization' of the higher clergy and their adoption of lay lifestyles, see F. Prinz, *Klerus und Krieg im frueheren Mittelalter. Untersuchungen zur Rolle der Kirche beim Aufbau der Koenigsherrschaft* (Stuttgart, 1971). An example of the critical reconsideration of ecclesiastical memory in the Carolingian age in a medieval city, see C. La Rocca, *Pacifico di Verona. Il passato carolingio nella costruzione della memoria urbana* (Rome, 1995).

A general overview on the ecclesiastical systems in the early medieval Italian countryside is A. Castagnetti, *L'organizzazione del territorio rurale nel medioevo. Circoscrizioni ecclesiastiche e civili nella 'Longobardia' e nella 'Romania'* (Turin, 1979). On the difficult perception of borders and relations with rural communities, see C. Wickham, *Dispute ecclesiastiche e comunità laiche. Il caso di Figline Valdarno (XII secolo)* (Florence, 1998).

A very recent overview on monasticism, with a useful bibliography, is V. Polonio, 'Il monachesimo nel medioevo italico', in Cantarella et al., *Chiesa, chiese, movimenti religiosi*. Brief introductions are G. Penco, *Storia del monachesimo in Italia. Dalle origini alla fine del medioevo* (Rome, 1961) and G. Picasso, 'Il monachesimo nell'alto medioevo', in *Dall'eremo al cenobio. La civiltà monastica in Italia dalle origini all'età di Dante* (Milan, 1987). On the relations between monastic centres and lay aristocracies, see G. Sergi, *L'aristocrazia della preghiera. Politica e scelte religiose nel medioevo italiano* (Rome, 1994). On southern Italy, see G. Vitolo, *Caratteri del monachesimo nel Mezzogiorno altomedievale (secoli VI–IX)* (Salerno, 1984) and H. Houben, 'Potere politico e istituzioni monastiche nella 'Langobardia minor' (secoli VI–X)', in Andenna and Picasso, *Longobardia e longobardi nell'Italia meridionale*. A glimpse into female monastic life is found in E. Pastor, 'Il monachesimo femminile', in *Dall'eremo al cenobio*, in G. Zarri (ed.), *Il monachesimo femminile in Italia dall'alto medioevo al secolo XVII a confronto con l'oggi* (Verona, 1997). Recent studies on specific cases are P. Delogu, F. De Rubeis, F. Marazzi, A. Sennis and C. Wickham, *San Vincenzo al Volturno. Cultura, istituzioni, economia* (Montecassino, 1996); A. Piazza, *Monastero e vescovado di Bobbio (dalla fine del X agli inizi del XII secolo)* (Spoleto, 1997); V. Carrara, *Reti monastiche nell'Italia padana. Le chiese di San Silvestro di Nonantola tra Pavia, Piacenza e Cremona, secc. IX–XIII*, (Modena, 1998); P. Golinelli (ed.), *Storia di San Benedetto Polirone. Le origini (961–1125)* (Bologna, 1998). On the influence of Cluniac monasticism in Italy, see G. M.Cantarella, *I monaci di Cluny* (Turin, 1993).

The link between reform movements in the Church and ecclesiastical institutions and Italic societies is examined in C. Violante, *La pataria milanese e la riforma ecclesastica*, I: *Le premesse (1045–1057)* (Rome, 1955), and in the collection edited by P. Zerbi, *'Ecclesia in hoc mundo posita'. Studi di storia e di storiografia medioevale raccolti in occasione del 70° genetliaco dell'autore* (Milan, 1993). For individual aspects of the reform movement, see N. D'Acunto, *I laici nella Chiesa e nella società secondo Pier Damiani. Ceti dominanti e riforma ecclesiastica nel secolo XI* (Rome, 1999).

Chapter 6

The literature on the papacy of late Antiquity and the early Middle Ages is vast. The works listed here are only some of the most essential and most recent publications. A complete work on the papacy is E. Caspar, *Geschichte des Papsttums. Von den Anfängen bis zur hoehe der Weltherrschaft* (Tübingen, 1933). For the period examined here, see P. Llewellyn, *Rome in the Dark Ages* (London, 1971) and W. Ullmann, *A Short History of the Papacy in the Middle Ages*, corrected edn., (London, 1974). An excellent short synthesis is G. Arnaldi, 'Profilo di storia della Chiesa e del papato fra tarda antichità e alto medioevo', *La cultura*, 35/1 (1997).

For the definition of the primacy of the bishop of Rome based on the inheritance of Peter, see the works by M. Maccarrone, in particular *Vicarius Christi. Storia del titolo papale* (Rome, 1952) and the collection of essays *Romana Ecclesia Cathedra Petri* (Rome, 1991). For the theoretical presuppositions and the developments of the basic questions involved in the relations between the papacy and the Christian Roman empire, see F. Dvornik, *Early Christian and Byzantine Political Philosophy: Origins and Background* (Washington, DC, 1966) and the essays collected in T. D. Barnes, *Early Christianity and the Roman Empire* (London, 1984).

An introduction to the relations between the papacy and the barbarian world is found in A. Paravicini Bagliani, 'Il papato medievale e il concetto di Europa', in G. Ortalli (ed.), *Storia d'Europa, iii: Il medioevo. Secoli V–XV*

(Turin, 1994). For relations with the Gothic kingdom in Italy, see T. F. X. Noble, 'Theodoric and the papacy', in *Teoderico il Grande e i Goti d'Italia* (Spoleto, 1993); for relations with the Lombards, O. Bertolini, *Roma di fronte a Bisanzio e ai Longobardi* (Bologna, 1941) is still the best text. On the life and works of Gregory the Great, see R. A. Markus, *Gregory the Great and his World* (Cambridge, 1997). Roman missionary activity is reconstructed by O. Bertolini, 'I Papi e le missioni fino alla metà del secolo VIII', in *Sett. CISAM*, 14, (Spoleto, 1967).

Building activities of the popes in early medieval Rome are illustrated in R. Krautheimer, *Rome: Profile of a City, 312–1308* (NJ, 1980), and also in the essays collected in L. Paroli and P. Delogu (eds.), *La storia economica di Roma nell'alto medioevo alla luce dei recenti scavi archeologici* (Florence, 1993) and in P. Delogu (ed.), *Roma medievale. Aggiornamenti* (Florence, 1998); see also P. Delogu, 'The rebirth of Rome in the eighth and ninth centuries', in R. Hodges and B. Hobley (eds.), *The Rebirth of Towns in the West: A.D. 700–1050* (London, 1988), and P. Delogu, '*Solium imperii-urbs ecclesiae.* Rome fra la tarda antichità e l'alto medioevo', in G. Ripoll and J. M. Gurt (eds.), *Sedes regiae (ann. 400–800)* (Barcelona, 2000). See also R. Coates-Stephens, 'Dark Age Architecture in Rome', *Papers of the British School at Rome*, 65 (1997).

On the constitution and management of the *patrimonia sancti Petri*, for which there exists a vast, albeit somewhat dated, literature (E. Spearing, *The Patrimony of the Roman Church in the Time of Gregory the Great* (Cambridge, 1918), see F. Marazzi, *I 'patrimonia sanctae Romanae ecclesiae' nel Lazio (secoli IV–X). Struttura amministrativa e prassi gestionali* (Rome, 1998); and P. Toubert, *Les structures du Latium médiéval: le Latium méridional et la Sabine du IXᵉ siècle à la fin du XIIᵉ siècle* (Rome, 1973). On the evolution of the papal *scrinium* into embryonic bureaucratic and administrative structures, with specific reference to the age of Gregory the Great, see E. Pitz, *Papstreskripte im frühen Mittelalter. Diplomatische und rechtsgeschichtliche Studien zum Brief-Corpus Gregors des Grossen* (Sigmaringen, 1990). An introduction to the *Liber Pontificalis* is O. Bertolini, 'Il *Liber Pontificalis*', *Sett. CISAM*, 17 (Spoleto, 1970).

On the succession of territory to the *patrimonium sancti Petri*, and the Frankish *promissiones*, see O. Bertolini, 'Il problema delle origini del potere temporale dei papi nei suoi presupposti teoretici iniziali. Il concetto di 'restitutio' nelle prime cessioni territoriali (756–757) alla Chiesa di Roma', in *Miscellanea Pio Paschini*, i (Rome, 1948). On the political and ideological implications of this pratice, see G. Arnaldi, 'Alle origini del potere temporale dei papi: riferimenti dottrinari, contesti ideologici e pratiche politiche', in G. Chittolini and G. Miccoli (eds.), *La Chiesa e il potere politico dal medioevo all'età contemporanea* (Turin, 1986). See also A. Angenendt, 'Das geistliche Buendnis der Päpste mit dem Karolingern (754–796)', *Historisches Jahrbuch*,

100 (1980). On the process of *translatio imperii* to Charlemagne, the essay by
G. Arnaldi, 'Il papato e l'ideologia del potere imperiale', in *Sett. CISAM*, 27
(Spoleto, 1981), is essential reading. An example of the approach that sees a
strong 'ideological' continuity in papal activity with respect to imperial
power from Gelasius I (or at least from Gregory the Great) to the Carolingian
age is W. Ullmann, *The Growth of Papal Government in the Middle Ages: A
Study in the Relation of Clerical to Lay Power*, 3rd edn. (London, 1970). On this
subject, see also C. Azzara, *L'ideologia del potere regio nel papato altomedievale
(secoli VI–VIII)* (Spoleto, 1997).

On the papacy in the Carolingian age, see T. F. X. Noble, *The Republic of St.
Peter: The Birth of the Papal State, 680–825* (Philadelphia, 1984); G. Tabacco,
Sperimentazioni del potere nell'alto medioevo (Turin, 1993). Finally, for an
introduction to the role played by the popes in the eleventh-century reform,
see the excellent studies by O. Capitani, *Immunità vescovili ed ecclesiologia in
età pregregoriana e gregoriana* (Spoleto, 1966), and G. Miccoli, *Chiesa gregoriana. Ricerche sulla Riforma del sec. XI* (Rome, 1966; new edn., Rome, 1999).

Chapter 7

A recent survey of early medieval archaeology in Italy is C. Wickham, 'Early
medieval archaeology in Italy: the last twenty years', *Archeologia medievale*, 26
(1999), pp. 7–20. Numerous comparisons of the studies in Italy have been
published in *Papers in Italian Archaeology i–iii* (Oxford, 1978, 1981, 1985). See
also E. Herring et al. (eds.), *Papers of the 4th Conference of Italian Archaeology*
(London, 1992) and N. Christie (ed.), *Settlement and Economy in Italy 1500
BC to AD 1500: Papers of the 5th Conference of Italian Archaeology* (Oxford,
1995). A wide study of Roman landscapes in the Mediterranean with specific
references to Italy is G. Barker and J. Lloyd (eds.), *Roman Landscapes: Archaeological Survey in the Mediterranean Region* (Rome, 1991); for the sixth
century, R. Hodges, W. Bowden (eds.), *The Sixth Century: Production, Distribution and Demand* (Leiden, 1998). On the processes of dissolution of the
rural sites, see G. P. Brogiolo (ed.), *La fine delle ville romane. Trasformazioni
nelle campagne tra tarda antichità e alto medioevo nel territorio gardesano*
(Mantua, 1996), and F. Cambi et al., 'Etruria, Tuscia, Toscana. La trasformazione dei paesaggi altomedievali', in R. Francovich and G. Noyé (eds.), *La storia
dell'altomedioevo italiano alla luce dell'archeologia* (Florence, 1994), pp. 183–
216. On the maritime villas in southern Tuscany: F. Cambi, 'Paesaggi d'Etruria e di Puglia', in A. Schiavone (ed.), *Storia di Roma*, 3/1, (Turin, 1993), pp.
229–54; M. Valenti, *Carta archeologica della provincia di Siena, i: Il Chianti
senese* (Siena, 1995); M. Valenti, *Carta archeologica della provincia di Siena, iii.
La Valdelsa* (Siena, 1999); F. Cambi and E. Fentress, 'Villas to castles: first
millennium AD demography in the Albegna valley', in K. Randsborg (ed.),
Archaeology and Social Development in the First Millennium AD (Rome, 1989),

pp. 74–86. On the Pisa area and northern Tuscany: G. Ciampoltrini, 'Ville, pievi, castelli. Due schede archeologiche per l'organizzazione del territorio nella Toscana nord-occidentale fra tarda antichità e alto medioevo', *Archeologia medievale*, 22 (1995), pp. 557–68; S. Menchelli, 'Contributo allo studio del territorio pisano. Coltano e l'area dell'ex palude di Stagno', *Studi classici e orientali*, 34 (1984), pp. 254–70. For Abruzzo, Puglia, and Sicily, see M. Aprosio et al., 'Il territorio di Segesta tra la tarda antichità ed i secoli centrali del medioevo', in S. Gelichi (ed.), *I congresso nazionale di archeologia medievale* (Florence, 1997), pp. 187–93.

The hypothesis of rural anarchy in the Longobard age related to the non-collection of taxes is set out in C. Wickham, *Italy and the Early Middle Ages*, in Randsborg, *Archaeology and Social Development*, pp. 140–51, and also in Wickham, 'Early medieval archaeology in Italy', pp. 16–22, where the generalizing importance is, however, weakened.

On early medieval castles, the most recent survey is G. P. Brogiolo and S. Gelichi, *Nuove ricerche sui castelli altomedievali in Italia settentrionale* (Florence, 1997). On the debate concerning 'incastellamento', essential works are: P. Toubert, *Les structures du Latium médiéval. Le Latium méridional et la Sabine du XIe siècle à la fin du XIIe siècle* (Rome, 1973); R. Comba and A. A. Settia (eds.), *Castelli. Storia e archeologia* (Turin, 1984); R. Francovich and M. Milanese (eds.), 'Lo scavo archeologico di Montarrenti e i problemi dell'incastellamento medievale. Esperienze a confronto', *Archeologia medievale*, 16 (1989); R. Francovich and C. Wickham, 'Uno scavo archeologico ed il problema dello sviluppo della signoria territoriale: Rocca San Silvestro ed i rapporti di produzione mineraria', *Archeologia medievale*, 21 (1994), pp. 7–30; R. Francovich and M. A. Ginatempo (eds.), *Castelli. Storia e archeologia del potere nella Toscana medievale*, i (Florence, 2000).

On Longobard settlement, some short publications have appeared over the last ten years which nevertheless contain all the reference literature: L. Jørgensen, 'Castel Trosino and Nocera Umbra: A chronological and social analysis of family burial practices in Lombard Italy (6th-8th cent. A.D.)', *Acta Archaeologica*, 62 (1992), pp. 1–58; L. Paroli (ed.), *L'Italia centro settentrionale in età longobarda* (Florence, 1997); G. P. Brogiolo and C. Bertelli (eds.), *Il futuro dei Longobardi. L'Italia nella costruzione dell'Europa di Carlo Magno* (Milan, 2000); see also S. Gasparri and P. Cammarosano (eds.), *Langobardia* (Udine, 1990); C. La Rocca, 'Segni di distinzione. Dai corredi funerari alle donazioni 'post obitum' nel regno longobardo', in Paroli, *L'Italia centro settentrionale*, pp. 31–54.

On the organization of rural settlements near ecclesiastical buildings: E. Cavada, 'Elementi romani e germani nel territorio alpino tra Adige e Sarca: aspetti e continuità dell'insediamento', in G. P. Brogiolo and L. Castelletti (eds.), *Il territorio tra tardoantico e altomedioevo. Metodi di indagine e risultati*

(Mantua, 1991), pp. 99–130. On the distribution of early medieval ceramics: R. Francovich and M. Valenti, 'La ceramica d'uso comune tra V–X secolo in Toscana. Il passaggio tra età tardoantica ed altomedioevo', in *La céramique médiévale en Méditerranée* (Aix-en-Provence, 1997), pp. 129–37. On the question of the sigillata pottery in victualling supplies: E. Zanini, 'Ricontando la terra sigillata africana', *Archeologia medievale*, 23 (1996), pp. 677–68; H. Patterson, 'The current state of early medieval and medieval ceramic studies in Mediterranean survey', in *Extracting Meaning from Ploughsoil Assemblages* (London, 2001), pp. 110–20.

On the debate regarding the stages of *incastellamento* through written sources, for the case of Italy, see some recent publications: V. Fumagalli, 'Strutture materiali e funzioni nell'azienda curtense. Italia del nord: secc. VII–XII', in *Per una storia delle dimore rurali*, (*Archeologia medievale*, 7, (1980), pp. 21–30; B. Andreolli and M. Montanari, *L'azienda curtense in Italia. Proprietà della terra e lavoro nei secoli VIII–XI* (Bologna, 1983); P. Toubert, 'Il sistema curtense. La produzione e lo scambio interno in Italia nei secoli VIII, IX e X', in R. Romano and C. Vivanti (eds.), *Storia d'Italia, Annali*, 6, (Turin, 1983), pp. 5–66; C. Wickham, *Il problema dell'incastellamento nell'Italia centrale. L'esempio di San Vincenzo al Volturno* (Florence, 1985); G. Sergi, 'Villaggi e curtes come basi economico-territoriali per lo sviluppo del banno', in G. Sergi (ed.), *Curtis e signoria rurale. Interferenze fra due strutture medievali* (Turin, 1993), pp. 7–24.

Chapter 8

On the debate on the decline and survival of the early medieval Italian city, see G. P. Brogiolo, 'La città tra tarda antichità e medioevo', in *Archeologia urbana in Lombardia. Valutazione dei depositi e inventario dei vincoli* (Modena, 1984), pp. 48–56; G. P. Brogiolo, 'A proposito dell'organizzazione urbana nell'alto medioevo', *Archeologia medievale*, 14 (1987), pp. 27–45; C. La Rocca, '"Dark Ages" a Verona. Edilizia privata, aree aperte e strutture pubbliche in una città dell'Italia settentrionale', *Archeologia medievale*, 13 (1986), pp. 31–78. For a decidedly negative view, see A. Carandini, 'L'ultima civiltà sepolta o del massimo oggetto desueto, secondo un archeologo', in A. Carandini, L. Cracco Ruggini and A. Giardina (eds.), *Storia di Roma. iii/2: L'età tardoantica. I luoghi e le culture* (Turin, 1994), pp. 11–38; a more nuanced view is to be found in R. Hodges and D. Whitehouse, *Mohammed, Charlemagne and the Origins of Europe* (London), pp. 24–33. An interesting series of ideas and summaries, covering early medieval cities as well, is to be found in C. Wickham, 'L'Italia e l'altomedioevo', *Archeologia medievale*, 15 (1988), pp. 105–24 and 'Considerazioni conclusive', in R. Francovich and G. Noyé (eds.), *La storia dell'alto medioevo italiano alla luce dell'archeologia*, (Florence, 1994), pp. 741–59. On the question of cities—including Italian cities—during the

Carolingian period, a recent discussion is to be found in R. Hodges, *Towns and Trade in the Age of Charlemagne* (London, 2000). A good recent synthesis on the development of the cities of Tuscia is the collection of essays *Archeologia urbana in Toscana. La città altomedievale* (Mantua, 2000). R. Balzaretti, 'Cities, emporia: local economics in the Po valley, c. 700–875', in N. Christie and S. J. Loseby (eds.), *Towns in transition: Urban Evolution in Late Antiquity and the Early Middle Ages* (London, 1996), pp. 212–34, discusses the cities of the Po valley in relation to economic factors. The question of the Christianization of cities and the problem of urban burial has been dealt with on more than one occasion by G. Cantino Wataghin; in particular in her '"Urbs" e "civitas" nella tarda antichità: linee di ricerca', in *La 'Civitas Christiana'. Urbanistica delle città italiane tra tarda antichità e altomedioevo* (Turin, 1991), pp. 7–42, and 'The ideology of urban burials', in G. P. Brogiolo and B. Ward Perkins (eds.), *The Idea and the Ideal of the Town between Late Antiquity and the Early Middle Ages* (Leiden, 1999), pp.147–80.

Chapter 9

A wide-ranging introduction to Lombard culture, with up-to-date bibliography, is to be found in the exhibition catalogue edited by G. P. Brogiolo and C. Bertelli, *Il futuro dei longobardi* (Milan, 2000). On Rothari's prologue, see B. Paradisi, 'Il prologo e l'epilogo dell'Editto di Rotari', *Studia et documenta historiae*, 34 (1968), pp. 2–3; for the Modena codex of the laws of the Lombards, see G. Russo, 'Leggi longobarde nel codice O.I.2 della Biblioteca Capitolare di Modena', in *Atti del 6° Congresso internazionale di studi sull'alto medioevo* (Spoleto, 1980), pp. 607–21.

On the movements of the Lombards in southern Italy, see P. Bertolini, 'Arechi I', in *Dizionario biografico degli italiani*, iv, pp. 68–71, and on ecclesiastical matters, H. Houben, 'Potere politico e istituzioni monastiche nella 'Langobardia minor' (secoli VI–X)', in *Langobardia e longobardi nell'Italia meridionale. Le istituzioni ecclesiastiche* (Milan, 1996), pp. 177–98; in the same volume see T. F. Kelly, 'La liturgia beneventana e la sua musica come testimonianza della cultura longobarda', pp. 239–47. An overview of the Lombard presence in Calabria is to be found in G. Fiaccadori, 'Calabria tardoantica', in S. Settis (ed.), *Storia della Calabria antica* (Rome, 1994), pp. 707–62; see also P. Peduto, 'Insediamenti longobardi del ducato di Benevento (sec. VI–VIII)', in S. Gasparri and P. Cammarosano (eds.), *Langobardia* (Udine, 1990), pp. 307–403. For Lombard influence on the Anglo-Saxons, see P. Scardigli, *Goti e longobardi. Studi di filologia germanica* (Rome, 1987), p. 222. On the activities of the *scabini* and the Franks' lay public archives, see E. Cortese, *Il diritto nella storia medioevale* (Rome, 1995), pp. 224, 233, 321.

An overview of eighth-century culture is in C. Villa, 'Cultura classica e tradizioni longobarde', in P. Chiesa (ed.), *Paolo Diacono e l'origine dell'Europa medievale. uno scrittore fra tradizione longobarda e rinnovamento carolingio* (Udine, 2000), pp. 575–600. The codex Palat. Lat. 1547 has been examined by P. Busonero, 'Un caso esemplare di antigrafo epografo nella tradizione di Seneca: il Pal. Lat. 1547 e il Reg. lat. 1529', in *Seneca e il suo tempo* (Rome, 2000), pp. 295–337. For the epigram that recalls Angilberga in the Piacenza Psalter, fo. 1ʳ, see A. Balsamo, *Catalogo dei manoscritti della Biblioteca Comunale di Piacenza* (Piacenza, 1910), p. 3; her biography is to be found in 'Engelberga' in *Dizionario biografico degli italiani*, xlii (1993), pp. 668–76. On the Benevento grammarians, see V. Brown, 'Where have all the grammars gone?', in *Manuscript Traditions from Antiquity to the Renaissance* (Cassino, 2000), pp. 389–414. On Salerno: A Petrucci and C. Romeo, 'Scritture e alfabetismo nella Salerno del IX secolo', in *Scrittura e civiltà*, 7 (1983), pp. 53–112.

John of Naples' Servius is described in entry no. 43 by A. M. Adorisio in M. Dell'Omo (ed.), *Virgilio e il chiostro. Manoscritti di autori classici e civiltà monastica* (Rome, 1996). The will of the bishop of Piacenza is in E. Falconi, 'Il testamento del vescovo Elbunco. Note sulla scrittura parmense nei secoli X e XI', in *Archivio storico per le province Parmensi*, 9 (1957), pp. 49–67. The codices cited of classical authors prior to the twelfth century are all described in B. Munk Olsen, *L'étude des auteurs classiques latins aux XIᵉ e XIIᵉ siècles* (Paris, 1982–5).

Chapter 10

A fundamental work on early medieval Italian documents is that by P. Cammarosano, *Italia medievale. Struttura e geografia delle fonti scritte* (Rome, 1991), pp. 39–111. The best manuals on diplomatics are C. Paoli, *Diplomatica* (1883), ed. G.C. Bascapè (Florence, 1942); H. Bresslau, *Handbuch der Urkundenlehre für Deutschland und Italien* (1899), ed. H. W. Klewitz, (Berlin, 1958); A. Pratesi, *Genesi e forme del documento medievale* (Rome, 1987); O. Guyotjannin, J. Pycke and B.-M. Tock, *Diplomatique médiévale* (Turnhout, 1993). Much material of documentary interest can be found in the collection *Typologie des sources du moyen âge occidental*, which is published in separate numbers, from 1972.

The quantitative data for the eighth century are based on the collection *Chartae latinae antiquiores: Fàcsimile-Edition of the Latin Charters Prior to the Ninth Century* (Lausanne and Zürich, 1954–93), (49 volumes in-folio, 21 of which on Italy, published between 1982 and 1993); the second series, on the ninth century, was begun recently. A general view of the Italian centres of preservation is in A. Petrucci, *Medioevo da leggere. Guida allo studio delle testimonianze scritte del medioevo italiano* (Turin, 1992). On 'private' Italian documents from the eighth–twelfth centuries, see C. Violante, 'Lo studio dei documenti privati per la storia medievale fino al XII secolo', in *Fonti medievali e problematica storiografica* (Rome, 1977), pp. 69–129. Excellent 'quantitative' analyses are proposed by F. Bougard, *La justice dans le royaume d'Italie de la fin su VIIIe siècle au début du XIe siècle* (Rome, 1995), pp. 79–108; 'Actes privés et transferts patrimoniaux en Italie centro-septentrionale (VIIIe–Xe siècles)', *Mélanges de l'Ecole Française de Rome. Moyen âge*, 111 (1999), pp. 539–64. In the same volume (pp. 499–537), see B.-M. Tock, 'L'acte privé en France, VIIe siècle-milieu du Xe siècle', which offers elements of comparison for the French territory; whereas for England (and for general evaluations) one may refer to M. T. Clanchy, *From Memory to Written Record: England 1066–1307* (London, 1979).

For Lombard documents, see S. Gasparri and P. Cammarosano (eds.), *Langobardia* (Udine, 1990), particularly the essay by L. Capo, 'Paolo Diacono e il problema della cultura', pp. 169–235, important for the 'Latin of the charters'. Many Italian-language historians deal with this topic: for an up-to-date picture, see G. Sanga, 'Italienische Koine—La koinè italiana', in *Lexicon der Romantischen Linguistik*, ii/2 (Tübingen, 1995), pp. 81–98. On the cursive of early medieval documents: G. Cencetti, 'Dall'unità al particolarismo grafico. Le scritture cancelleresche Romane e quelle dell'alto medioevo', in *Sett. CISAM*, 9 (Spoleto 1962), pp. 237–64; E. Casamassima, *Tradizione corsiva e tradizione libraria nella scrittura latina del medioevo* (Rome 1988); A. Bartoli Langeli, 'Scritture e libri. Da Alcuino a Gutenberg', in *Storia d'Europa*, iii: *Il medioevo (secoli V–XV)*, ed. G. Ortalli (Turin, 1994), pp. 935–83, esp. pp. 941–6. Of basic importance regarding the writings of notaries and subscribers is the book by A. Petrucci and C. Romeo, *'Scriptores in urbibus'. Alfabetismo e cultura scritta nell'Italia altomedievale* (Bologna, 1992).

The bibliography on the *charta* is very ample, and includes the top names in German and Italian diplomatics in the last 150 years: cf. the survey by S. P. P. Scalfati, 'Alle origini della *Privaturkundenlehre*', in C. Scalon (ed.), *Libri e documenti d'Italia dai longobardi alla rinascita delle città* (Udine, 1996), pp. 129–51. Some recent Italian titles: A. Pratesi, 'Appunti per una storia dell'evoluzione del notariato' (1983), repr. in A. Pratesi, *Tra carte e notai. Saggi di diplomatica dal 1951 al 1991* (Rome, 1992), pp. 521–35; G. Nicolaj, 'Il documento privato italiano nell'alto medioevo', in Scalon, *Libri e documenti d'Italia*, pp. 153–98. As for the corroboration by witnesses, see P. Supino Martini, 'Alfabetismo e sottoscrizione testimoniali al documento privato nell'Italia centrale (sec. VIII)', in A. Petrucci and F. M. Gimeno Blay (eds.), *Escribir y leer en Occidente* (Valencia, 1995), pp. 47–61.

The clearest description of the two models of the *charta* and of the *breve* or *notitia* is found in S. P. P. Scalfati, '*Forma chartarum*. Sulla metodologia della ricerca diplomatistica', in *La forma e il contenuto. Studi di scienza del documento* (Pisa, 1993), pp. 51–85, esp. pp. 59–63. A summary of document types from the south is offered by A. Pratesi, 'Il notariato latino nel mezzogiorno medievale d'Italia', in *Scuole diritto e società nel Mezzogiorno medievale d'Italia*, (Catania, 1987), pp. 137–68.

Chapter 11

Early medieval epigraphy in Italy still need a synthesis. The most important essay, from a palaeographical perspective, is still N. Gray, 'The palaeography of Latin inscriptions in the eight, ninth, tenth century', *Papers of the British School at Rome*, 16 (1948), pp. 38–170. Epitaphs are studied in a general perspective by A. Petrucci, *Le scritture ultime. Ideologia della morte e strategie dello scrivere nella tradizione occidentale* (Turin, 1995); for the Lombard tradition, see F. De Rubeis, 'La tradizione epigrafica in Paolo Diacono', in P. Chiesa (ed.), *Paolo Diacono. Uno scrittore fra tradizione longobarda e rinnovamento carolingio* (Udine, 2000), pp. 139–162, and F. De Rubeis, 'Le epigrafi dei re longobardi', in F. Stella (ed.), *Poesia dell'alto medioevo europeo: manoscritti, lingua e musica dei ritmi latini* (Florence, 2000), pp. 233–240. On bookscripts and lay literacy: G. Cavallo, 'Libri e continuità della cultura antica in età barbarica', in *Magistra Barbaritas* (Milan, 1984), pp. 603–62, and the seminal work of R. McKitterick, *The Carolingians and the written word* (Cambridge, 1989), and of A. Petrucci and C. Romeo, *'Scriptores in urbibus'. Alfabetismo e cultura scritta nell'Italia altomedievale* (Bologna, 1992). On the early Christian tradition in Rome: C. Carletti, '*Viatores ad martyres*. Testimonianze scritte altomedievali nelle catacombe Romane', in G. Cavallo and C. Mango (eds.), *Epigrafia medievale greca e latina. Ideologia e funzione* (Spoleto, 1995), pp. 197–226. Book-scripts and display scripts in southern Italy are examined by: F. De Rubeis, 'La scrittura a San Vincenzo al Volturno fra manoscritti ed epigrafi', in P. Delogu, F. De Rubeis, F. Marazzi, A. Sennis and C. Wickham, *San Vincenzo al Volturno. Cultura, istituzioni, economia*, (Montecassino, 1996), pp. 21–40; J. Mitchell, 'Literacy displayed: the use of inscriptions at the monastery of San Vincenzo al Volturno in the early ninth century', in R. McKitterick (ed.), *The Uses of Literacy in Early Medieval Europe* (Cambridge, 1990), pp. 186–220; J. Mitchell, 'The display of scripts and the uses of painting in Longobard Italy', in *Sett. CISAM*, 41 (Spoleto, 1994), pp. 887–954.

Chronology

593–4	King Agilulf and the Lombards invade central Italy
595	Theodelinda founds the church of St John in Monza
598	Peace treaty between Lombards and Byzantines with the intervention of Gregory the Great
601–2	King Agilulf conquers Padua and Monselice, still under Byzantine control
602	Birth of Adaloald, son of Theodelinda and Agilulf, in the palace of Monza, built by Theodelinda
604	Adaloald is elected associated king of the Lombards in Milan
	Death of Gregory the Great
606	Schism of the 'Three Chapters': Severus is elected patriarch in Aquileia for the Lombards, Candidianus is elected patriarch in Grado for the Byzantines
610	The Avars invade Friuli
612	Foundation of the monastery of St Colombanus at Bobbio
616	Death of King Agilulf; accession of Adaloald
616–19	Revolts of John of Conza and of the Exarch Eleutherius in Byzantine Italy
626	Death of King Adaloald
	Arioald, duke of Turin, is elected king of the Lombards thanks to his marriage with Gundiperga, daughter of Agilulf and Theodelinda
636	Death of King Arioald
	Rothari, duke of Brescia, is elected king of the Lombards thanks to his marriage with Gundiperga, daughter of Agilulf and Theodelinda and wife of the previous king
643	Rothari, king of the Lombards, issues his law code
652	Death of King Rothari; accession of his son Rodoald, who dies a few months later
653	Aripert is elected king of the Lombards
	Official conversion of the Lombards to the Catholic faith
661	Death of King Aripert; the Lombard kingdom is divided between his two sons, Godepert and Pertarit
662	Grimoald, duke of Benevento, kills King Godepert in Pavia and is elected king. King Pertarit escapes to the khan of the Avars, then (663–5) to the Franks
671	Death of King Grimoald; accession of his son Garipald

	Pertarit kills King Garipald in Pavia and is elected king of the Lombards
679	After rebelling against King Pertarit, Alachis, duke of Trento, is forgiven by the king and elected duke of Brescia
	Cunipert, Pertarit's son, is elected associated king
680	Synod in Rome condemns monotelism
	Peace is concluded between Byzantium and the Lombards
685	Foundation of the private monastery of St Fredianus, near Lucca
688	Death of Pertarit; Cunipert is elected king of the Lombards
698	Synod in Pavia under King Cunipert ends the schism of the Three Chapters
700	Death of King Cunipert; accession of his son Liutpert, under the regency of Ansprand
c.700	Foundation of the monasteries of Farfa and S. Vincenzo al Volturno
701	After the revolt of Ragimpert, duke of Turin, his son Aripertus II is elected king of the Lombards. Ansprand escapes to Bavaria with his son Liutprand
712	Ansprand and Liutprand defeat Aripert II in Pavia; Ansprand is elected king of the Lombards, but dies a few months later
	Liutprand is elected king of the Lombards
713	Liutprand makes the first of his many additions to the Lombard law code
722	The English monk Boniface is consecrated as a missionary bishop by Pope Gregory II and sent to Germany
726	Emperor Leo III of Byzantium comes to the throne and orders the destruction of all icons in the Byzantine empire (726–30)
727–8	Revolts in Byzantine Italy: independent dukes are elected in the *Venetiae*, Ravenna, and Naples
728–9	Liutprand, king of the Lombards, conquers towns and villages in Emilia, in the *Pentapolis*, and the castle of Sutri which after is given back to the pope; the rebel dukes of Spoleto and Benevento submit; Liutprand travels to Rome, where the royal insigna are placed on St Peter's grave
735–6	Because of ill health Liutprand associates his nephew Ildeprand to the Lombard throne

741–52	Papacy of Zacharias
742	After the rebellion of Trasmund, duke of Spoleto, Ansprand, Liutprand's nephew, is elected duke; Gisulf, loyal to Liutprand, is elected duke in Benevento
	Peace treaty between the pope and Liutprand
744	Death of Liutprand and deposition of Ildeprand: Ratchis, duke of Friuli, is elected king
745	King Ratchis promulgates new additions to the Lombard law code
749	After a military expedition in the *Pentapolis*, Ratchis abdicates in favour of his brother Aistulf, and becomes a monk at Montecassino
749–56	Kingdom of Aistulf, who promulgates new additions to the Lombard law code
*c.*750	Anselmus, already duke of Friuli, founds the monastery of Nonantola
751–2	The Lombards capture Ravenna, the Exarchate, and the *Pentapolis* from Byzantium
753	Aistulf and the Lombards move against Rome, imposing a tribute on the inhabitants of the city
754	Pope Stephen II goes to France to ask King Pippin for assistance against the Lombards, and obtains the *Promissio Carisiaca*
754 and 756	Pippin twice defeats Aistulf, king of the Lombards, who swears to give the captured territories back to the pope
756	Death of King Aistulf
757	Desiderius is elected king of the Lombards, with the favour of Pippin, king of the Franks
757–67	The forged *Constitutum Constantini* is produced in Rome during the papacy of Paul I
758	Desiderius refuses to give the captured territories back to the pope and invades the *Pentapolis*
759	Adelchi, Desiderius' son, is associated to the Lombard throne
759–71	Peace between the Lombards and the pope
761	Foundation of the monastery of S. Salvatore in Brescia by King Desiderius and his wife, Ansa
768–814	Reign of Charlemagne, king of the Franks (774 king of the Lombards, 800 emperor)

770–71	Charlemagne marries and then repudiates a daughter of King Desiderius
772	Adrian I (772–795) is elected pope. He asks Desiderius for the restitution of the occupied territories, but Desiderius attacks the *Pentapolis*, Emilia, and southern Tuscany
773–4	Charlemagne conquers the kingdom of the Lombards and is elected king
775–6	A revolt against the Franks, organized by Adelchi, Desiderius' son, fails
	Repression of the Lombard rebels in Veneto and Friuli
776	Issue of the first Frankish Capitulary for Italy
781	Carloman, Charlemagne's son, is baptized in Rome under the name of Pippin
781–810	Reign of Pippin, king of the Lombards
c.783	Paul the Deacon writes his *History of the Lombards*
796	Pippin, king of the Lombards, defeats the Avars and destroys their Ring
800	Charlemagne crowned emperor by Pope Leo III in St Peter's, Rome
806	Charlemagne's *Divisio regnorum*: Pippin is given the kingdom of the Lombards, Istria, Dalmatia, Bavaria and Sclavonia
810	Pippin tries to capture Venice and attacks Dalmatia
	Death of Pippin
811	On the islands of Rialto, Agnellus Particiacus is elected duke of Venice under the protection of Byzantium
812	Peace treaty between Byzantium and the Franks with regard to Dalmatia and Venice, which remains under the protection of Byzantium
813	Charlemagne crowns his son Louis as emperor
	Bernard, Pippin's son, is elected king of Italy
813–40	Louis the Pious rules as emperor
814	Death of Charlemagne and accession of his son Louis the Pious
817	*Ordinatio imperii* of Louis the Pious: the kingdom of the Lombards is assigned to his eldest son, Lothar, who is made co-emperor

Pactum Lodovicianum: Louis confirms the pope in the possession of his territories and patrimonies and guarantees the freedom of papal election

Revolt of Bernard, king of Italy, against his uncle Louis. After its failure Bernard is blinded and dies

823	Lothar is crowned emperor and king of Italy in Rome by Pope Paschal I
824	The *Constitutio Romana* gives the emperor the right to control papal election
824–30	Muslim raiders seize strongholds in Sicily
833	Deposition of Louis the Pious
	Public penance of Louis the Pious
834–40	After the restoration of Louis the Pious, Lothar is confined in Italy
840	Death of Louis the Pious
	Civil wars between Lothar and his brothers Louis the German and Charles the Bald
841	Muslim emirate established in Bari
843	Treaty of Verdun and division of the Frankish empire: Italy and the emperial crown are assigned to Lothar
844	Louis II, Lothar's son, is crowned king of Italy in Rome by Pope Sergius
848	First military expedition of Louis II against the Muslims in the Beneventan territory: the principality of Benevento is divided in two, creating the principality of Salerno
850	Louis is anointed co-emperor in Rome
855	Death of Lothar; accession of Louis II
860–1	Louis II officially marries Angilberga, providing for her the first written *dotalicium* for a queen. The document was initially dated 861 but was later backdated to the year 851
866	Louis II's military expedition in southern Italy
871	Louis II reconquers Bari, but is captured by Adechi, prince of Benevento

875	Death of Louis II, without male heirs
	Charles the Bald, king of the west Franks (840–77), is crowned emperor in Rome by Pope John VIII
875–6	Byzantines reoccupy Bari and other strongholds in southern Italy
877	Death of Charles the Bald
878	Syracuse falls to Muslims
879–87	Reign of Charles the Fat (884 emperor)
881 and 883	The monasteries of S. Vincenzo al Volturno and Montecassino are abandoned after Saracen raids. Both were later restored in the tenth century
888	Death of Charles the Fat, who was succeded by Arnulf, the illegitimate son of Charles the Fat's brother, Carloman
	Berengar, marquis of Friuli and grandson of Louis the Pious, is elected king in Italy
889	Wido of Spoleto defeats Berengar on the river Trebbia and is crowned king of Italy
891	Wido of Spoleto is crowned emperor in Pavia
892	Lambert, Wido's son, is crowned emperor
894	Death of Wido of Spoleto
896	Arnulf is crowned emperor by Pope Formosus
897	The synod of the 'corpse': the corpse of Pope Formosus is exhumed and tried for perjury by his successor, Pope Stephen VI. Declared guilty, the body was flung into the Tiber
898	Death of Lambert, without male heirs
	The Magyars invade northern Italy up to the river Brenta
899	The Magyars invade Pavia and sack northern Italy
	Death of Arnulf
900	Louis of Provence is offered the kingdom of Italy by Berengar's enemies; Louis is crowned king in Pavia
901	Louis of Provence is crowned emperor in Rome
902–5	Berengar is re-elected king of Italy; Louis escapes then settles in Pavia again, but is blinded and killed by Berengar's supporters

915	Berengar I is crowned emperor by Pope John X
923	Ralph, king of Bourgogne, defeats Berengar at Fiorenzuola d'Arda
924	Berengar I is murdered in Verona
926	Hugh of Provence is elected king of Italy
945–51	Berengar II, Marquis Anscarius' son, defeats Hugh, but Hugh's son Lothar is still recognized as king
949 and 968	Liutprand of Cremona's embassies to Constantinople respectively for Berengar II and Otto (described in his *Antapodosis* and his *Relatio de legatione Constantinopolitana*)
950	Berengar II is crowned king in Pavia together with his son Adalbert
951	Otto I is crowned king of Italy and marries Adelheid, widow of Lothar, king of Italy
951–66	Struggle between Berengar II and Otto I, which ends with the imprisonment and death of Berengar II
962	Otto I is crowned emperor in Rome by Pope John XII
	Privilegium Othonis: reconfirm the donations of Pippin and Charlemagne, papal possessions, and the imperial control on papal election
972	Marriage in Rome of Otto I's son Otto II to Theophanu, niece of the Byzantine emperor John I Tzimisces
973	Death of Otto I
973–83	Reign of Otto II
982	Otto II is defeated by the Saracens at Capo Colonne, Calabria
983–91	Regency of Theophanu for her son Otto III
991–6	Regency of Adelheid, Theophanu's mother-in-law, for her grandson Otto III
996	Otto III is crowned emperor in Rome
	Bruno, Otto III's cousin, is elected pope as Gregory V
998	Otto III, during his second visit to Rome, deposes the anti-pope John Philagatus

999   Otto III's former tutor, Gerbert of Aurillac, archbishop of
            Reims, becomes Pope Sylvester II

1002   Death of Otto III

Map section

FRANKS

AVARS

BYZANTINE EMPIRE

Chiavennao
Adige
Bolzano
Belluno
Cividale
Drava
Sava
Danubio
Drava
Aosta
ai Franchi
575
Ivrea
Como
Bergamo
Trento
Ceneda
Aquileia
Trieste
Istria
Stura
Novalesa
Vercelli
Milano
Brescia
Verona
Vicenza
Treviso
Oderzo
Altino
Grado
Susa
ai Franchi
575
Torino
Asti
Novara
Pavia
Cremona
Mantova
Padova
Venezia
Pola
Alba
Acqui
Tortona
Piacenza
Parma
Reggio
Modena
Adria
Ferrara
Genova
Albenga
Luni
Pistoia
Bologna
Imola
Faenza
RAVENNA
Rimini
Nizza
Lucca
Fiesole
Urbino
Pesaro
Fano
Ancona
Pisa
Firenze
Arno
Pentapoli
Esino
Lesi
Volterra
Siena
Arezzo
Gubbio
Camerino
Fermo
Elba
Populonia
Chiusio
Perugia
Todi
Nocera
Norcia
Trento
Vomano
Pescara
Marianao
Amelia
Spoleto
Chieti
Viterbo
Farfa
Sutri
Porto
ROMA
Larino
M. S. Angelo
Ostia
Sora
Alfedena
Terracina
Venafro
Lucera
Canosa
Bari
Gaeta
Benevento
Capua
Acerenza
Brindisi
Aiactio
Napoli
Salerno
Taranto
Gallipoli
Otranto
Olbia
Amalfi
Paestum
Potenza
Grumento
Porto Torres
Cassano
Tirso
Amantea
Cosenza
Crotone
Cagliari
Tropea
Squillace
Carini
Palermo
Milazzo
Messina
Trapani
Reggio C.
Marsala
Belice
Taormina
Platani
Enna
Catania
Agrigento
Salso
Lentini
Siracusa
Modica
Malta

	Byzantine territory in 603
	Lombard territory in 603
	Lombard territory by 616
	Lombard territory by 638
	The Exarcate in 744

0   50   100   150   200
km

Map 1 Lombard Italy (568–774)

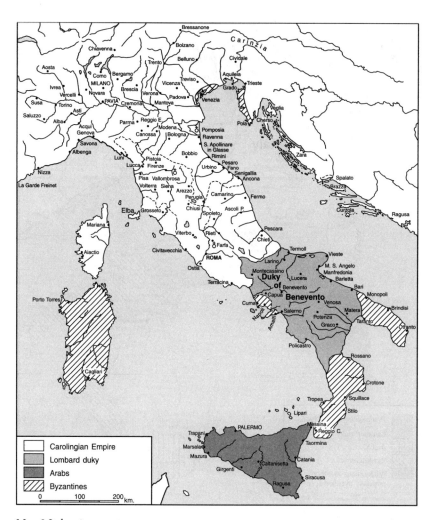

Map 2 Italy *c.*850

Legend:
- Carolingian Empire
- Lombard duky
- Arabs
- Byzantines

0   100   200 km.

Map 3 Italy *c.*1000

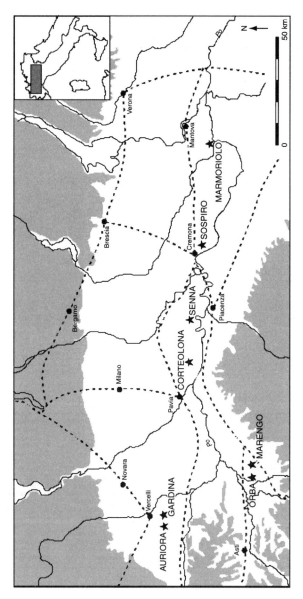

Map 4 Royal palaces in northern Italy

Map 5 Early medieval excavated rural sites

1 Rodengo Saiano	18 Calvatone	35 Manzano	52 S. Salvatore al Monte
2 Villandro	19 San Tomé di Carvico	36 Santo Stefano Belbo	Amiata
3 Cavalese	20 Monte Barro	37 Orba	53 Heba
4 Varone	21 Milano	38 Modena	54 Cosa Ansedonia
5 Ledro-Volta de Besta	22 Castelseprio	39 Russi	55 La Selvicciola
6 Monselice	23 Locarno, Muralto	40 Lucca	56 Aterni (Terni)
7 Verona	24 Angera	41 Volterra	57 Statonia
8 Monzambano	25 Sizzano	42 San Vincenzino	58 Viterbo
9 Desanzano	26 Carpignano	43 Rocca San Silvestro	59 Poggio Smerdarolo
10 Padenghe	27 Belmonte	44 Scarlino	60 Mola di Monte Gelato
11 Sirmione	28 Trino Vercellese	45 Poggia Imperiale	61 Rignano Flaminio
12 Pieve di Manerba	29 Ticineto	46 Galognano	62 Casale San Donato
13 Nuvolento	30 Pecetto	47 San Marcellino in	63 Santa Cornelia
14 Brescia	31 Centallo	Chianti	64 Ostia
15 Iseo, San Martino in	32 Castelvecchio	48 Siena	65 Castrum Truentinum
Prada	33 Breolungi di	49 Montarrenti	66 Castrum Novum
16 Pontevico	Mondovi	50 Santa Cristina	67 Hortona (Ortona)
17 Piadena	34 Bene Vagienna	51 Pantani-Le Gore (Torrita)	68 Histonium
			69 San Vincenzo al Volturno
			70 Santa Maria in Civita
			71 Benevento
			72 Melfi-Leonessa
			73 San Giusto
			74 Avicenna
			75 Barletta
			76 Trani
			77 Bari
			78 Rutigliano-Purgatorio
			79 San Miserino
			80 Santa Maria dell'Alto
			81 Contrada Fontanelle
			82 Eraclea Minoa
			83 Entella
			84 Segesta
			85 Calathamet
			86 Monreale

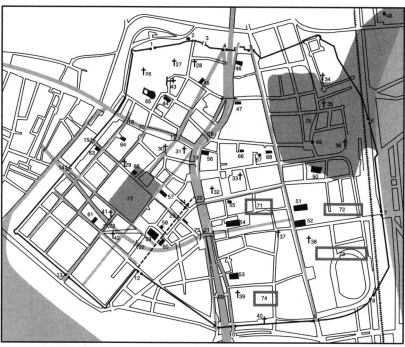

1 *PORTA TEGURIENSIS*	29 Ecclesia S. Demetrii	51 S. Apollinare Nuovo
2 *TURRIS UMBRATICA*	30 Ecclesia S. Paterniani	52 S. Salvatore ad Calchi
3 *POSTERULA AUGUSTI*	31 Ecclesia S. Mariae in Gallope	53 S. Agata Maggiore
4 *PORTA S. VICTORIS*	32 Monasterium S. Stephani	54 Basilica Apostolorum
5 *PORTA SERRATA*	junioris	55 S. Giorgio de porticibus
6 *PORTA ARTEMIDORIS*	33 Ecclesia S. Vincentii ad	56 S. Michele in Africisco
7 *PORTA PALATII*	monetam	57 S. Agnese
8 *PORTA WANDALARIA*	34 S. Andrea dei Goti Ecclesia	58 Battistero Neoniano
9 *PORTA CAESAREA*	Gothica	59 Cattedrale Ursiana
10 *PORTA URSICINA*	35 Ecclesia S. Mariae in horris	60 Episcopium
11 *PORTA S. MAMAE*	36 Ecclesia SS. Sergi et Bacchi	61 S. Andrea Maggiore
12 *PORTA DI GAZZO*	37 Ecclesia S. Mariae in Pace	62 S. Maria in foro
13 *PORTA AUREA*	38 Ecclesia S. Stephani ad	63 SS. Giovanni e Paolo
14 *POSTERULA LATRONUM*	fundamentum regis	64 S. Eufemia ad arietum
15 *POSTERULA S. ZENONIS*	39 Ecclesia S. Mariae in	65 S. Vittore
16 *PONS S. STEPHANI*	Chartilario	66 SS. Nicandro e Marciano
17 *PONS AUGUSTI*	40 Ecclesia SS. Philippi et Iacobi	67 Battistero
18 *PONS MARINUS*	41 Monasterium S. Severini	68 Cattedrale e rini degli Ariani
19 *PONS S. MICHAELIS*	42 Monasterium S. Martini	69 *FLUMEN PADENNAE*
20 *PONS APOLLINARIS*	post ecclesiam maiorem	70 *FLUMISELLUM PADENNAE*
21 *PONS CAPITELLUS*	43 S. Croce	71 *PALATIUM di Odoacre(?)*
22 *PONS CANDAVARIAE*	44 S. Maria Maggiore	72 *THEODORICIANUM*
23 *PONS CALCIATUS*	45 S. Apollinare in veclo	73 *PALATIUM AD LAURETA (?)*
24 *PORTA ASIANA (?)*	46 S. Vittore	74 *CIRCO (?)*
25 *POSTERULA VINCILEONIS (?)*	47 S. Giovanni ad naviculam	75 *PORTA PLUVIENSE*
26 Basilica S. Stephani Maioris	48 Mausoleo di Teodorico	76 *Antico basino del PORTUS*
27 Monasterium SS. Iohannis	ad Farum – necropoli gota	*CORIANDRI bonificato de*
Baptistae et Barbatiani	49 S. Stefano ad balnea Gothorum	*Teodorico (?)*
28 Monasterium S. Laurentia in	50 S. Giovanni Evangelista	77 *PORO*
Pannonia	necropoli romano-gota	

Map 6 Ravenna from the fifth to the eighth century

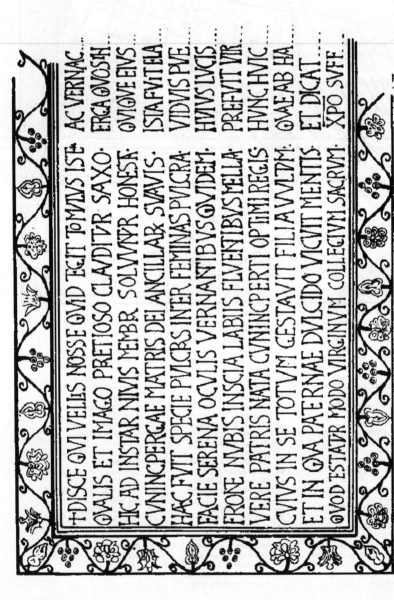

Map 7 The epigraph of Cuniperga (early 8th century)

Index